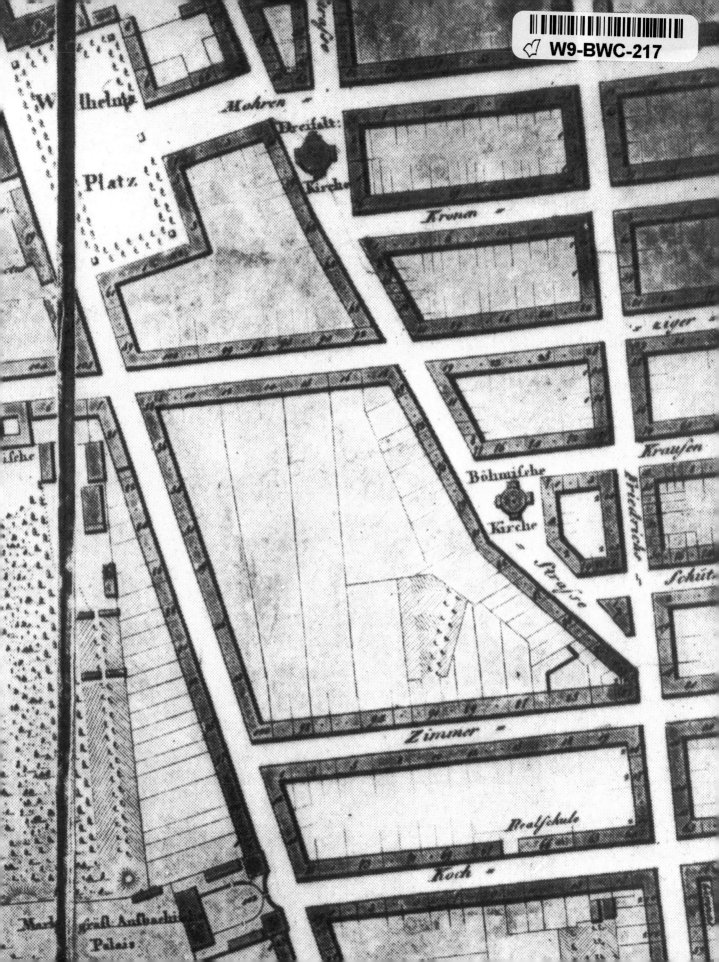

BERLIN

THE POLITICS OF ORDER

1737 – 1989

BERLIN

THE POLITICS OF ORDER

1737 – 1989

Alan Balfour

RIZZOLI
NEW YORK

First published in the United States of America in 1990 by
Rizzoli International Publications, Inc.
300 Park Avenue South, New York, NY 10010

Library of Congress Cataloging-in-Publication Data

Balfour, Alan
    Berlin: The Politics of Order: 1737 – 1989/Alan Balfour
        p. cm.
    Includes bibliographical references
    ISBN 0-8478-1271-5
        1. City planning--Berlin (Germany) 2. Architecture and state--Berlin (Germany)
3. Neoclassicism (Architecture)--Berlin (Germany)
I. Title: Berlin: The Politics of Order: 1737-1989
NA9200.B4B35 1990
720′,1′03--DC20

ISBN 0-8478-1271-5

Design: Group C; New Haven, Connecticut
        (B.C., G.S., D.K., S.H.)
Printed and bound in Japan

FOR ANNE, SARAH, AND DAVID

ACKNOWLEDGMENTS

This work developed over a number of years and was strengthened through the help of many colleagues and friends. I am particularly indebted to: Florian von Buttlar, Merrill Elam, David Elwell, Kenneth Frampton, Ronald Lewcock, Angel Medina, and Barry Russell for their willingness to read and advise; Dirk Förster and Eberhard Schröter, my guides to Berlin; colleagues Mack Scogin, Douglas Allen, Robert Segrest, James Williamson, and Jennifer Bloomer for their persistent and critical stimulus; and Josephine Buddel and Jeff Attwood for their invaluable creative assistance.

Field research was made possible by a grant from the National Endowment for the Arts, and made pleasurable through the help and assistance of many libraries and archives in Berlin, particularly the Akademie Der Kunste, Kunstbibliotek Preussischer Kulturbesitz, Ullstein, and the Landesbildstelle.

CONTENTS

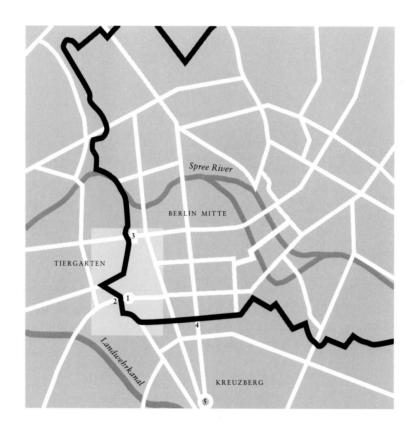

1
Leipziger Platz
2
Potsdamer Platz
3
Brandenburg Gate
4
Checkpoint Charlie
5
Hallesches Gate

Border between
East Berlin and West Berlin

Area of Detail

Spree River

BERLIN MITTE

TIERGARTEN

Landwehrkanal

KREUZBERG

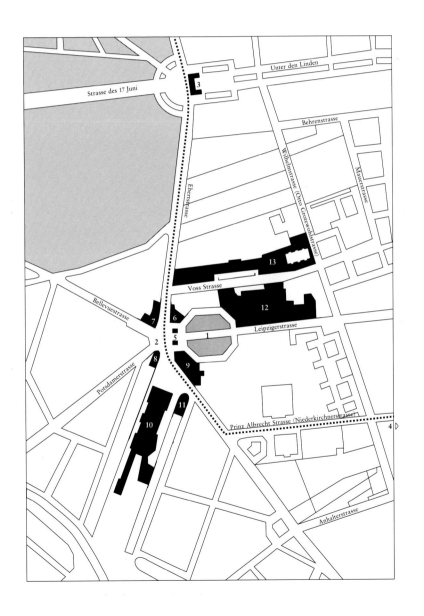

1
Leipziger Platz
2
Potsdamer Platz
3
Brandenburg Gate
4
Checkpoint Charlie
5
Schinkel's Potsdam Gates
6
Palast Hotel
7
Columbus Haus
8
Pschorr Haus
9
Hotel Der Fürstenhof
10
Potsdamer Bahnhof
11
Haus Vaterland
12
Wertheim Department Store
13
Reich Chancellery
▪▪▪▪
The Wall

Leipziger Platz and Potsdamer Platz
from the air in 1915.

This is a study of the ideals, myths, and fictions of a culture seen through the reflections of architecture, architects, and artists.

The city is Berlin. The document is of one place: a rectangle of land a thousand meters deep and a thousand meters wide on either side of Leipziger Platz, at the heart of the city. It was chosen to reveal the extremes in the shifting ideas that have shaped Western culture since the eighteenth century.

This work assembles all the layers of surviving residue around this place – texts, drawings, photographs – from two hundred and fifty years of dreams and catastrophes, like a plug drilled from a tree, to uncover the nature and subsequent impact of past seasons and past events. It is a section through the landscapes of desire.

Projects for the future are caught in the midst of such complex accumulations of history that they are often undermined and diminshed by them. Looking closely at the contiguous events around one place – particularly one as tragic and mysterious as Leipziger Platz – reveals a deep disorder unseen or ignored in those projects of our temporal desire. It is important to read the evidence of the layers and stages very carefully, for in them lies the only tangible clues to the fleeting promise of their plays.

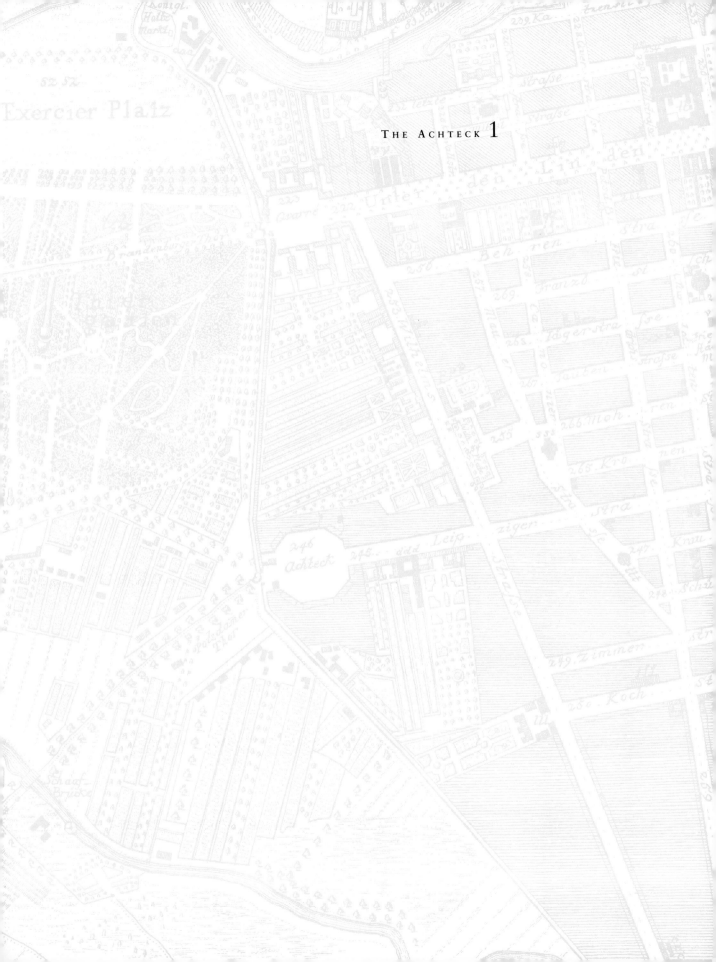

The platform on Potsdamer Platz, a few hundred yards south of the Brandenburg Gate, was the most popular place for viewing the Wall and the Eastern Sector from the West. There was conflict between seeing and understanding. From the platform there was little to see: a clear space with grass, an access road, a cobbled street with rails. At the extreme left lay a triangle of land whose vegetation was returning to the scrubby forest of the Prussian plain. So adept was nature at eroding man's work that there was a time when wildlife flourished in this wilderness at the center of the city. It was a piece of the East German nation too inconvenient to govern. It was nowhere. The green fields to the left were the gardens of the Reich Chancellery, where Bismarck and his court and Hitler and Hindenburg strolled and reflected on summer afternoons, and where Hitler's body would be burned. In the distance, to the left,

1.1
Berlin, November 12, 1989.
East German workers removing sections
of the Berlin Wall at Potsdamer Platz,
once the city's thriving center.

still stands a small mound covered in grass beneath whose earth lies the rubble of Hitler's bunker and, deeper down, the concrete floor where he, Eva Braun, Joseph Goebbels and his wife and six children all took their lives.

Straight ahead, the trace of an octagonal figure can still be seen in the stones that once lined the road's edge. It is the mark of the Achteck at Leipziger Platz. Even its slender outline produces a spinning sensation in the mind trying to place value and extract meaning from this place. It is the simultaneous experience of what is concrete, yet abstract, of what is knowable, yet unknowable. While the imagination struggles to recreate what was, the intellect is conscious of what is. The Achteck represents literally the passage of death within life, an interval within reality.

There is a poignant desire to revise all the events and objects in the past of this place. The mind plays with the senses, teases the ear to hear lost voices and street sounds, to reconstruct with the eye and the imagination the grand houses and the elaborate social performances that have been played out here for more than two hundred years. Here Napoleon, hidden in his carriage, rushes to Sans Souci and sips brandy laced with laudanum. Here the elderly Goethe weeps with pain at the approach of winter. Here Chopin gives a recital in a drawing room and complains about the noise of the steam trains. Here, on the steps of the gatehouse, Brecht and Piscator argue about the movies of D.W. Griffith, and Josephine Baker plays peekaboo with Max Reinhardt. Here workers rise up against their government only to be forced into submission by Russian tanks. Here in August of 1961 the heart of this city is physically divided by a wall. The seeds of division lie deep in the history of this place.

The year is 1737. The place is the westward edge of Berlin. A sector is being created to provide an ordered reality for a newly emerging urban aristocracy. It will symbolize the emergence of German culture from rural feudalism into an appearance of "enlightenment" and reason. At the same time the last expansion of the fortifications that had enclosed the city since its foundation in 1237 is being set out. This first ordering of a nondescript piece of land will become both the actual and conceptual reference for a range of political and social visions that will follow. It is the projection of an octagonal figure onto the open fields. The name in German is "Achteck," or eight corners.

Imagine a panoramic drawing, an amateur drawing. The artist is sitting on raised land overlooking a city. On the left he has drawn a forest. Through the trees are glimpsed hunters on horses with dogs. Part of the hunt rests by a creek. Fishermen, marked by rod and line, dot its marshy border. The city in the background bristles with towers and spires and flags, and in the foreground sheep graze, cattle are driven, and great tumbling wagons roll toward the city. On the right, in careful ink lines, the artist has placed the surveyors of the king laying out a large octagonal space on newly drained and cleared land. In the center, between the forest edge and the octagon, between savage nature and reason, he uses a wooden rule to mark the line of a new city wall. It will be a customs wall, three meters high, constructed to tax trade and regulate entry into the city. Only a few years separate this simple structure from the last line of moats and ramparts built for serious military defense. It establishes a line that will ultimately divide the city.

1780

1.3
Detail from J.F. Schneider map
of Berlin and environs, 1802.

1802

Beginning in the 1700s under the Prussian King Friedrich I (1657-1713) and continued by Friedrich Wilhelm I (1688-1740), a series of new districts had been laid out on the west of what had remained a largely medieval city. They were formed in intense grid patterns, unrelieved by open space or public monument. The district to the southwest was named Friedrichstadt, and the expansion of 1737 advanced the city wall and the idea of the new city sufficiently far to establish three great public spaces at the three major gates [1.3]: on the south a circle marked the Hallesches Gate, on the north a square marked the Brandenburg Gate, and between, on the west, an octagon marked the Potsdam Gate, the entry into the city from the road to Potsdam. Square, circle, octagon – these self-conscious embellishments were to represent a higher level of thought than the grid of the military surveyor. Inspired in envy of the reconstructions at the center of Paris by Louis XIV, these were the projections of reason and idealized order on the fields of a provincial monarchy.[1] The Potsdam Gate had an especially royal significance – it was the point of entry into the city from Sans Souci, the favorite country palace of the king. This led the surveyors of Friedrich Wilhelm I to recreate in the Achteck the octagonal form used in the most fashionable of the royal squares of Paris, Place Louis Le Grand, completed some forty years earlier in 1699.[2]

These figures differed, however, from the squares of Paris. The Achteck and its companion plazas were pure definitions of abstract idealized space without concern for surface or image. The circle and crescent in the English town of Bath, exactly contemporary, were fantasies about the image of Rome in which the experience had to do with the classical illusion carried in the architecture. The Achteck, in contrast, was solely a demonstration of the desire for a rational autocratic order, free from the confusion of history. The great achievements of Friedrich Wilhelm I were in disciplining the army and in centralizing the government, and these new city districts were the stage for his consolidation of power. They were peopled by all the wayward elements of Prussia's ancient and independent feudal aristocracies, drawn to city life by royal decree, and thereby brought within the King's power. The nature of the new city was not unlike a spider's web with the King and his palace at the center, the new protected urban class caught between its strands and shaped to conform to the King's imposed order. The spaces by the gates allowed for the massing of his troops and the anonymous streets in uniform grids allowed for the visible reduction of the individual personalities of his courtiers.

The new plan was in direct opposition to the medieval city. It was an autocratic imposition projected to make the city controllable. It molded reality in relation to rational prediction and to simple notions of universal order, demanding that the city be the project of ideas rather than random incident. The medieval city, anchored by the great monuments of the church and crown, was controlled from the past. Those shaping the new city recognized the possibility of controlling the physical order of the future.

They could now promote the conscious social and political structuring of reality. The project of the court would be made explicit. From the earliest maps the octagon was inscribed "Achteck Markt Platz" [1.4]. The idea of a marketplace on the edge of the city presented a radical change in the relation between the peasant and the city dweller. The peasant farmers who had brought their produce to the city since its foundation were being held at the gate. Keeping the peasants at the edge acknowledged the deep division between country life and life in the new city. Keeping the peasants at the edge separated the new rational world from their unreasonable and savage nature.

These ideal orders in space, through which an absolute monarchy attempted to control the future and physically structure time, were the critical first marks in the conflicting political utopias that grew from the Enlightenment. In the old city the social order had been subjective; in the new city it would become objective. What appeared on the surface of the new city as unity and coherence contained beneath it elements of deep division – division not only between the peasants and the new urban aristocracy, but between the order of circumstance and the power of ideals. In a simple sense it reflected a future transplanted from the will of God into the will of man.

1.4
Achteck Markt Platz,
Berlin, from the Dusableau
Plan of 1737.

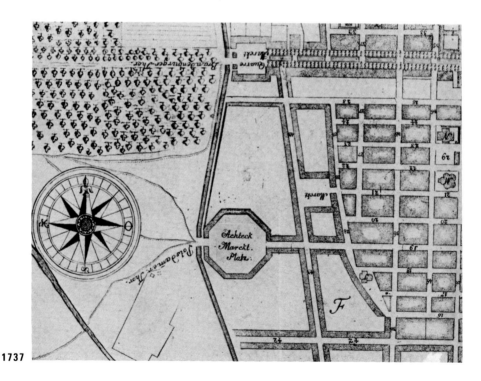

1737

Projecting the future of the city helped determine the fate of the culture, and all that followed was, in some measure, a result of idealizing and abstracting the order of reality [1.5].[3]

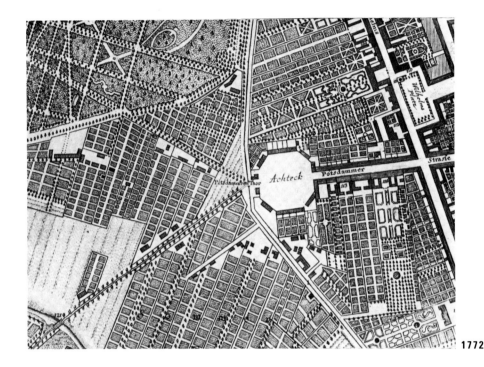

1772

FRIEDRICH GILLY AND THE MONUMENT TO FREDERICK THE GREAT

Frederick II, the son of Friedrich Wilhelm I, ruled Prussia from 1740 to 1786. In ways both enlightened and despotic, he had forced Europe into complex wars and alliances and expanded the territory and power of Prussia. At his death he was called Frederick the Great and mourned as the most powerful leader of the German people since Charlemagne. In his life he had expressed the wish to be buried with his pet whippets, unmarked beneath the garden terrace of his Palace of Sans Souci, but after his death members of the Royal Academy voted to erect a monument to his memory.

In 1797 Friedrich Gilly prepared a design. He was twenty-five years old, and already the intensity of his imagination and the elegance of his draftsmanship had been recognized by Friedrich Wilhelm II (1744-1797), nephew of Frederick the Great who inherited the Prussian throne in 1786.[4] The young man was aware of his role as the medium for the royal production of an "enlightened" reality. Friedrich II proposed to the Royal Academy that the monument to his uncle be placed in the middle of the

Achteck.[5] Here, he argued, it would be framed by the city and the memory of the King would lie on the path to the palace he most loved. Gilly's notes and drawings for the monument provide a revealing window into the imagination and the desires of the German Enlightenment; their significance and their power were to lie in the distant future [1.6]. They have a freshness and intelligence that allow even now an intimacy with the character of their creator. Along with sketches of architectural forms there are notes, fragments of thoughts, and fleeting ideas on the visual qualities of classical temples, many of which had only recently been excavated. He never visited these places, yet from the work of archaeologists and others, they had an independent existence in his imagination:

> *Climb up to the cella as in Paestum?*
>
> *The floor in Nismes*
>
> *Korinth-*
>
> *What were the old temples?*
>
> *No temple. Heroum? (?Place of Heroes? Surround of Heroes?)*
>
> *It must be entirely open, not a cella, also not round from the outside.*
>
> *No example except in Pozzuoli[6]*
>
> *Roman temple. Pantheon the cosmos.*
>
> *Quadrilateral*
>
> *The columns not too widely spaced one must be able to see in but not*
>
> *see through; same from in out.*
>
> *Great also in mass.*
>
> *Justifiably the largest in the city.*
>
> *Jupiter's temple of Agrigent.[7]*

This is a conversation between words and images. As he writes he draws. He draws literally from memory and imagination. It is a critical discourse narrowing down the choices until he selects a form with a virtue appropriate to the idea. In this he is closely guided by the writings of Johann Winckelmann,[8] the archaeologist and aesthete whose work placed classical art and architecture as the supreme achievements of Western culture. Winckelmann evoked the spirit of the hero:

For it demands a lofty understanding to express the significant and speaking stillness of the souls: for

the imitation of the violent as Plato says, can be made in different ways; but a calm wise demeanor can

neither be easily imitated nor when imitated easily be comprehended.[9]

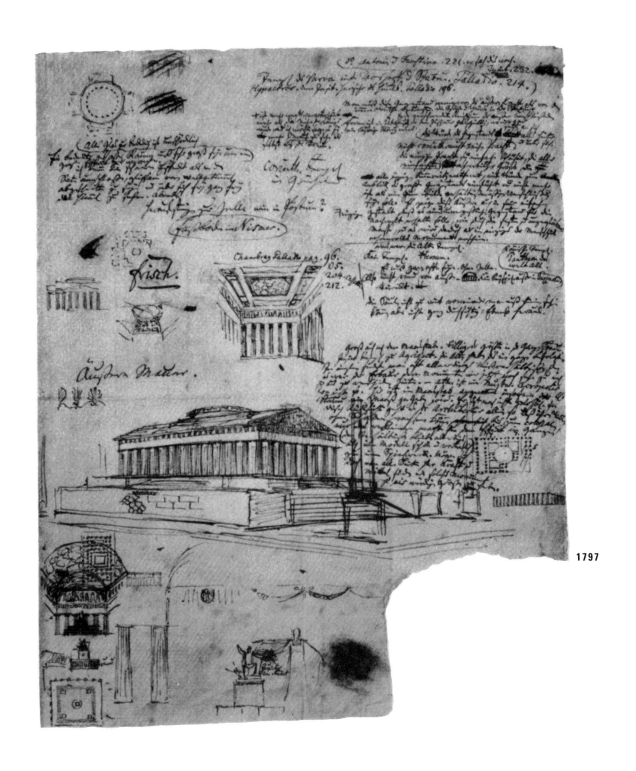

1797

1.6
Friedrich Gilly, studies and notes for the
Monument to Frederick the Great, 1797.

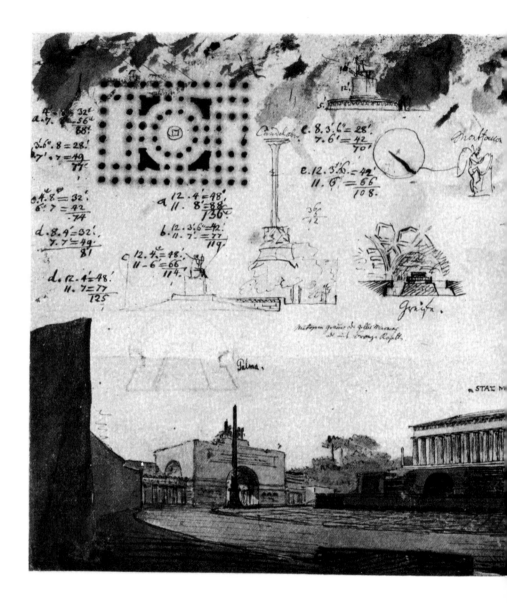

These thoughts resonate in Gilly's notes on the meaning embodied in the temple:

. . . the dignity of this object sits in itself and must subject everything to itself. The opulence of the temple is in its simple beauty, in its reverential magnitude it banishes all arrogant sensuous stimulation. . . . I know of no more beautiful experience than being enclosed on all sides and cut off from the world's tumult and within this to see about one, freely, entirely free, heaven's evenings.[10]

The temple would have simplicity, clarity, grace, and a secret sadness – a representation of the duality between a longing for night and a

1797

longing for day in an age which loved tragedy more than comedy. The
temple would refuse to accept the descent from light into darkness. The
temple would transform ambiguous presence into ubiquitous idea – an
object-word, a place to be, a place for meditation, a place of lightness,
clarity, and reason against its antithesis in darkness and mystery, the
cathedral. The temple alone held the speaking stillness of the soul, and
remembered a time when it was at one with the cosmos.[11]

From the desolation of the Achteck today imagine what might have
been. The gate to the city was to have been approached through an oval
drive cut from a block of trees [1.7]. The gate in the drawing is massive and
plain and in the form of a triumphal arch carrying on its crest a bronze

1.8
Friedrich Gilly,
exhibition perspective of the
Monument to Frederick the Great,
gate detail, 1797.

quadriga, facing the city as if arrested on the journey back from Potsdam [1.8]. The carriage is driverless but a strange plume fixes the reins and holds the memory of the lost hero. The massive outer arch provides a solemn frame for the temple. All who entered Berlin by this gate would pay tribute to the memory of Frederick the Great. Into the city, cradled in two gently arching groves of trees, the monument in the drawing triumphs over the Achteck [1.9]. The form of the trees is echoed in a low, curving stone wall which holds the temple platform as if in clasped hands. From a distance it is an object of wonder, effortlessly rising above all else, its layers of ascending color – from black basalt to red granite to white marble – brilliant and inspiring in the midday sun. The eye continually moves from the outline of the sarcophagus in the black vault to the serene purity of the temple.

1.9
Friedrich Gilly, final plan
for the Monument to Frederick
the Great, 1797.

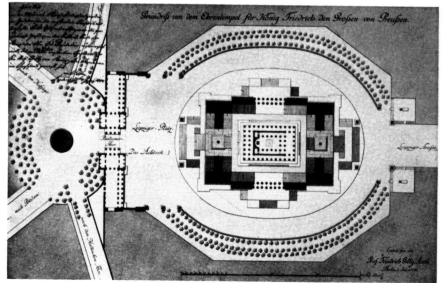

1797

The vault must be entered. A vast coffered passage in dull black basalt joins with a perfect sphere at the center of which lies the tomb of the hero [1.10]. The tomb, resting on a base of sheer black marble, rises from an unfathomable pool. The slightest sound echoes and wounds the senses. All movement is with obsessive care and in absolute silence. It is the vivid presence of death that elevates the spirit:

As the bottom of the sea lies peaceful beneath a foaming surface, a great soul lies sedate beneath the strife of passions in Greek figures.[12]

The stair to the temple platform cuts through the massive base, a representation of the ascent to the oracle at Delphi. The temple is revealed. The journey is a lonely passage, an act of homage. Purifying smoke drifts from a brazier. It was from Winckelmann that Gilly learned that "Longing for the fatherland is a noble symbol in the figure of Ulysses, who wishes he could see the smoke rising in Ithaca from afar. . . ."[13]

The movement is exhilarating. Through a line of Doric columns into the pronaos and through a double colonnade into the naos, it is a progression of the most fundamental Greek forms. A blinding shaft of light from a square oculus obscures the exedra [1.11]. One must pass through the light and be cleansed, sanctified, and charged with the awareness of a transcendental reality to confront the presence of the hero. The memorial

1797

compels order, yet it is willing to exist in a changing external reality. In the great vaults below the temple the tomb of Frederick is always seen in relation to the changing city. The temple is above the real, inspiring not interfering. Though armies can march to its door, the tomb is open only to the individual; it demands a personal relationship with the memory of the King. In death the hero is as all other men. The struggle between darkness, light, and the promise of eternity is resolved in the inspiration of the transcendent spirit of the hero.

But in this most reasonable of times all the gods have left. Underlying all the nostalgia and the pictorial evocation of ancient Greece, these drawings search for a fundamental architecture, for the affirmation of an essential reality, for a new beginning. They are the marks of a young man, practical and idealistic, whose deeper vision is distorted by the insecurity of his religious inheritance. Gilly was a Huguenot, a Protestant whose ancestors

had been continually persecuted by the French court and who had been forced by Louis XIV out of France by the hundreds of thousands at the end of the seventeenth century.[14] Beneath his courtly demeanor he dreamed not for the deification of the king but for a transcendent symbol of a victory over Catholic persecution and dispossession. Behind all the pomp and ordered circumstance his visions were founded in Huguenot desire.

There is one page from the notebook where the drawings display brilliant insight [1.12]. They present the signs of a purely modern sensibility.[15] There are two drawings on the page. They are both fragments of thought from the initial designs for the monument. At the top, a tomb lies within a columned hall at whose center is a great circle. In the lower Pfeilerhalle, or pillared hall, a complex colonnade covers a flight of steps. Despite its modesty it is a work of startling prescience. It is not a simple description of structure but an abstract reflection on the meaning and potential of an essential geometric order. The formative order of architecture was understood to be derived from a combination of reason and myth, but for the "enlightened" mind the essence of order lay only in reason. Divorcing the order of any object from its roots in myth and nature would transform its essential character, moving it into the realm of abstraction shorn of any metaphysical or historical connection. In such a condition, an object such as a column would become concerned only with itself and its own nature, free from repeating the imperfectly understood myths and gods of dead cultures. Gilly, through the drawing, was considering what would happen if the concept of a column was to be freed from the burden of representing classical meanings. In this simple colonnade over a flight of stairs the column becomes a ubiquitous rectilinear volume, repeated throughout the structure, and able to interweave into a wholly new and abstract interaction of space and experience. The colonnade presents opposing lines of force, involved only in its own spatial ambiguity, opposing its historical origin. It is as if the numerous terms that defined all the separate elements of the classical column, all the refinements in decoration and modulation, had been silenced. Freedom from representing the myths and harmonies of history meant that architecture no longer needed to be a record of the past but could become an accord of place, a pure force, a pure circumstance, a project of infinite meaning and no meaning at all. Architecture could become self-possessed.

Desire for fundamental change led Gilly to reject the texts of history, to detach the idea of space from that of ancient gods, and to reconnect the idea of beauty to that of ideal order. With reverberations of the French and American revolutions growing ever stronger throughout Europe and cries for freedom and equality heard on all fronts, it must have been inevitable that Gilly would see in such conceptions a direct connection between the act of freeing architecture from the bonds of history and the cause of political freedom. Liberation from the structures of past autocracies could mean liberation from a constraining social order.

Such reflections on perceptual revolution, however, had no place in

1.12
Friedrich Gilly, studies for the Pfeilerhalle in the Monument to Frederick the Great, 1797.

the Monument for Frederick, and Gilly reestablished the old gods in glory [1.13]. Consider the effect on Gilly of a critical position which rejected the inheritance of history in a culture which was validated by it. Perhaps this explains the all-pervasive sadness that permeates the final perspective prepared for the Royal Academy in 1797 [1.14]. It is an oblique view of a still, silent place as empty as a stage set. Reason is smothered in antique sentimentality:

The true feeling for beauty is like the liquid plaster cast which is poured over the head of Apollo.

Touching every single part and enclosing it. The subject which evokes this feeling is not what instinct,

friendship and the courteous praise, but what the innermost refined sense feels when purified of all

other purposes for the sake of beauty.[16]

But such stifling aristocratic sensibilities were dying with the century and the monument was set aside in the increasing and disquieting passions rippling from the acts of Napoleon.

All projections into external reality are as much projections of ignorance as of knowledge, but the brilliance of Gilly's imagination promised insights into the reformation of architecture which could have altered the shape of the nineteenth century. Tragically, in 1800 while travelling abroad, he caught a chill and died soon after returning to Berlin. He was twenty-eight.

1797

1.13
  Friedrich Gilly, model of the
  Monument to Frederick the Great,
  1797.

1.14
Friedrich Gilly, perspective of the
Monument to Frederick the Great,
1797.

1797

KARL FRIEDRICH SCHINKEL: PROJECT FOR THE MONUMENT TO FREDERICK THE GREAT
AND THE CATHEDRAL TO THE WARS OF LIBERATION

In 1814 a new monument was conceived for the Achteck. It would be the Cathedral to the Wars of Liberation and was proposed by the architect Karl Friedrich Schinkel[17] in memory of Gilly. As one of the first teachers at the newly founded Berlin Building Academy, Gilly had formed a close friendship with the young Schinkel,[18] and in later years Schinkel wrote that it was the drawing for the Monument to Frederick the Great, on exhibition in Berlin in 1797, that led him into architecture.

Although the site of this new monument was to be the Achteck, the intention was fundamentally different. A spirit of revolution against the inherited monarchies and their claim of God-given power swept Europe at the end of the eighteenth century, shaped in reaction to Napoleon and leading, in the first decades of the new century, to essential changes in the nature and structure of European society. Thus, when Schinkel came to the Achteck sixteen years after Gilly's exercise in imperial heroics, Prussia had been irrevocably changed. The task now was to celebrate not only victory over Napoleon, but the end of the absolute power of the monarchy and the promise of political freedom in a united Germany. In May of 1804, Napoleon

Bonaparte had been crowned Emperor of France. In December of 1804, he defeated Austria and Russia at the battle of Austerlitz. On the Prussian throne was the son of Friedrich Wilhelm II, Friedrich Wilhelm III (1770-1840). Napoleon viewed him as "no less false, than stupid," and the Prussian state was compelled in 1805 to enter into a formal treaty of alliance with France. From this followed the formation of the Rheinish Confederation of sixteen German principalities which were forced to recognize Napoleon as liege lord.[19] In reaction, Friedrich Wilhelm declared war on France and suffered overwhelming defeats at the battles of Jena and Auerstädt. In October of 1806, Napoleon entered Berlin welcomed by the city fathers. The nation was humiliated. All the achievements of Frederick the Great had been undone.

The seed for Schinkel's vision of a great symbol for the German people was formed by the philosopher Johann Gottlieb Fichte and planted in the midst of the occupation.[20] On December 13, 1807, Fichte began a series of lectures in the amphitheater of the Berlin Academy entitled "Addresses to the German Nation," which considered with great urgency and force the question of national identity. He exhorted the audience to envisage the epic project to be fulfilled by the German race. In the concluding lecture he said:

If you continue in your dullness and helplessness, all the evils of serfdom are awaiting you; deprivations, humiliations, the scorn and arrogance of the conqueror; you will be driven and harried in every corner, because you are in the wrong and in the way everywhere; until, by the sacrifice of your nationality and your language, you have purchased for yourselves some subordinate and petty place, and until in this way you gradually die out as a people. If, on the other hand, you bestir yourself and play the man, you will continue in a tolerable and honorable existence, and you will see growing up among and around you a generation that will be the promise for you and for the Germans of most illustrious renown. You will see in spirit the German name rising by means of this generation to be the most glorious among all peoples; you will see this nation the regenerator and re-creator of the world.[21]

This challenge to the suffering national spirit was meant to cause a deep disturbance. With foreign troops guarding the doors, the monarchy discredited, and discontent and dissolution throughout the culture, Fichte offered a vision of Germany as recreator of the world if only the spirit of the German people could be harnessed. To an audience dominated by the disaffected intelligentsia, such inspiring thoughts would be held for the appropriate field of action.[22]

In 1812 Napoleon invaded Russia with an army of 500,000 men, most of whom were forced conscripts and mercenary aliens. The expedition was a disaster; less than 50,000 returned. In 1813, first Prussia and Austria, then Russia, Sweden, and Britain came together for the effort which became known in Prussia as the War of Liberation. Between the 16th and 18th of

October 1813, Napoleon was challenged and defeated at the Battle of Leipzig. His dispirited armies were pushed across France and in March of 1814 the Allies entered Paris in triumph. In that summer the Congress of Vienna began work on a settlement of the conflict, and Schinkel began to consider the creation of a great symbol to be a lasting monument to the Wars of Liberation. He would begin with the model of Strasbourg Cathedral. Within the flow of ideas that informs Leipziger Platz, Prussian culture, in less than two decades, moved from the project for a monument to the memory of an absolute monarch to a symbol of the prospect of political freedom; and with it the architectural model moved from a Greek temple to a medieval cathedral. These are the first signs of instability in the play of the culture. The conservatism of the weakened court was being met by incipient liberalism.

Strasbourg Cathedral could be seen to embody in its texture an apt form for Fichte's challenge to make Germany the regenerator and recreator of the world, but the inspiration for it as an appropriate symbol came to Schinkel from the writings of Johann Wolfgang von Goethe.[23] The elderly Goethe, whose aura permeated the culture in these unsettled years, believed in architecture: "the highest purpose [it] undertakes" he wrote, is "the super satisfaction of the senses and the raising of the cultivated mind to astonishment and rapture." And for him Strasbourg Cathedral, above all other structures, embodied the essential virtue of the German people in architecture:

And now I ought not to be angry . . . if the German art expert, on the hearsay of envious neighbors, fails to recognize his advantage and belittles [Strasbourg Cathedral] with that misunderstood word 'Gothic.' For he should thank God he can proclaim this is German architecture, our architecture.[24]

It was not only profoundly German but also had the virtue of opposing the prevalent taste for the classical among Prussia's neighbors. Goethe was passionate on this issue:

'It is in a niggling taste,' says the Italian, and passes on. 'Puerilities,' babbles the Frenchman childishly after him, and triumphantly snaps open his snuff box 'a la Greque.' What have you done, that you should dare to look down your noses? Has not the genius of the ancients risen from its grave to enslave yours, you dagoes?[25]

In this same essay, written in 1772, he evokes the emotional presence of the minster and suggests it as a metaphor for a new nation:

How freshly the minster sparkled in the early morning mist, and how happily I could stretch out my arms towards it, and gaze at the harmonious masses, alive with countless details. Just as in the external works of nature everything is perfectly formed down to the meanest thread, and contributing purposefully to the whole.[26]

1812

1.15
Karl Friedrich Schinkel, west facade
of Strasbourg Minster with south
tower addition, engraving, 1812.

And in the political turmoil of 1812 he returned again to Strasbourg for reassurance:

The more I investigated the more I was astonished and the more I busied myself with measuring and

drawing . . . . I spent a good deal of time studying what was available and restoring in my imagination

what was missing or incomplete, especially the towers.[27]

Because it carried in its form the complete metaphor of the political ideal, the dream of a perfect Strasbourg was for Goethe a vision capable of restoring confidence in the renewal of German culture even in the midst of war and social confusion.[28] The cathedral symbolized the natural idea of the nation formed out of a myriad of intersecting interests and strengths. Schinkel, in tribute, created a brilliant engraving of the cathedral's west facade which, with the addition of the missing south tower, had been made whole [1.15].[29]

Schinkel's first studies for the new cathedral were done in the summer of 1814 [1.16]. The perspective presents the building at the center of Leipziger Platz, enclosed by a vast public cloister which extends from the transepts. His task, with the will of the nation, was to construct a monument that would advance the idea of liberty for all the people. In the drawing, the great public space represents the power of a forum for the people in the presence, not of the idea of God, but of the idea of the nation [1.17]. The cathedral in the drawing corresponds piece by piece to Goethe's critical analysis of Strasbourg. He called on the imagination to abstract the west facade: "Imagine this enormous wall without ornament − with solid buttresses, and openings only in so far as they are necessary." He then rejected this notion as "depressing and inartistic." Yet, Schinkel used this simplification to establish a strange

1.16
Karl Friedrich Schinkel,
ink study for the Monument and
Cathedral to the Wars of
Liberation, 1814.

1814

middle ground between the medieval and the ancient. At the crossing of the transepts an ideal spherical space would occupy the center of this German church. Guided by Goethe, for whom the fusion of the rational with the romantic was an explicit task for the time,[30] he would contain classical order within gothic structure to create a fusion between the natural order of the German people and the rational state represented by the perfect geometry of the sphere. It also holds an echo of Fichte's subjective idealism where the "ego" becomes aware of its own freedom and its unity with the absolute. Schinkel writes of his exact intention:

If one could, grasping the spiritual principle of ancient Greek architecture, intend them to the

conditions of our new epoch, within which lies simultaneously the harmonious blending of the best of

1.17
Karl Friedrich Schinkel,
plan of the Monument
and Cathedral to the
Wars of Liberation, 1814.
A vast colonnade extends
the Achteck through the
original customs wall
to the west.

all the intermediate periods, then one would have found possibly the most unified solution for the

architectural problem.[31]

In the drawing the cathedral turns its back to the city and offers this prospect toward those burdened by a thousand years of feudalism. This was to be their cathedral.

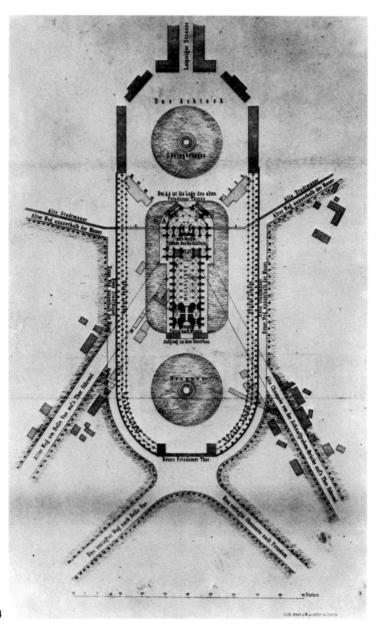

1814

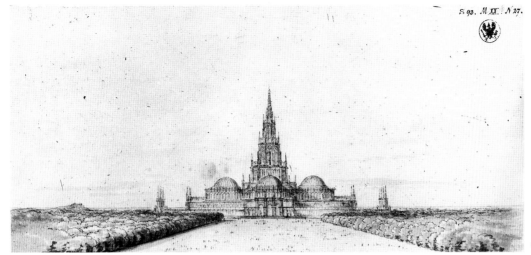

S 93. M XX. N 27.

1814

Only one drawing survives of Schinkel's second project for the monument [1.18].[32] It is an astounding vision of stupendous and unequaled scale. The view is from the west. The cathedral is approached down a vast avenue cut through a forest, uniting the city with the country. It overwhelms the octagonal confines of Leipziger Platz. Its spire, more than a thousand feet in height, would have overshadowed all else in the city and in the imagination of the nation. It would have been seen for miles across the Prussian plains, and individuals would have been reduced to dust in its vastness.

"The best [work of art] chains our feelings and imagination," wrote Goethe. It "robs us of our will power, for we cannot do what we please with the perfect, we are compelled to surrender to it in order to receive ourselves again, raised and ennobled."[33] Here, the spirit of the new nation is all. The plan is a cross. The arms – north, south, east, and west – are symmetrical and self-centered beneath domes whose forms owe nothing to history. The spire, like an effusion of nature, rises out of the crossing, terracing through layers of gothic strata to its pinnacle. It is intoxicated with the significance of its presence. It would obey the Fichte dictum: "Art is part of divine revelation, art provokes change." It was a raging creative act addressing the passionate desire for liberation and unity at a point in time when it appeared that the Crown would make freedom and representation a constitutional right, and Schinkel, in his imagination, could almost touch and feel the repressed popular power and creativity this would release.

With the death of the language, wrote Fichte, the supersensuous part of culture becomes "a tattered collection of arbitrary and totally inexplicable symbols for ideas that are just as arbitrary."[34] Yet, in the death of the language, the ideas that had distinguished the culture would remain alive in the material object of art. Here, in this cathedral, he believed that the language of freedom would have been nurtured. It would have become the

1.18
Karl Friedrich Schinkel,
ink study for the Cathedral to
the Wars of Liberation, 1814.

persistent symbol of the genius of the German spirit. It would have become a continual inspiration to the liberated forces of the culture to control the future. Its presence would have changed the course of history. Schinkel wrote:

The encouragement of art must be considered and no omissions must arise in the progress of an active

state, because as a result of omission, barbarism will again gain entry to the culture.[35]

Does the failure to establish an ideal lie at times in the failure to build the building?

1.19
Karl Friedrich Schinkel,
section-elevation of the Monument and
Cathedral to the Wars of Liberation, 1815.

1815

1.20
Karl Friedrich Schinkel, plan of
the Monument and Cathedral to
the Wars of Liberation, 1815.

In March of 1815, the proceedings of the Congress of Vienna were interrupted by Napoleon's flight from Elba and his landing at Cannes. The French people immediately rallied to his side and reclaimed him as emperor. There was confusion and dismay throughout Europe, and in Prussia some in military and political circles argued for Napoleon. These supporters were rejected however, and the military alliance which had produced the victory at Leipzig was re-established. On June 18, 1815, Napoleon was finally defeated in the field at Waterloo, the field of "La Belle Alliance."

1.21
Karl Friedrich Schinkel, elevation
of the Monument and Cathedral
to the Wars of Liberation, 1815.

In the aftermath, the Congress of Vienna considered a request by the German states for the restoration of the expanded Germany that had been created by Frederick the Great, but this was firmly blocked by Austria. Instead, the Congress devised a new and loose federal union bearing the name Deutscher Bund (German Confederation), which included all parts of the old empire but with an Austrian as its hereditary president. The Congress also refused to return Strasbourg and Alsace to Germany, and Strasbourg Cathedral, the embodiment of the German *geist*, was to remain captive in France.

In 1815 Schinkel returned to the Cathedral and the Monument to the Wars of Liberation [1.19-21]. From the drawings, it is as a balloon deflated, the energy and the passion gone, though what remains is intense and aggressive. This is no longer a challenge to history, yet it is compact and powerful like some instrument of war. There is less certainty over what has been achieved. It may celebrate victory in the war, but it seems to symbolize more hope than success in the

1815

1817

struggle for freedom and unity. The single spire is unambiguous on the idea of unification, but is much reduced from the soaring spirit of 1814. The classical presence is not all lost; the figures that decorate the tympanum appear more the product of Greek myth than of medievalism. Over the central door a winged Pegasus springs, it can be inferred, from the blood of Napoleon. Where the transept and choir should have been, a space has been created to hold once again the figure of a sphere. In a sensuous feat of imagination, the dome of the sphere has become trapped in the fibrous tissue of gothic tracery, a perverse marriage of the sacred and the cosmic.[36] From within, the assembled masses would look to the altar of reason for the path to freedom.[37]

Goethe wrote in 1816, recommending Schinkel to a colleague, that he wished "such a rich talent may be granted an equally broad spirit of action." Schinkel was to emerge as the most gifted and influential architect within the court of Friedrich Wilhelm III.[38] In only one other project did he display such intense passion over the divided soul of the culture in the conflict between an absolute monarchy and the desire for democracy, and more fundamentally, between the forces of reason and nature. The setting was again Leipziger Platz.

In 1817, in a dream vision for Leipziger Platz, the choir of the Cathedral to the Wars of Liberation became the central element in a painting which Schinkel entitled *Triumphbogen* (Triumphal Arch). It is a painting made by the architect for his patron Crown Prince Friedrich Wilhelm III [1.22]. Though the stage is large the players are small. Schinkel's patron, the Crown Prince, stands at the center on the stage below the arch. The occasion is the returning to Berlin of the Quadriga, the symbolic bronze chariot pulled by four horses. In reality, this great work by the sculptor Johann Gottfried Schadow had been removed from the Brandenburg Gate and taken to Paris after the defeat of 1806. The return of the chariot would mark the restoration of independence and dignity to the nation. Although it is placed at the center, the chariot is an insignificant detail within the painting. The subject of the work is elsewhere. It was made to be a lesson to the Crown Prince on the dangers of withdrawing from the promise of freedom and representation that had been so overwhelmingly expressed in the autumn of 1814, a warning to a crown prince who had joined in 1815 with the emperors of Russia and Austria to form a "Holy Alliance." By 1817, that alliance was emerging as the instrument for the reestablishment of the absolute power of the monarchy. All the promises of the Wars of Liberation were fading and the commitment of the Crown, made in the stress of occupation, to constitutional rights, freedom, and political representation was being withdrawn.

The composition can be seen conceptually as a representation of Hegel's notion of a "dialectical moment," a moment of metaphysical and dynamic conflict on the path to universal reason.[39] In the disillusion of the aftermath of war there appears in the work the realization that the path to reason is not necessarily the path to freedom. In the middle distance, random gatherings of people can be seen moving toward the great arch. On the path, in procession, a great bronze quadriga is being drawn towards the foreground. The ordered ranks give way to scenes of orgiastic disorder and emotion. Some in the crowd are in classical dress. There is a sense of anticipation. Something is about to happen on the platform in front of the arch. Within the arch, overwhelming everything, two mounted figures ride from light into darkness, from day into night – Kurfürst the Grand Elector and, at his left, Frederick the Great. Both are dressed in medieval robes. In contrast, the arch within which they are placed and all elements within it appear Roman. The arch marks an edge between an end or a beginning. Two mythical figures ride together out of the light and into a world unknown. A break in the passage of time leaves all in the past; it is the viewer who literally stands now in the future and knows the rider's fate, sees the need to return to the past, to the light, to nature, and to the great medieval cathedral.

The symbols, large and small, are complex and deliberate. The tendrils decorating the archivolt flow from a winged youth, representing the guardian spirit of the state. Within circular medallions are the heads of great warriors and statesmen of antiquity – Lykung, Solon, Perikles, Timoleon, Alexander, Hannibal, Pompeus, Caesar, Titus, Marcus Aurelius, Constantine, Karl dem Grossen, and Maximillian – offered by Schinkel to the Crown Prince as the models for his future reign. On the bas-relief at the base a procession of Roman statesmen and soldiers demonstrate confidence in the imperial state.[40] Within the arch, Justice, in classical mythology the most important virtue in a king, is represented by the Roman figure of Genius, with tablets of law open for the instruction of seekers. The arch is founded on a base of lions for strength, and eagles mark the springing point, German eagles or Greek eagles of the apotheosis, the rising to the status of a god. The witness to the painting stands in the foreground, confronting the mouth of the spring that flows into the future. It is surrounded by the figures of a man, woman, and child. The water of life and the family of life form the vitality on which rest the welfare and the future of the state. But the source is dry.

It is a complex and prescient document of Germany's past and future, a symbolic text filled with irony, and a dialectic moment in the presence of reason and experience pitting the absolute power of kings against the faith of the people. Each element has been pondered and placed with care. The heroic figures frozen on the march have left behind their medieval heritage in striving for power and empire. The arch of their triumph frames an ominous and foreboding present. They have turned their backs on the great cathedral, yet it alone offers hope and light in the ancient and natural spirit of the German people. The witness must ask what kind of place lies past the foreground, what kind of place could create such dreadful darkness. This arch is not free-standing and triumphant, but is part of a vast structure within which the witness is placed. All the events in the foreground predict a deceitful future and the dreadful burden of absolute power; the spring, the life force of the people, has been crushed by an overwhelming imperial order.[41]

The painting was exhibited at the Berlin Academy in 1818 and was found too subjective and too opaque. It was described by one critic as "a fantasy piece of Berlin with a new cathedral and gate which appear similar to *A Midsummer Night's Dream* if the proportions and purposes of the project are analyzed."[42] With the passing of time the desire for a great national cathedral faded along with the promise of political freedom. Six years after his dream of a thousand-foot spire constructed to change the course of history, Schinkel produced his final design for the Monument to the Wars of Liberation. It was an iron obelisk sixty-two feet tall, which was finally unveiled on June 18, 1821, the sixth anniversary of Napoleon's surrender at Waterloo, in the Victory Park in the Berlin district of Kreuzberg.

ANSICHT DES THORS VON AUSSEN·

1823

In 1823, Schinkel designed the new city gates at Leipziger Platz. Here, his project was simple and direct. The customs wall and gate had existed for eighty years, and it was his task to rehouse the customs post and police station and give distinction to the entry to the city. The work possesses an almost archaeological correctness [1.23]. All desire for transcendent significance is gone, replaced by a style of genteel imperialism. The nation had settled down and the dreams of reform had been suspended, leaving in their place a sense of complacency and uneasy quiet. The Achteck, intended as a marketplace, had become Leipziger Platz, a private park for the new bourgeoisie [1.24]. Schinkel's passionate visions for the Achteck end in this modest bridge to the nineteenth century, at the threshold to industrial culture and the new commercial city. It marks the decline of the metaphysical, the demise of romanticism, and the inception of pragmatism and socialism.

1.24
The Potsdam Gates in 1833 from
a popular collection of Berlin views.
The gates and the garden have
just been completed.

1830s

Around the constraining figure of the Achteck a pattern begins to emerge that reveals an increasing instability in the ordering of reality. Gilly's abstraction of place from the influences of myth and nature was met by its antithesis in the towering metaphysics of Schinkel's thousand-foot spire. Yet both were visions of freedom. The underlying problem was in the limits of the language of architecture, limits to its ability to represent ideology and influence political progress and revolution. By what means could these elaborate and ancient harmonies of forms and symbols, devoted throughout their histories to the power of kings or gods, enhance the projects of reason or liberty? Where were the artistic and institutional forms that would reflect and shape the movement of the masses?

Gilly conceived of removing all past meanings from architecture to create a universal structure of pure geometry and reason, free to find its significance in the order of the new age. But in his desire he could not escape the limits of an autocracy. The rational order in his project would simply have replaced the order of gods and kings in its dominance over the culture. He could not have anticipated that the struggle for liberty would retain little connection to the project of reason. Schinkel, with subtlety and precision, attempted a complex transformation in architecture through the marriage of reason to the natural "gothic" order of the people. But in *Triumphbogen* he seems to have recognized that architecture could only be a servant to the plays of political culture, an emblematic background to the more complex realities of social upheaval.[43]

Yet, as time moved around this place, past intentions remained continually present. The flourish of liberalism released in the aftermath of war withered as the Crown reestablished its authority. It withered but did not die, and the struggle to keep alive the demands for free institutions and political representation led to decades of destructive urban unrest. As the liberals met with increasing political suppression they turned their concern to the conditions of the Berlin poor where disease fed on the rapidly forming slums, and the omnipresence of death turned desperation into violence. These were people weakened by the dependency of feudalism.

It all came to a bloody climax in the Revolution of 1848.[44] The heaviest street fighting was among the barricades and slums east of the city. Schinkel's gates were undefended but Leipzigerstrasse was blocked to the east. It was a popular uprising repeating the cries for political freedom and for German unity. It united the disaffected liberals with the urban poor. Gottfried Semper, a protégé of Schinkel,[45] Richard Wagner, and many other notables were to be seen building the barricades shoulder to shoulder with the nameless proletariat. The act of building the barricades, of taking and ripping up all the moveable objects in the city – wagons, furniture, sheds, posts, fences, paving slabs, and cobbles – and recombining them into walls behind which the battles could be fought, anticipated both physically and symbolically the intense desire of the masses to oppose the absolute power of the monarchy. The project of freedom by necessity had to attack and undermine autocratic structure in every form, particularly in the order and architecture of the new city.

The revolution was brutally suppressed by the king's troops to the horror of the liberals, severing the fragile relationship they had established with the Crown since the Wars of Liberation. While the Crown became increasingly conservative and removed from the new city life, the liberal cause was divided. Many deserted when faced with the prospect of sharing power with the poor and uneducated. Many idealists, however, dissatisfied with the narrowness of the cause, turned to socialism and the vision of Karl Marx. Kaiser Wilhelm I (1797-1888), upon succeeding his brother in 1861, undid the modest gains in freedom that had settled the turmoil of 1848. By 1870 he had united the German states and reclaimed belief in his divine right and holy mission to reestablish an omnipotent German empire, a project intensified by his grandson Kaiser Wilhelm II (or "Darling Billy," as his aunt Queen Victoria might have it) when he came to power in 1888 in the fortuitous and expedient alliance of the Crown with industrial capitalism.

Toward the twentieth century, it was the growth of commerce and the production of new wealth, directed by the order of industry,[46] that temporarily eased the deprivations stemming from the ancient concentrations of wealth and power. In Berlin, beginning at the Potsdam Gates, the railway revolutionized migration, swelling the population with rural workers carrying to the city dreams of liberty and prosperity and little else, an ever-expanding stream of migrants dammed in place with a constantly disaffected proletariat [1.25].[47] To the conflict posed in *Triumphbogen* between imperialism and the will of the people was added the project of industry, and all the notions of a stable reality held by architecture were being lost as the products of the factories began to entertain and order the masses to their own end.

1.25
In this drawing by an unknown artist from 1860, Berlin's first railway line, established in 1838, runs into Potsdamer Platz from the north on tracks placed just within the old customs wall. The railroad became the basis of Berlin's industry. Here, the city has become increasingly occupied by trade and the populace has moved westward.

1860

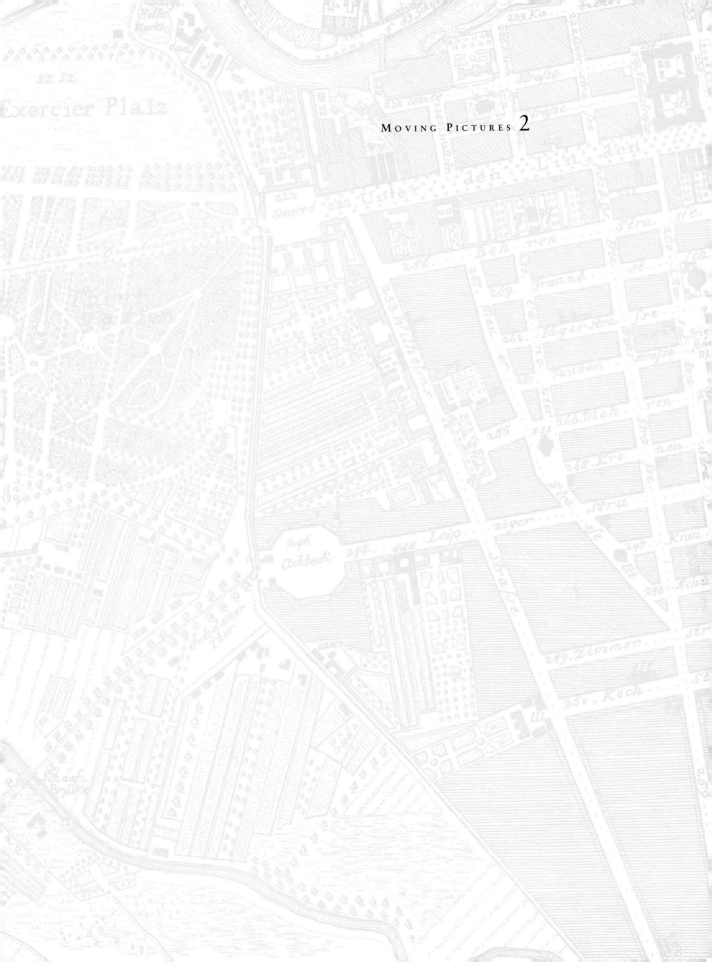

1915

2.1
Leipziger Platz and
Potsdamer Platz from
the air in 1915.

What follows are as images and notes from a scrapbook. So little survives of the past that any attempt at recollection is by necessity an assortment of scraps. They are documents of a passage through time in and around Leipziger Platz and its alter ego on the west side of the gates, Potsdamer Platz, which were shaped not from abstraction and idealism but out of the demands of commerce. Together, they reveal the hidden nature of change. And these were to be times of disturbing change, indeed. Wrote one critic of Berlin culture, Walter Benjamin:

Just as all things, in a perpetual process of mingling and contamination, are losing their intrinsic character while ambiguity displaces authenticity, so is the city.[1]

If one considers the perception of reality as a wave-like force, changed as it is refracted through the different mediums of power and faith, then architecture is its disordered residue, a residue made increasingly relative by time. The progression of realities from the nineteenth into the twentieth century can be examined as layers of this residue, surviving for the most part in photographs. These are presented along with the few drawings and paintings that seem to represent extremes of emotion unseen by the photographs. In contrast, however, the photographs offer evidence of time passing, disturbing the imagination with a direct sense of loss. They are representations of reality from one place at one time which can never be reconstructed. Photographs of places become, in time, complex documents of the conflicting ideals in the order of reality. They provide painful evidence of the uncontrollable and often unacknowledged forces below the surface of experience, which may erupt when least expected to destroy the promise of a time and weaken the strength of desire.

2.2
The Potsdam Gates
in 1900.

1900

1913

A VIEW DOWN POTSDAMERSTRASSE TOWARD LEIPZIGER
PLATZ

2.3
Potsdamerstrasse,
looking north towards
Potsdamer Platz, 1913.
In the foreground is
the bridge over the
Landwehrkanal where
it passes under
Potsdamerstrasse,

Potsdamerstrasse could be a
street in any of the new commercial cities [2.3]. It is defined by the rails of
the streetcars, and is as much a product of industry as the factories, a place
shaped to house, service, and entertain the increasingly expanding and
consuming bourgeoisie. It mimics the boulevards of Paris as a convenient
path for troop movements and trolley cars.

This is a street constructed in its every detail to support and
encourage trade. All who grew up here following the last decades of the
nineteenth century know the city only as a theater of purchases, and within
its streets products are thrust at passersby and the walls speak.[2] The texts on
Potsdamerstrasse that day in 1913 still read clearly: Max Dryer, Pianos and
Grand Pianos; Stutterheim and Company, Mortgages and Building Loans. On
the next block Neufeld's offers more pianos and Rosenfeld's enameled
bronzes. The office of Lanzsch and Co. is in the trees, as are the stationers,
the silk mercers, the photographers, the linen drapers, the milliners, and
costumiers. Above the shops in the many old homes, the owners are content
to co-exist with commerce. There is nothing to be lost in trade. Their
incomes are all connected to the activities of the street below and the public
face of their apartments is worn like a good coat.

On the surface of this fortunate part of the city, nothing is
enhanced save a complacent consumption of the products of industry.
Underneath, however, in the interiors of the apartments, a profound change
is taking place. These newly affluent citizens – freed for the first time in their
history from the burden of mere survival, confident and self-aware and
married to all the many new products of industry – construct in their private

rooms a personal universe. In it they gather scenes and objects from remote places and pasts. Drawing rooms, dining rooms, and bedrooms all have become boxes in a world theater.[3] Behind the image of the photograph personal realities are being constructed to ease repression and externalize desire, to stimulate erotic or exotic dreams, and to provide safe passage to the comforts of a dream world. Within the limits of things manufactured, domestic reality has become the property of individual consciousness, composed of objects freed from singular notions of virtue or progress, and no longer dependent on faith or the dictates of an aristocracy.

Yet many interiors, as in the dark sanctuaries of ancient temples, indulge not in fantasy but in the illusion of an ordered reality, of time suspended. Some whisper in their desire for a selfish and godless immortality. Invisible in the photograph, but underlying and constraining the existence of all things within it, is the conservatism and the imperialism of the kaiser's world order.

The people in the photograph seem so familiar and full of character – uniformed maids, civil servants, carters, coachmen, and soldiers, walking or riding on trolleys, horses, buses, automobiles, carriages, trucks, and bicycles, all held in a confidence and energy appropriate at this insignificant moment in time. It is confidence made buoyant in the shift from a feudal order to an order of industrial capital. Yet, this manufactured world veils profound divisions between the extremes of affluence and poverty confused by the products of industry, a fissure between the conservative project of nationalism and royal predestination and the Marxist socialism uniting the laboring masses. Trapped in the divide, the middle classes seek security in privacy and invisibility.

2.4
Potsdamerstrasse, 1980.

1980

THE LATE AUTUMN

The city is like a chimera and the pursuit of its essential nature can be seen as a process of successive approximation. The photograph is of a narrow field of grass bordered by leafless trees [2.4]. It appears to be in a suburban area where the country and the city meet. The land on each side of the field is fenced. There are small buildings in the fields; they appear to be garages or workshops. To the right, mostly hidden by the trees, is a tall structure of an ambiguous nature. This is a nondescript place, without distinction, and only through the use of words and the telling of stories can it be given significance. But words only remotely represent reality. Words present not an approximation, but an independent existence which may entertain the imagination but which essentially create their own reality.

The photographer is a deceiver and he seeks to shock. We have seen this great street before; it has been reclaimed by nature. Trees preserve a memory now replanted, for this was once a grand boulevard in imitation of Paris; beneath the grass galloped horses, pulling carriages and carts, while trolley cars rolled by shops and cafes beneath the balconies of grand apartments. Fragments of the cobblestones and rails, the drains and sewers, and the curbs and conduits still lie beneath the grass, and out of view in the distance a wall blocks what was once a gateway to the city. A trace of the road moves through the wall and expands into the outline of an octagon. The significance of this photograph lies in the mind and in the imagination. This is Potsdamerstrasse in 1980.

1909

THE WILHELMINE PLAY

This is a drawing of an imaginary scene across Leipziger Platz to Potsdamer Platz [2.5]. It presents a fragment of Berlin in the dreams of Kaiser Wilhelm. Though gothic arcades extend around every face of the octagon, the restaging of Potsdamer Platz is Roman. Great temples would be built to house the many servants of royal capitalism. The road through Leipziger Platz is widened and marked along its ceremonial way by a parade of monuments from sacred and civic life. As it enters Potsdamer Platz, two votive columns carry tributes to the greatness of German kings.

The drawing was made by Bruno Schmitz, the kaiser's favorite

2.5
Bruno Schmitz, study for
the reconstruction of
Potsdamer Platz, 1909.

architect. Dominating his thoughts on Leipziger Platz is his major creative work, the Völkerschlacht in Leipzig.[4] It was to be the final mark of victory in the Wars of Liberation, but above all it would embody the metaphysics of the Wilhelmine Empire. As a compliment to the revival of Rome on Potsdamer Platz, the Völkerschlacht sought to resurrect the memory of earthly gods. It is a bell-like mountain carved from solid rock, enclosing a vast cave ringed by a circle of giant medieval warriors. Each warrior is embedded in a huge primeval head. It is the intense physical expression of the desire to regain the Holy Roman Empire of Karl dem Grossen, or Charlemagne, to forge a German nation preeminent in Europe and the world.

The monument was completed in the first months of 1914, and on July 28, 1914, Germany invaded Belgium; the war to end all wars had begun.

FRAUEN AM POTSDAMER PLATZ

On Potsdamer Platz, unconcerned with war, Ernst Ludwig Kirchner confronted what he both loathed and yet found irresistible – street life in the corrupt city. In Dresden he had painted in nature, seeking the expression of emotional freedom, seeking to be cleansed from the pollution of materialism.[5] To hold the immediacy of the moment this woodblock view south from the center of Potsdamer Platz was cut with the knife directly into the wood; sensual expression is all [2.6]. In the background is the Potsdamer Bahnhof, the railway station through which so many thousands have come to the city. A random array of predatory males circle the two women who stand on Schinkel's circle. Nothing is certain or clear – the print from the block is the reverse of reality. The Wilhelmine dream of an everlasting order is an absurdity in the face of the disturbed realities of everyday city life. Only an autocracy removed from circumstance could sustain such a fantasy. Only a plutocracy seduced by the illusions of the new materialism could be so blind.

From two million in 1900, Berlin's population began to soar. At the brink of war in 1914 it neared three million. Kirchner's city has become a voracious and pitiless organism, sucking the rural populations into its all-consuming maw – people drawn not so much by opportunity as by the pure spectacle of automobiles and elevated railways and department stores, the brilliant shows of wealth and invention, and electric lights and neon displays. They still dream of liberty and free association among a diverse mass of millions, far from the suffocating conventions of provincial life.

1914

2.6
Ernst Ludwig Kirchner,
Frauen am Potsdamer Platz
(Women on Potsdamer Platz),
woodcut, 1914.

2.7
The Wertheim Department
Store, 1914. Begun in 1896
and designed over several
years by the architect Alfred
Messel, it was completed
with great fanfare in 1904.

1914

THE WERTHEIM DEPARTMENT STORE FROM THE POTSDAM
GATES
The women in Kirchner's print
look through the Potsdam Gates and across Leipziger Platz to the view in the
photograph of Wertheim's Department Store, to some the greatest theater of
trade in pre-war Europe [2.7]. The Baedeker Guide of 1901 noted:

Wertheim's Emporium, erected by Messel in 1897 and enlarged in 1899, is an excellent type of modern

German commercial house. The front of the building which covers 9,000 square yards is 320 feet long

and consists throughout of granite pillars ornamented with metalwork; the back of the building in the

Voss Strasse is also worthy of notice. The interior well repays a visit; visitors need not make any

purchase. The glass-covered inner court contains a statue of industry by Manzel and pictures of

harbors by Koch and Gehrke; in the west portion of the building is an art salon.

Nowhere in the Western world is the act of buying elevated to such
a refined experience; no stage so perfectly enhances what Marx called "the
theological whims of goods," the process by which the exchange value of
commodities is glorified by illusion, eclipsing their intrinsic value. The
massive arcade on the Achteck carries what appears to be a place of public
assembly beneath a great roof, a recollection of the medieval hall of the craft
guilds and a subtle symbol of a time when labor was dignified in the national
history. Wertheim's is, in all its parts, illusion in the service of consumption.

There is all around an absurd proliferation of unnecessary things
existing merely to be consumed. For those who can afford to buy, consumption requires a new form of obedience to authority and, in a paradox of
freedom, it nurtures the lower classes into conservatism. But for those too
poor to buy, it pushes their already marginal position within the new scheme
of things to a breaking point.

The Wertheim Department Store,
interior view of the Grosser Lichthof,
the great roof-lit hall at the center
of the store, 1914.

1914

WERTHEIM'S ENSHRINES THE PRODUCTS OF INDUSTRY

In the interior of Wertheim's the illusion
changes [2.8]. The noble public face is a mask behind which is concealed a
sensual pleasure palace. In cultivating the aura in which the value of goods is
glorified, the merchant has surrounded the objects of desire with feelings of
the exotic, the delightful, the slightly mysterious, and the sinful. The interior
is a brilliant fusion of realities drawn from the world's expositions and

advances in science and engineering, garnished with a hint of the oriental bazaar. Under the great roof-lit halls, soft-voiced salesmen serve as intermediaries in elevating the worth of objects, and the act of buying and selling is performed as an act of worship.

Architecture has moved far from the simple, heroic constructions of Friedrich Gilly. It has moved from being an art capable of making the transitory permanent to become itself a product of the transitory. Yet, some believe the power to invent complex allegories and to tell rich and wonderful lies, for whatever reason, is architecture's greatest strength. Architecture, after all, has always sought to coerce and deceive in the interest of the ambitions of one minority or another, and the amorality of this cause has rarely detracted from the pleasure in the experience.

1917 - 18

2.9
Georg Grosz,
Widmung an Oskar Panizza
(Requiem for Oscar Panizza)
oil on canvas, 1917-18.

WIDMUNG AN OSKAR PANIZZA

Requiem for Oscar Panizza is everywhere in the center of Berlin in deliberate chaos, in a riotous dance of death and life [2.9]. Georg Grosz was discharged in madness from the army so he could contemplate the madness in the world. He said he began this painting in 1917 and completed it before the war's end. It anticipates not just the defeat of Germany but the shattering of bourgeois confidence. It is the dialectical act of the cynic undermining any path to reason. It is the whining of the deceived bourgeoisie.

While the paint is still wet the kaiser has fled, and the veil of Wilhelmine desire has been swept away.[6] The exhausted German war machine conceded defeat in the signing of the armistice on November 11, 1918. In the end, the war killed and maimed forty million people. It utterly destroyed one illusion only to provoke a thousand others.

2.10
A map of revolutionary
activity throughout
Berlin between November
1918 and January 1919

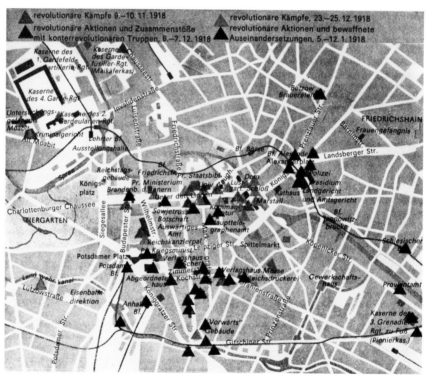

1918 - 19

THE SPARTACIST UPRISING

A political map of Berlin in turmoil shows
the revolutionary bases and barricades around Leipziger and Potsdamer Platz
between November 1918 and January 1919 [2.10].[7] The city in the days after
the end of the war is in shock and near madness. For the many returning
from years of battle, the collapse of social order in the city is like the
bursting of a dam. All the pent up anger and frustration rages in a torrent of
violence led by the Socialists under the Spartacist banner of Karl Liebknecht
and Rosa Luxemburg. They rise to prevent the forces of capitalism from
occupying the center of power. They rise for the idea of a worker's state.
They are defeated by a government militia of co-opted ex-soldiers.
Liebknecht and Luxemburg are arrested and killed by their military captors,
their bodies found in the Landwehr Canal near where it passes under
Potsdamerstrasse.

VISIONS FROM POTSDAMER PLATZ I

A watercolor painting by Hans Scharoun and a charcoal drawing by Mies van der Rohe are visionary images from two young architects in the spring of 1919, monuments to be seen across the city from Potsdamer Platz [2.11-12]. They are reflections of the desire to create objects whose powerful and virtuous presence would reform and restore society. They are "stadtkrone," city crowns, cathedrals of a new beginning and a new age.

Scharoun's drawing burns with the intensity of ecstatic revelation; it is an object of sensual freedom, of solitary genius, of purification – a biblical burning willing the age of Dionysus. The drawing by Mies is a silent scream for reason and order in the midst of chaos. Utterly devoid of sensuality, its passions lay in the belief in an ultimate reality. Both architects believe they have created allegories of the ideal political structure. Both refuse to speak with the language of history, yet in their silence they present a thesis and anti-thesis in reality. For Scharoun, the future is to be founded in sensual experience, in an existential fusion of the social masses. For Mies, the future is to be disciplined by the past in the ordered harmonics of geometric reason.

2.11
Hans Scharoun,
study for a monument
watercolor, 1919.

2.12
Ludwig Mies van der Rohe,
elevation study for the
Friedrichstrasse Office Building
project, 1919.

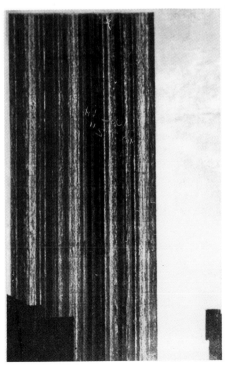

1919

2.13
Adolf Hitler,
studies for a triumphal arch
and a great hall, 1924.

VISIONS FROM POTSDAMER PLATZ II

In the summer of 1924, while dictating *Mein Kampf* in the Landsberg Fortress, Adolf Hitler makes a number of small drawings. Some are simply doodles of personal dreams, but two in particular are conceived and framed in his imagination as a counter to the disorder destroying the nation [2.13]. The economy has collapsed under the crushing burden of reparations,[8] and the collapse of all order releases the nation into a world without constraints, encouraging extremes of degradation, sensual experimentation, and exploitation. Hitler dreams, like Scharoun and Mies before him, of creating vast symbolic constructions to compel unity among the people, reform the state, and restore strength to the idea of Germany. The imperialism of his project differs from the Wilhelmine enterprise only in the pretense of displacing the will of the kaiser with the will of the masses. The great pantheon of his imagination is to become a "weldkrone," the crown of a new world order; the triumphal arch is to celebrate the victory and to remember all who would die for this cause. Architecture, above all, is to provide the order and the symbol for the redemption of the West.

2.14
Frames from Walter Ruttmann's
documentary film *Berlin, Die
Sinfonie der Grosstadt* (Berlin,
Symphony of a Great City), 1927.

These frames from Walter Ruttmann's film *Berlin, Symphony of a Great City* were taken from all around Potsdamer Platz [2.14]. In the film, Potsdamer Platz becomes the fulcrum in the acceleration of disjointed experiences in a day in the life of the city, a city moving out of the control of authority. Passages of experience and movement are assembled to present the dissonance of the new city life, a dissonance deeply disturbing to the predictable notions of order in the dreams of the petit bourgeois. Ruttmann's city no longer embodies any one simple idea. It cannot be known, save through the continually changing kaleidoscope of autonomous rhythms arising from the machines and their masters. Against the silhouette of Wertheim's, a specter of another age, the insane passage of cabs, buses, steam trains, and subways overwhelms all else in the play of the city. Slaves to the order of automation, the actors around the octagon dodge traffic, seek shelter from the rain, and fall back from the rush of the fire engines. In the vortex of motion and text, Potsdamer Platz frames the only words that move out of the action onto the screen: MORD, BÖRSE, HEIRAT . . . GELD, GELD, GELD (MURDER, STOCK MARKET, MARRIAGE . . . MONEY, MONEY, MONEY).[9]

The liberal capitalism of the Weimar Republic is creating a giddy and unstable freedom. Nothing has compensated for the loss of place and meaning. Although it has been ten years since the end of the war, the people still feel broken, and as disconnected as the rubble in the streets. City life can no longer be understood in terms of personal relationships but only in the random association between changing objects of desire; it has become a life of vicarious and empty excitement in time and movement. Architecture, history's most forceful instrument of permanence, disintegrates into commodification along with all else.

1927

DER KAUFMAN VON BERLIN

The opening was clearly a success. The theater
was crowded, but it was the vast photo-montage filling the whole stage that
left the deepest impression [2.15]. Laszlo Moholy-Nagy, a gifted teacher at the
Bauhaus, set the scene for Walter Mehring's *The Salesman from Berlin*,
publicly proclaiming the replacement of a singular dominant reality with the

2.15
Laszlo Moholy-Nagy,
photo-montage set for Walter
Mehring's *Der Kaufman von Berlin*
(The Salesman from Berlin),
1929.

1929

multiplicity of events and acts that have overwhelmed city life. He depicts a
fragmented city of actions and objects all mutually dependent, yet independent, and meaningful only in terms, some say, of their relativity in the
passages through space and time. For others, the set resembles a great barricade blocking the way to an ordered future. For the state to regain its purpose,
a clear and dominating order will have to be imposed on all things again.

1930

ON THE SOUTH SIDE OF POTSDAMER PLATZ

The photographer working in Berlin during the 1920s confronted a city that was becoming less and less able to be photographed. Persistent movement was eroding the idea of place. He stands exactly where Kirchner stood before him and sees a place of many realities [2.16]. On the right, the Pschorr Haus is met and opposed by the powerful lines of the Telschow Haus in which architecture has become a neutral presence whose surfaces carry the messages of a commercial city.[10] On the left, in the distance behind the city's first traffic light, between the Hotel Der Fürstenhof and the Potsdam Station, stands Haus Vaterland.

PICTURE POSTCARD OF HAUS VATERLAND FROM POTSDAMER PLATZ

The House of the Fatherland opened on the south side of Potsdamer Platz in September of 1928. The signs, brightly lit in the evening, read "Kempinski's House of the Fatherland" [2.17]. It is the creation of the great Jewish impresario and restaurateur Hans Kempinski, who took a dull collection of Wilhelmine entertainment halls and cafes and transformed them into a fantasy world. It is a sexual object; like a bordello, it allows for the purchase and consumption of sensual experiences. Masked balls are held in the court of the metallic palms, the gender of the guests as ambiguous as the vegetation. Movies are shown in a drum ringed by neon lights, insulated and isolated from the outer world. Despite Germany's travails, love of the fatherland can still be glorified for commercial gain. The whole concept, though vulgar, is full of the Wilhelmine spirit. In the view from Potsdamer Platz, Haus Vaterland almost looks like the work of Bruno Schmitz.

There is enough of a sense of indignation with the way the world has treated Germany that only nations which supported the kaiser's grand illusions have been allowed to take part in this fantasy – with the exception, that is, of the bounteous United States of America. France, Britain, and most of northern Europe have been excluded in favor of the Turkisches Cafe, a Spanish bodega under vast romanesque vaults, and a suitably rustic Hungarian village inn, the Puszta Czarda. The exuberance of the illusions grows in intensity the closer they come to the heart of the fatherland. In the Grinzinger Heuriger, a cafe, we sit in a wine garden in front of the painted Vienna woods looking at the evening panorama of the city. A model of Vienna in meticulous detail shows the city reconstructed, complete with tiny motor vehicles that move down the great boulevards under electric lamps the size of match sticks. In the Löwenbräu Bavarian beer hall we watch the sun rising on the Zugspitze mountain through a great window, capturing with radiant effect the rose veil that briefly seems to envelop all the world. And in the Rheinterrasse Cafe our hearts pound as we are subjected to a furious artifical storm that is staged every hour on the hour. And late at night, after wandering the city, we end up at the Wild West Bar and pretend to be Tom Mix. Those who may mistake all this for the pursuit of trivial entertainment will fail to see behind the theatrics the most alluring promise of modern technology and the gratification of the senses.

In all its deception, this is the authentic face of the modern age. In the cinemas and in the multiple illusions of Haus Vaterland, the people can forget or ignore the unresolved conflicts in the life of the city. What is, for the overly serious bourgeois intellectual, an all-consuming vortex of mindless illusion spiraling towards

1929

the fragmentation of city life, remains for the producers of the commercial city a wonderful explosion of synthetic realities relieving and veiling the actual conditions of life and work. The power of illusion satisfies and gratifies while offering sensual and unthreatening realities to be used and consumed by all. Loss of place and loss of meaning have been replaced by the commodification of reality, a much less ambitious project for the culture as a whole than the restoration of world order.

2.17
Picture postcard of Haus Vaterland
from Postdamer Platz, 1929.

1901

2.18
Potsdamer Platz, view
toward the north, 1901.

LOOKING NORTH FROM POTSDAMER PLATZ

These two photographs, taken thirty years apart, offer essentially the same perspective and contrast the radical shift in cultural perspectives [2.18]. In the first photograph, Schinkel's gate pavilions leading to Leipziger Platz are present but obscured by trees. On the right is the Hotel Der Fürstenhof, a building whose world view belongs to the middle of the previous century, a modest place content to lie in the background. On the corners opposite are two very similar hotels, the Bellevue and the Palast. Compared with the Fürstenhof, these are places that ask to be noticed and wear the masks of commercial enterprise. All of the objects in view are linked by a classical perspective with its promise of permanence and stability.

The players on this stage of desire wander casually across the streets, among traffic whose pace is little faster than footsteps. The tower of the Reichstag can be seen above the roofs of Bellevuestrasse. The mood is relaxed. There is clear diversity of style and class. Even in busy places people such as these know each other; shopkeepers wave, the carters and coachmen and drivers of trolley cars pass and greet and tease each other each day. All walk in different directions under the guidance of the Emperor.

1932

Looking North from Potsdamer Platz

In the view of 1932, the apartment building to the left has given way to a product of commerce, the beer hall, constructed by the Pschorr brewery and built in the form of a town hall, with tower, flag, and heraldic device over the entrance [2.19]. Drinking and eating are thus ennobled by the association with civic life. On the right, the Hotel Der Fürstenhof has metamorphosed into the fat child of consumerism. Competition with the Hotel Palast has driven architecture to consume space and to wear a modish dress. It is more concerned with energy and presence than with significance. Its surfaces are not made to be read, but merely to entertain. They stimulate the consumption of architectural language until it loses all meaning or reference. They convey the transformation from a literate architecture to a physical architecture, a passage from mind to body. A first reading sees its swollen form as a direct product of the demand for hotel accommodations resulting from the railway. But what lies behind the mask? Out of what desire has it been formed? The great new roof gives a late-medieval cap to the walls, which form a strange blend of the classical and the mechanical. This is a deliberate fantasy that destroys the constraints of language and style, and destroys the narrow frames within

2.19
Potsdamer Platz, view
toward the north, 1932.

which scholarship had limited the inheritance from past ages. It is a violation and a heresy, consuming the forms of past realities and giving freedom to our recollections of history. A second reading sees in the architectural form an act of cultural subversion, an act that makes possible a compounding of realities, an act that destroys the autocratic power of architecture and mocks its mysteries.

The Hotel Palast remains undisturbed. But the Grand Hotel Bellevue, sister to the Palast, has failed. Competition has driven it into bankruptcy. It has been replaced by an alien object, wholly in opposition to all that surrounds it. It will be called Columbus Haus. The new name conveys the promise of a new world.

Columbus Haus is the fruit of a deep dissatisfaction and of a desire for reform. The fantasies of Haus Vaterland no longer satisfy the dreams of an aggressive avant-garde willing the advent of a new age. The children of the conservative bourgeois seem driven to expiate an inherited guilt from their parents in their obsession to construct a future in the antithesis of Wilhelmine permanence.[11] They have revived in an extreme form the pre-industrial vision of modernism – the desire to abstract experience and reality from the polluting language and influence of commerce, and to reestablish what has never existed, a carte blanche for the future. The midnight revelers, after playing Tom Mix in the Wild West Bar, are confronted across the trolley rails of Potsdamer Platz by the zealous presence of Columbus Haus glowing under brilliant floodlights.

Yet, there was more substance to Haus Vaterland with its insignificant illusions than the intelligentsia recognized. The ephemeral pleasures and allegorical fantasies of Haus Vaterland and the other objects of the commercial city were not merely entertaining; in them, the illusion of reality was shaped for the first time to seduce rather than dominate a mass audience.

1932

2.20
Erich Mendelsohn,
Columbus Haus, 1932.

COLUMBUS HAUS

Into this vortex of mechanized consumption, of rocks and rivers, of conservatives and radicals, Columbus Haus serves as an object of redemption, a spatial synthesis through which the path to pure reason can be rediscovered [2.20]. It is the ultimate object of negation, conceived in rejection of the degeneration that obsessive consumption has caused to the culture. Its presence attempts to break the conspiracy between architecture and the persistence of the memory of Rome, the dangerous and uncontrollable evocation of ancient gods and mysteries. It is as if architecture had become naked, shedding all deception to purify itself and the city.

To the question "What time was this place?" the architect would answer "future time." To the question "What culture was this place?" the architect would answer "all cultures," an honest answer that belies the more complex philosophical dimension in his desire for a new order. The architect is Erich Mendelsohn, the most successful commercial architect in Berlin and a Jew.

2.21
George Hoyningen-Huene,
Josephine Baker, black-and-white
photograph, 1929.

GEORGE HOYNINGEN-HUENE'S *JOSEPHINE BAKER* IN BERLIN
In the popular imagination she is a slightly naughty cabaret dancer who dresses in bananas, but her raw sensuality and freedom to experience is the essence of the intellectual dreamer's romance with America [2.21]. Le Corbusier is obsessed with her body and even Vienna's moralizing architect, Adolf Loos, designs her a house in black and white, of a barely concealed sexuality. She gives tangible form to the character of the new order for the new age – the age of Columbus Haus.

1934

THE VIEW FROM POTSDAMER PLATZ

A military band is marching into Potsdamer Platz past Schinkel's Gates and crossing in front of Columbus Haus [2.22]. Hitler has moved into the old Chancellery on Voss Strasse, one block north of Leipziger Platz. It is winter and there is snow on the ground and already the imperial style of the new regime is emerging.

THE VIEW FROM POTSDAMER PLATZ

On the Hotel Palast, the facade of Wertheim's, and from the roofs and walls of every building down the length of Leipzigerstrasse hang the red, white, and black symbol of the state, the swastika [2.23]. Throughout the city center thousands upon thousands of swastikas redress reality. Its ancient mystical character gives a metaphysical dimension to the cultural revolution. Hitler's administration has occupied Columbus Haus, taken the assets of Haus Vaterland from the Kempinski family, and will remove the name from the walls.[12]

HAUS VATERLAND AT NIGHT

Haus Vaterland is no less an object of illusion than is Columbus Haus [2.24]. They are both rivers of a kind, flowing in opposition to autocratic order, both searching for the furthest extension of modern experience. Both emerge from Berlin's Jewish culture. The strength of Haus Vaterland is in its amoral speculation in all the pleasures of the modern age. The strength of Columbus Haus is in its desire for a state of clarity that has never existed. Dimly, behind the street sign on the left, a kiosk marked by an eagle and a swastika demands the help of all in the struggle against hunger and cold.

If architecture is all that remains when a culture fades away, it frequently leaves very little, and what survives can only provide an imperfect representation of those who built it. Yet, in its imperfection, architecture persists in touching the mind and placing the body in the world. A reality below the surface of things is continually felt, experienced, and interpreted. Experientially, architecture can indicate the paradigms by which we choose to live – between the plowed field and the forest, between a forced march and the freedom to wander, between walking and running and rioting and dancing. Evolution in nature is

imperceptibly slow. It is man's artifacts and acts which create the appearance of progress or regression. It is man's actions that extend the idea and experience of time beyond the rhythms of nature. In forty years the ideas that have shaped this double place of Potsdamer and Leipziger Platz have moved from the resurrection of the authority of history to the consumption of history to the rejection of history – from armor, to costume, to nakedness in which each change of garb leaves an ever-increasing state of confusion. Despite the passionate actions of Mendelsohn and others, the idea of architecture in this place has shifted from the desire for objects of eternal worth to the fabrication of genteel masks, disposable skins continually changing their form in the process of speculation and consumption. Architecture has begun to deceive in either abstraction or picturesque illusion, comforting and concealing the gathering opposition to the idea of freedom.

The city is thus dividing, but the nucleus of its power remains intractably conservative. A hundred years of refusal to resolve the conflict between the autocrats and the masses is blurred in the drunken frenzy that propels Berlin into the 1930s, stimulated by the indulgence of industrial capitalism, blurred until refocused by Hitler and the project of national socialism.

The segment of Albert Speer's plan
for the reconstruction of Berlin around
Leipziger Platz, 1940. Speer's plan is
darkly shaded.

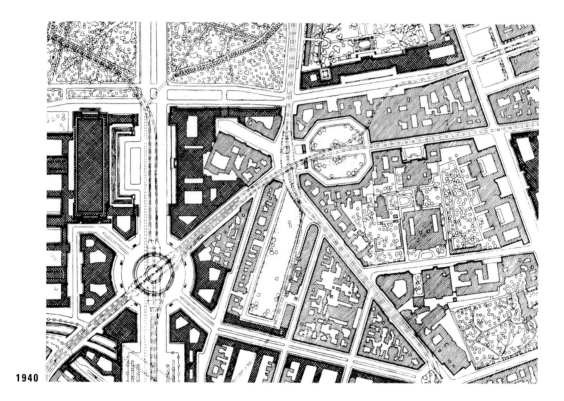

1940

Between the eighth and ninth of November 1923, a small group
from the National Socialist German Workers' Party attempted to seize the
government of Bavaria. They declared a new republic under the presidency of
Adolf Hitler.[1] The Beer Hall Putsch proved to be a fiasco and was quickly
put down by the militia. In February of 1924, Hitler was put on trial for high
treason. The motives of the conspirators found sympathy with the judiciary,
and Hitler served only nine months of a five-year sentence in the Landsberg
Fortress. In detention, with the help of prison colleagues, he dictated the first
volume of his political philosophy, *Mein Kampf* (My Struggle). The forces of
materialism corrupting the city were vividly in his mind:

*Yet, how truly deplorable the relationship between state buildings and private buildings has become
today! If the fate of Rome should strike Berlin, future generations would someday admire the department stores of a few Jews as the mightiest work of our era and the hotels of a few corporations as the
characteristic expression of the culture of our times. . . .*

Thus our cities of the present lack the outstanding symbol of national community which, we must therefore not be surprised to find, sees no symbol of itself in the cities. The inevitable result is a desolation whose practical effect is the total indifference of the big city dweller to the destiny of his city. This too is a sign of our declining culture and our general collapse. The epoch is stifling in the pettiest utilitarianism, or better expressed, in the service of money.[2]

As he wrote of the chaotic condition of German culture and argued for *lebensraum* (living space) for the German peoples in the east, not just words but images filled his mind, images of the great buildings that would be the fruits of the mission that lay ahead. He made two drawings – one of a domed hall, the other of a triumphal arch – which were to remain with him till the last hours of his life [3.2]. It seems that they almost drew themselves, such is the ease and confidence with which the architecture is described. They made Hitler's political project concrete and set the stage for the future. The hall would be at the center of the new political order, and the arch would pay tribute to the victims of the struggle by which the new order would be established. Their style was imperial; their scale, judged by the ant-like creatures marching toward their bases, was astounding. Their site was to be the center of Berlin. Years later Hitler would share these two drawings with the architect Albert Speer.[3]

From the early days several architects played a formative role in the National Socialist movement. Professor Paul Schultze-Naumberg was an architect and a rabid anti-semite. He led the League of Struggle for German Culture, and designed buildings in a dull romanticized vernacular. Alfred Rosenberg, who studied architecture in Riga and later in Moscow under German professors, was the Nazi Party Reichsleiter for Ideological Indoctrination and editor of the official party paper *Der Voelkische Beobachter* (The Racist Observer). "Architecture," he wrote, "is the first art on its way to becoming honest again." He was one of Hitler's earliest followers and as savage an opponent of Christianity as he was of Judaism. His book *The Myth of the 20th Century*, published in 1930, sold over 300,000 copies and established him in the popular imagination as the Party's grand visionary. However, Hitler claimed only a passing knowledge of the work. He called it "stuff nobody can understand" written by "a narrow-minded Baltic German who thinks in horribly complicated terms" and "a relapse into medieval notions!"[4] Though many played a part in orchestrating the vision of national socialism, Hitler was the conductor.

1924

3.2
Adolf Hitler,
studies for a triumphal arch
and a great hall, 1924.

Throughout his life Hitler preserved the feeling of being the architect "manqué." In *Mein Kampf* he wrote that in the years 1909 and 1910 "I painted to make a living and studied architecture for pleasure . . . [and] my faith grew that my beautiful dream for the future would become reality after all, even though this might require long years. I was firmly convinced that I should someday make a name for myself as an architect."[5] He applied to the Vienna Academy but was denied admission. The problem was not a lack of skill, but inadequate high school preparation. Yet, fate could have interceded in other ways, as Speer observed much later. If, before the Great War of 1914-1918, instead of drawing city views for picture postcards, Hitler had been offered even a modest building commission, the history of the world might have been profoundly different.

There is in all of his writings a strong use of metaphor and idea construction. His words vividly represent the physical order underlying the character of his global project. The style of its architecture would, by necessity, be classical – not only for the use of heroic forms, but because the Greeks and the Germans were racially linked:

It is . . . no wonder that each politically heroic age in its art immediately seeks bridges to a not less heroic past. The Greeks and the Romans suddenly become very near, because all their roots lie in a founding race, and therefore, the immortal accomplishments of the ancient peoples have an attractive influence on their racially related descendants. Therefore, since it is better to imitate something good than to produce something new but bad, surviving intuitive creations of these peoples can today doubtless fulfill their educative leading mission through style." [6]

It would also be classical because the Roman ideal had been destroyed by Jews and Christians and their degrading promotion of equality under the worship of a single God:

It's since St. Paul's time that the Jews have manifested themselves as a religious community, for until then they were only a racial community. St. Paul was the first man to take account of the possible advantages of using a religion as a means of propaganda. If the Jew has succeeded in destroying the Roman Empire, that's because St. Paul transformed a local movement of Aryan opposition to Jewry into a supra-temporal religion, which postulates the equality of all men amongst themselves and their obedience only to God. This is what caused the death of the Roman Empire. [7]

Only Imperial Rome had opposed the multiple corruption of Judeo-Christian Bolshevism:

Christianity is a prototype of Bolshevism: the mobilization by the Jew of the masses of slaves with the object of undermining society. Thus one understands that the healthy elements of the Roman world were proof against this doctrine. [8]

The lessons of history showed that:

A very large measure of individual liberty is not necessarily the sign of a high degree of civilization. On the contrary, it is the limitation of this liberty within the framework of an organization which incorporates men of the same race, which is the real pointer to the degree of civilization attained.[9]

Explicitly from the texts, Hitler saw himself as the recreator of the material world, an architect-demiurge called upon by the forces of history and culture to undertake the salvation of Western civilization. Among the notes from 1924 for *Mein Kampf* are:

> *Parliamentarianism as*
>
> *vocation and trade*
>
> *Salvation through Parliament*
>
> *impossible*
>
> *Changing the foundations*
>
> *The programme of a new*
>
> *Movement – the D.A.P.*
>
> *Minority not majority makes*
>
> *world history*
>
> *Not the majority will save Germany*
>
> *Not the dictatorship of the Jews*
>
> *but the dictatorship of genius*
>
> *See Rome*
>
> *Today we take our stand as apostles*
>
> *We aim to build a new age*
>
> *And hope, that whoever now declares*
>
> *I must make a clean break*
>
> *will also declare I am a German.*[10]

"The dictatorship of genius" is precisely how Hitler conceived of his calling. It echoes Nietzsche's call for the new "lords of the earth" in the *Will to Power*:

A new vast aristocracy based upon the most severe self-discipline, in which the will of philosophical men of power and artist-tyrants will be stamped upon thousands of years: a higher species of man which, thanks to their preponderance of will, knowledge, riches, and influence, will avail themselves of democratic Europe as the most suitable and supple instrument they can have for taking the fate of the earth into their own hands, and working as artists upon man himself. Enough! The time is coming for us to transform all our views on politics.[11]

The idea of re-shaping humanity occurs frequently in nineteenth-century German texts. Schiller wrote that when an artist sets his hand to material he:

. . . has no qualms about doing violence to it; he merely avoids displaying that violence. He will however seek to deceive any defender of the freedom of the material by pretending to respect it.

It is a quite different matter with the pedagogical and political artist, who uses human beings both as his raw material and as his project. Here purpose returns to the material, and only because the whole serves the parts may the parts lend themselves to the whole.

Thus the artist of the state must have a quite different respect for his materials than the sculptor pretends to have for his. He must protect the peculiarity and personality of his material, not subjectively, in order to produce a deceiving effect in the senses, but objectively for its true inner-self.[12]

This echoes Goethe in calling for the artist of the state to protect the personality of the material and to reveal its "true inner-self," whereas Hitler would reform the state with the procrustean imposition of imperial order unconcerned with its natural character. "Politics, too, is an art," wrote Joseph Goebbels,[13] Nazi Minister of Propaganda, in 1933, "perhaps the highest and most far reaching one of all, and we who shape modern German politics feel ourselves to be artistic people, entrusted with the great responsibility of forming out of the raw material of the masses a solid, well-wrought structure of a *volk*."[14]

Architect as demiurge, or demiurge as architect, Hitler's actions can all be seen as aspects of artistic construction. He envisioned himself first as architect of the reconstruction of the German people, then as architect for the reconstruction of the world. The destruction of people and places he considered undesirable was equivalent to the demolition of useless or dangerous structures. His armies moving into battle were, in his imagination, as construction crews setting forth to lay the foundation for an eternal future. The waste of great cities was an effective by-product, cleansing reality of regressive memory. His great project would end instability in the culture of the state, end the progressive waste of time, and establish an eternal past against which all future actions could be measured. "In the midst of peace time," Speer wrote after the war, "while continually proclaiming his desire for international reconciliation [Hitler] was planning buildings expressive of an imperial glory which could be won only by war."[15] They were wars waged for empire, but beyond empire lay the true object of Hitler's desire — to be the architect of the salvation of Western man.

The two drawings from the Landsberg Fortress, made in the midst of an intensity of visions, reveal the desire of an architect. They are windows into the soul. "I never doubted," Hitler told Speer, "that someday I would build those two edifices."[16]

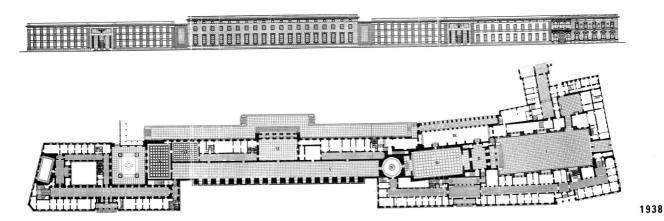

1938

3.3
Albert Speer,
Reich Chancellery,
elevation and plan,
1938.

On January 30, 1933, German President Paul von Hindenburg appointed Hitler chancellor, and Hitler moved into the old Chancellery north of Leipziger Platz on Voss Strasse. On June 30, 1934, Hitler purged all rivals both in the Party and in the state. On the death of Hindenburg on August 2, 1934, Hitler proclaimed himself head of state.

Eva Braun, Hitler's mistress, wrote in her diary on February 15, 1935: "Berlin seems to be on the cards at last. But until I'm in the Chancellery I shan't believe it. Let's hope it's going to be fun." Then on the 28th of May, 1935, she wrote: "Dear Lord, I am afraid he won't answer today. If only someone would help me, everything is so terrible and hopeless. Perhaps my letter reached him at the wrong moment. Perhaps I oughtn't to have written at all. Whatever happens uncertainty is more unbearable than a sudden end. Dear Lord help me, let me speak to him this day, tomorrow will be too late. I have decided on 35 pills, this time I want to make 'dead certain.' If only he would ring me."[17]

In January of 1938, Hitler commissioned the architect Albert Speer to design a new Reich Chancellery [3.3]. The commission was for an extension of the old Chancellery which had housed the chief minister of the state since the nineteenth century, and by Hitler's decree all aspects of the new construction had to be completed within one year. Speer ordered demolition on the site within hours of receiving the commission and quickly established his reputation as a brilliant manager. Over 4,500 workers of all trades labored on the site for two shifts every day throughout the year, and many thousands more throughout the nation worked with equal intensity to produce the furnishings and decorations.

It was a mature design for the thirty-four-year-old Speer. The land north of Voss Strasse had been occupied since the eighteenth century, first by the large palaces of the urban aristocracy, and subsequently by the many branches of the Prussian state government. Speer's plan gave unity not only to Voss Strasse, but also created a formal garden and garden facade. The central grouping of offices linked the two main wings in an order of restrained classicism. The western end faced Columbus Haus [3.4]. The wings were dominated by brutally powerful portals, showing a clear debt to Hitler's first architect, Paul Troost [3.5]. Their spare classical forms carrying the great rising eagle have come to be seen as the quintessential expression of the order and character of national socialism.

1939

3.4
Albert Speer,
Reich Chancellery,
Voss Strasse facade,
1939.

3.5
Albert Speer,
Reich Chancellery,
Voss Strasse portal.

The plan was an explicit presentation of the tactics of power. All was secondary to constraining the passage through time and space for visitors to Hitler's chamber. Speer wrote of his intention:

The oblong site was an invitation to string a succession of rooms on a long axis. I showed Hitler my design: From Wilhelmplatz, an arriving diplomat drove through great gates into a court of honor [3.6]. By way of an outside staircase he first entered a medium-sized reception room from which double doors almost seventeen feet high opened into a large hall clad in mosaic [3.7]. He then ascended several steps, passed through a round room with a domed ceiling, and saw before him a gallery four hundred and eighty feet long [3.8]. Hitler was particularly impressed by my gallery because it was twice as long as the Hall of Mirrors at Versailles. Deep window niches were to filter the light, creating that pleasant effect I had seen in the Salle de Bal at the Palace of Fontainebleau.[18]

3.7
Albert Speer,
Reich Chancellery,
The Mosaic Hall.

3.8
Albert Speer,
Reich Chancellery,
The Marble Gallery.

Hitler's impression was quite specific: "On the long walk from the entrance to the reception hall they'll get a taste of the power and grandeur of the German Reich!"[19] He particularly enjoyed the highly polished marble floor. "That's exactly right," he said. "Diplomats should have practice moving on a slippery surface."[20]

Construction began in January 1938, and on March 13, 1938, German troops marched into Austria. The work was essentially complete by November 10, 1938, the date of Kristallnacht, when Jewish shops were smashed and synagogues burned throughout the nation. To mark the completion of the work on January 9, 1939, several days earlier than scheduled, Hitler addressed the thousands of assembled artists, craftsmen, and construction workers:

I stand here as representative of the German people. And whenever I receive anyone in the Chancellery it is not the private individual Adolf Hitler who receives him, but the Leader of the German nation – and therefore it is not I who receive him but Germany through me. For that reason I want these rooms to be in keeping with their high mission.

Every individual has contributed to a structure that will outlast the centuries and will speak to the posterity of our times. This is the first architectural creation of the new, great German Reich! [21]

The Chancellery's great gallery appears immediately after passing through the circular vestibule. In the distance, the door is open. It is not Hitler's office but the reception room. Hitler's study is behind the third door on the right. The experience is one of anticipation and surprise [3.9].

There is a paradox in the attempt to create in less than twelve months a symbolic construction embodying a nation's history and culture. Hitler's office [3.10] is a profoundly substantial place – marbles in black and red, bronze doors, exquisite furniture, objets d'art, tapestries, paintings, and medallions, all convey a complex and forceful mythology. Behind the desk is a door leading to a small study. Only in this retreat is the Führer at one with his dreams and desires. The portrait bust in the corner is of Hindenburg. There is absolute silence.

Hitler is standing behind his chair [3.11] looking towards the infor-

mal seating arranged around the fireplace. Over the mantel is a portrait of Bismarck by Lenbach. The medallions above the doors represent allegorical premonitions of war and the inevitability of death. On the great marble table in the months and years to come, he would clear space for Speer's drawings of the project for the rebuilding of Berlin, and they would spend hours together dreaming of the possible. "When one enters the Reich Chancellery," Hitler told his friends, "one should have the feeling that one is visiting the master of the world."

Hitler's armies occupied Prague in March of 1939, and invaded Poland on the first of September, forcing Britain and France, on September 3, 1939, to declare war on Germany.

Speer was an architect of exceptional competence, and a perfect complement to Hitler's desire. Skilled, sensual, erudite, and willing to surrender his own ego and his own vision to those of Hitler's, he must have seemed a godsend. He had demonstrated his power as the orchestrator of the Reichsparteitag, the annual National Socialist Party rally held on Zeppelinfield in Nuremberg. His design for the Haupttribune on Zeppelinfield was completed in 1934 [3.12], and in the rallies of 1935 and 1937 the imagination of the world was touched by a theatrical construction conceived by Speer in which more than a hundred search lights were beamed skywards, creating what the press called a "Cathedral of Ice" [3.13].[22] Speer reflected on these events much later: "I feel strangely stirred by the idea that the most successful architectural creation of my life is a chimera, an immaterial phenomenon."

1937

3.12
Albert Speer,
Haupttribune, Zeppelinfield,
Nuremberg, 1937.

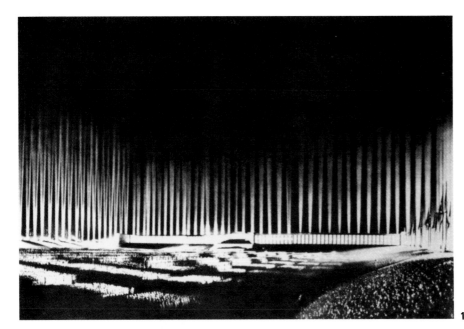

3.13
The Cathedral of Ice, Speer's
production of a Nazi Party rally at the
Zeppelinfield, Nuremberg, 1937.

1937

BERLIN PLAN

In the summer of 1937, Hitler commissioned Speer to prepare plans for the construction of a new Berlin. Hitler had a clear historical sense of the role of the omnipotent leader in reforming the city. He is recorded as remarking: "It may well be that it is impossible for any city to achieve an appearance which is pleasing to our sense of culture, unless at sometime or other some great man has breathed his inspiration into its walls."[23]

At a dinner party on October 21, 1941, where the special guest was Reichsführer Heinrich Himmler,[24] Hitler discussed frankly the making of war in relation to the role he would play after his victory. His goal was the shaping of a world culture:

The means I shall set in operation to this end will far surpass those that were necessary for the conduct of this war. I wish to be a builder . . . . My reaction is that of a peasant whose property is attacked and who leaps to arms to defend his patrimony. This is the spirit in which I make war. For me it's a means to other ends. A day will come when battles will be forgotten. But the monuments we shall have built will defy the challenge of time . . . . Berlin will one day be the capital of the world.[25]

3.14
    Albert Speer,
    plan of the Nordsüd Achse,
    or North-South Axis, 1940.
    Leipziger Platz appears just
    to the east of the Runder Platz,
    the circular plaza along the
    great drive that connects
    the Triumphal Arch and the
    Great Hall.

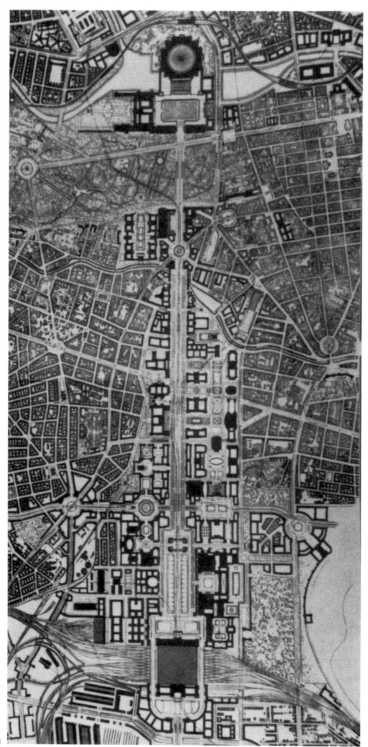

1940

On his vision for Berlin he was explicit:

What is ugly in Berlin, we shall suppress. Nothing will be too good for the beautification of Berlin . . . .

One will arrive there along wide avenues containing the Triumphal Arch, the Pantheon of the Army,

the Square of the People – things to take your breath away! It's only thus that we shall succeed in

eclipsing our only rival in the world, Rome . . . . Let [the center of the new Berlin] be built on such a

scale that St. Peter's and its Square will seem like toys in comparison!

It was the vision from the Landsberg Fortress:

For material, we'll use granite. The vestiges of the German past, which are found on the plains to the

North, are scarcely time-worn. Granite will ensure that our monuments last forever. In ten thousand

years they'll be still standing just as they are, unless meanwhile the sea has once again covered our

plains.[26]

In 1933, the city planners for Berlin had proposed a master plan for
the city under the title Nordsüd Achse (North-South Axis). Speer carried
many elements of this plan forward, including a series of circular and square
plazas,[27] but his program differed from the city's in one fundamental way –
the North-South Axis would not become a traffic artery, but a great ritual
passage through the city [3.14]. "A thing," as Hitler said, "to take your breath
away," and a place to eclipse the memory of Rome:

As Hitler told me, his conception of an enormously wide avenue went back to the early twenties, when

he began to study the various plans for Berlin, found them all inadequate, and was impelled to develop

his own ideas. Even then, he said, he had decided to shift the Anhalter and Potsdam railroad stations

to the south of Tempelhof Field. This would release broad strips of trackage in the center of the city,

so that with only a little further clearing, a magnificent avenue lined with impressive buildings could

be built, three miles long.

Speer continued:

To be sure, all the architectural proportions of Berlin would be shattered by two buildings that Hitler

envisaged on this new avenue. On the northern side near the Reichstag, he wanted a huge meeting hall,

a domed structure into which St. Peter's Cathedral in Rome would have fitted several times over . . . .

To balance this structure Hitler wanted an arch of triumph four hundred feet high. 'At least that will

be a worthy monument to our dead of the world war. The names of our dead, all 1,800,000 of them,

will be chiseled in the granite,' said Hitler . . . . He handed me two sketches drawn on small cards.

'I made these drawings ten years ago. I've always saved them, because I never doubted that some day I would build these two edifices. And this is how we will carry it out now.'[28]

By 1939, a great model for the project had been built [3.15], and in the midst of a rapidly escalating war Hitler's vision for Berlin became his ruling passion:

Hitler's favorite project was our model city, which was set up in the former exhibition rooms of the Berlin Academy of Arts.[29] *In order to reach it undisturbed, he had doors installed in the walls between the Chancellery and our building and a communicating path laid out . . . . Sometimes he invited the supper guests to our studio. We would set out armed with flashlights and keys. In the empty halls spotlights illuminated the models. There was no need for me to do the talking, for Hitler, with flashing eyes, explained every single detail to his companions . . . he loved to 'enter his avenue' at various points and take measure of the future effect. For example, he assumed the point of view of a traveler emerging from the south station or admired the great hall as it looked from the heart of the avenue. To do so, he bent down, almost kneeling, his eye an inch or so above the level of the model, in order to have the right perspective, and while looking he spoke with unusual vivacity* [3.16].[30]

"Do you know what you are?" a colleague asked Speer. "You are Hitler's unrequited love!"

Speer's master plan defined the overall style for the architecture, and many architects designed the individual pieces.[31] His large professional team prepared meticulous construction documents covering all aspects of the project, from materials to engineering, from manpower to art. The great model was continually revised as the design evolved. Separate models were made of the major buildings which became larger and larger, employing skilled teams of carpenters and craftsmen working in ornamental plaster. Some huge symbolic pieces were constructed at full size. The schedule called for the construction of every new building shown on the great model by the summer of 1950. A world exposition would be held to mark the event, in which all the nations and the major industries and institutions on earth would come together to be the first players on this eternal stage.

1938

The city had to be demolished to make way. Beginning on the west side of Potsdamerstrasse in 1938, whole streets of sound and elegant homes were purchased and torn down [3.17-18]. Construction of the first building on the great axis, the House of Tourism, began immediately.

3.17
Potsdamerstrasse in 1938 with demolition begun to make way for Runder Platz and for the House of Tourism.

1939

3.18
Potsdamerstrasse in 1939 with demolition complete.

1940

1941

Four major elements of Hitler's Berlin would have been visible from Leipziger Platz: the House of Tourism on Runder Platz, where construction of the North-South Axis began; the Palace for Reich Marshal Hermann Goering; the Hall of the Soldier, a pantheon for the army; and the Great Hall, to be the center of a new world order.

Runder Platz appears on the plan where the North-South Axis would have crossed Potsdamerstrasse [3.19]. It would have marked the division between the political and symbolic city to the north and the commercial and social city to the south. The House of Tourism [3.20] by the architects Rottcher and Dierksmeier, completed in 1940, was the only structure on the axis to be occupied. Its form was representative of the public character Hitler and Speer desired for their eternal city. Architecture's primary use would be to give gravity and order to the public stage, to solemnize public experience. Above all, this was to be a city for the exercise and demonstration of power.

Until the outbreak of the war, Speer maintained that his work for Hitler and for the Party had been performed as a private architect. A curious example of this was the commission from Reich Marshal Hermann Goering for a personal palace.[32] The first steps in its conception came when Hitler and Goering joined in a plot to remove Field Marshal of the Army Werner von Blomberg. Hitler needed to increase his influence over the army, and Blomberg was not sympathetic to national socialism. The plot involved a woman whom Blomberg met and married in 1938 at a ceremony in which Hitler and his court were present. Shortly thereafter, evidence was made public that the woman had been a prostitute. Hitler immediately demanded Blomberg's resignation, and elevated Goering from Air Minister to Reich

Marshal of the Armed Forces.

Hitler kept exclusive control over the plans for the city, much to the irritation of Goering who believed that his distinction in the national culture merited a place in the re-creation of Berlin. His appointment as Reich Marshal provided the excuse, and he privately appointed Speer architect of the Palace of the Reich Marshal. Speer recalled Hitler's reaction: "The building is too big for Goering. He's puffing himself up too much. All in all, I don't like his taking my architect for that purpose."[33]

Speer described his project for the Palace:

3.21
Albert Speer, elevation model of the Palace of the Reich Marshal, 1939.

1939

This part of the Ministry, with its eight hundred feet of frontage on the grand boulevard, was supplemented by a wing of equal size, on the Tiergarten side, which contained the ballrooms Goering had stipulated as well as his private apartment.

I situated the bedrooms on the top story. Alleging the need for air raid protection I decided to cover the roof with thirteen feet of garden soil, which meant that even large trees would have been able to strike root there. Thus I envisioned a two and a half acre roof garden, with swimming pools and tennis courts, fountains, ponds, colonnades, pergolas, and refreshment rooms, and finally a theatre for two hundred and forty spectators above the roofs of Berlin.

Goering was overwhelmed and began raving about the parties he would have there.

'I'll illuminate the great dome with bengal lights and provide grand fireworks for my guests.'[34]

"This was a decisive step in my personal development," wrote Speer, "from the Neo-classicism I had first espoused, and which was perhaps still to be seen in the new Chancellery, to a blatant nouveau riche architecture of prestige."

It is a design [3.21] loosely based on Roman palazzi from the fifteenth century. The grand facade on the North-South Axis would have gained its force from a compression of five different layers of composition which set up

contradictions between rational order and the symbolic form. Abstract planes of granite would form geometric frames around the classical molding opening the wall, and entertain the notion of a double fiction [3.22-23]. The interior, however, would have presented a much less thoughtful archi-tecture, owing as much to Hollywood as to Rome. It was, in Speer's own words, "blatantly nouveau riche." The powerful harmonic orchestration of the public facade collapses into confusion and indulgence, a gaudy flamboy-ance perfectly suited to the reputation of the Reich Marshal [3.24]. Goering was satisfied:

An entry for May 5, 1941 in my office journal records that the Reich Marshal was highly pleased with the model of his building. The staircase especially delighted him. Here he would stand, he declared, when he proclaimed the watchword of the year for the officers of the Air Force . . . . 'In tribute to this, the greatest staircase in the world,' Goering continued, 'Breker must create a monument to the Inspector General of Buildings [Speer]. It will be installed here to commemorate forever the man who so magnificently shaped this building.'[35]

Nothing can explain or excuse the small niches on either side of the great stair, presumably to contain statues of cupids urinating. As a response to Goering's theatricality and indulgent sensuality, Speer's use of models to convey his ideas reached a climax in the Palace of the Reich Marshal. The model of the entrance hall stood six feet in height and was presented to the audience as a theatrical stage. One bay of the main facade was constructed at full scale.

3.22
Albert Speer, full-size model
for a section of the facade of the
Palace of the Reich Marshal,
1939.

3.23
Albert Speer, model of the
Palace of the Reich Marshal,
1939.

1939

3.24
Albert Speer, model of the
entrance court in the Palace of
the Reich Marshal, 1939.

3.25
Albert Speer, model of the
Tiergarten facade of the Palace
of the Reich Marshal, 1939.

The Tiergarten facade with its rustication [3.25] would have re-
sembled the palaces of Florence more closely than those of Rome. It would
have caused the destruction of all the existing buildings on Bellevuestrasse
save one – Columbus Haus. Speer and Goering knew Mendelsohn and his
work. Goering personally supervised the construction of the Luftwaffe
Headquarters on Leipzigerstrasse in 1938 with the architect Ernst Sagebiel,
Mendelsohn's chief assistant on Columbus Haus.[36]

1939

Albert Speer, the Berlin Plan
surrounding Leipziger Platz.

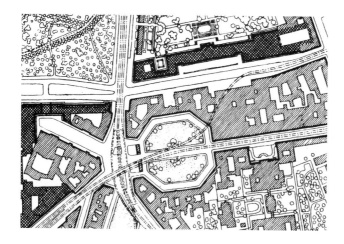

The outline of Columbus Haus appears, wraith-like, on Speer's
drawing [3.26]. It would have established the scale of Goering's Palace which,
in turn, would have reduced to a meaningless fragment what Mendelsohn
believed would be a universal reordering of the city in the modern spirit. It is
thesis and anti-thesis, the search for inner truth against the authority of
autocratic history. No object could offer a more complete opposition to
Mendelsohn's vision [3.27].

3.27

Detail view of the Berlin
Plan model, with Leipziger
Platz in the foreground.
The Wertheim Department
Store and Schinkel's Potsdam
Gates remain present, as
does Columbus Haus which
is integrated into Speer's
designs.

3.28
Wilhelm Kreis, model of the
Hall of the Soldier, 1940.

1940

The Hall of the Soldier [3.28] was to be placed on the Great Axis, opposite the Palace of the Reich Marshal, its forms responding point-counterpoint to Speer's facade. Here would be enshrined an eternal representation of the supreme virtue – the willingness to die for the state. The design by architect Wilhelm Kreis conveys a great physical presence. Here, within monolithic walls representing the power and permanence of the state, he would have revived and transformed Gilly's Monument to Frederick the Great into a hall of vast dimensions [3.30]: 820-feet-long, by 295-feet-deep, by 262-feet-high. In the crypt [3.29] he would have placed not just the tomb of Frederick but all the heroes of German history. This was to be the German Pantheon. Joseph Goebbels wrote in his diary:

3.29
Wilhelm Kreis, the crypt of
the Hall of the Soldier, 1940.

The Führer characterized it as nothing short of absurd that Frederick the Great was buried under the cupola of the Potsdam Garrison Church, contrary to his wish to be interred beside his dogs in the park of Sans Souci. Thank God, English air raids have compelled us to end this condition . . . . The coffin of Frederick the Great has been placed where it is safe from bombs. The Führer will never restore it to the Potsdam Garrison Church. Either an imposing mausoleum in Greek style is to be built for Frederick the Great in the park of Sans Souci, or he is to be laid to rest in the great Soldiers' Hall of a new War Ministry . . . .[37]

3.30
Wilhelm Kreis, the shrine of
the Hall of the Soldier, 1940.

The Great Hall was conceived to be the most powerful and permanent construction in the history of architecture. Speer wrote:

Hitler liked to say that the purpose of building is to transmit a time and its spirit to posterity. Ultimately all that remains to remind men of the great art epochs of history is their monumental architecture. What remains of the emperors of Rome? What would still bear witness to them today, if their buildings had not survived?

. . . Periods of weakness are bound to occur in the history of nations, but at their lowest ebb, their architecture will speak to them of former power. Naturally, a new national consciousness cannot be awakened by architecture alone. But when after a long spell of inertia a sense of national grandeur is born anew, the monuments of man's ancestors are the most impressive exhortations.[38]

3.31
Albert Speer,
model of The Great Hall.

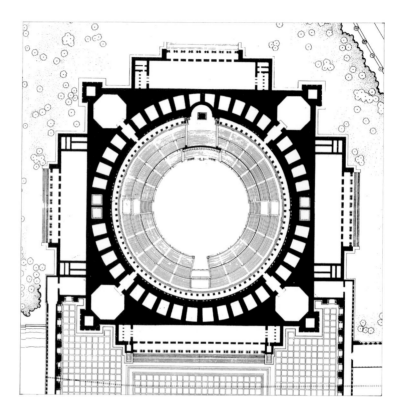

Speer, in his autobiography, described the Hall in the same flat
tone he used to describe his trial at Nuremberg:

*A round interior was to have the almost inconceivable diameter of eight hundred and twenty-five feet.
The huge dome was to begin its slightly parabolic curve at a height of three hundred and twenty-three
feet and rise to a height of seven hundred and twenty-six feet . . . . In a sense the Pantheon in Rome
had served as our model. The Berlin dome was also to contain a round opening for light, but this
opening alone would be one hundred and fifty-two feet in diameter, larger than the entire dome of the
Pantheon (142 feet) and of St. Peter's (145 feet). The interior would contain sixteen times the volume
of St. Peter's [3.31-32].*[39]

A thousand feet high, it would be a man-made mountain. Hitler
could approach the plans with a sense of amusement. He observed to his
colleagues one evening when discussing the benefits of such an epic building:
"All we need to do is tell the Americans how much the Great Hall costs.
Maybe we'll exaggerate a bit and say a billion and a half instead of a billion.
Then they'll be wild to see the most expensive building in the world."[40]

Speer said that the interior appointments:

. . . were to be as simple as possible. Circling an area four hundred sixty-two feet in diameter, a three-tier gallery rose to a height of one hundred feet. A circle of one hundred rectangular marble pillars – still almost on a human scale, for they were only eighty feet high – was broken by a recess opposite the entrance.

This recess was one hundred and sixty-five feet high and ninety-two feet wide, and was to be clad at the rear in gold mosaic. In front of it on a marble pedestal forty-six feet in height perched the hall's single sculptural feature: a gilded German eagle with a swastika in its claws. This symbol of sovereignty might be said to be the very fountainhead of Hitler's grand boulevard. Beneath this symbol would be the podium for the Leader of the nation; from this spot he would deliver his messages to the peoples of his future empire . . . .

I tried to give this spot suitable emphasis, but here the fatal flaw of architecture that has lost all sense of proportion was revealed. Under that vast dome Hitler dwindled to an optical zero [3.33].[41]

There is throughout Speer's memoirs a disingenuous quality as he distanced himself from the projects or downplayed their significance. To suggest that the visual power center of the Great Dome was flawed ignores his stage management of the great rallies in Nuremberg, in which, by Speer's design, Hitler was also an optical zero, yet his power and influence were never more magnified. Speer wrote in his memoirs that "I felt myself to be Hitler's architect, political events did not concern me." Yet the means by which the state would create the city of world domination was slavery, and Speer was fully supportive. As the war expanded and intensified through 1940, Speer complained that there was not enough building material for the project:

[Himmler] when he heard of the threatening shortage of brick and granite offered to employ his prisoners to increase production. He proposed to Hitler that an extensive brickworks be set up in Sachsenhausen, near Berlin under SS direction and as SS property.[42]

3.33
Albert Speer,
the interior of the Great Hall.

Himmler further offered "to supply granite blocks for the buildings in Nuremberg and Berlin using the labor of concentration camp prisoners." And Speer in response complained about the quality of materials supplied. As Hitler began the Russian campaign he called Speer into his study one evening and said "now we will have all the granite and marble in any quantities we want."[43]

While rejecting all religions, Hitler wished to retain within his city and his culture the idea of divine presence, because it can be presumed he foresaw his deification:

One may ask whether the disappearance of Christianity would entail the disappearance of belief in God. That's not to be desired. The notion of divinity gives most men the opportunity to concretise the feeling they have of supernatural realities. Why should we destroy this wonderful power they have of incarnating the feeling for the divine that is within them?[44]

In his will of 1938, Hitler had explicitly asked to be buried in Munich beneath one of the two temples of the Eternal Watch designed by his friend, the architect Paul Troost, on Königsplatz [3.34].[45] However, with the emergence of the Great Hall there was an implicit understanding among Hitler's inner circle of its eventual purpose. Speer wrote:

In spite of Hitler's negative attitude toward Himmler's and Rosenberg's mystical notions, the hall was essentially a place of worship. The idea was that over the course of centuries, by tradition and venerability, it would acquire an importance similar to that St. Peter's in Rome has for Catholic Christendom. Without some such essentially pseudo-religious background the expenditure for Hitler's central building would have been pointless and incomprehensible.[46]

Speer could not remain apolitical while directing the largest and most permanent construction of architectural and political power ever conceived, a project which he knew would become the eternal tomb for the man who sought to master the world. Reichsführer Heinrich Himmler was more specific:

Right after the war we shall build a house which will be the largest and most magnificent house in the world. We started with plans as early as 1938. It will be built on Königsplatz Berlin. The cost is estimated at 50 billion marks. The height will be 355 meters; the diameter 1500 meters. The foundation alone will cost 3 billion marks . . . . It will be a house such as the world has never seen. It will contain rooms and halls with space for two to three-hundred thousand people . . . . In the cellar we shall build a vault more gigantic and magnificent than the Pharaohs ever dreamt of and built. And this will one day be Adolf Hitler's tomb.[47]

The existing drawings show no evidence of a crypt. Perhaps Himmler was mistaken. Hitler was reported to have said to friends in 1942 that "I especially wouldn't want our movement to acquire a religious character and institute a form of worship. It would be appalling for me, and I would wish I had never lived, if I were to end up in the skin of a Buddha!"[48]

Until 1942, Speer's plan for the creation of the capital proceeded at full pace. The House of Tourism, the only building to be completed within the Great Axis, was ready for occupation by the fall of 1941. In February 1942, after the death in an air crash of Hitler's Minister of Armaments and Munitions, Dr. Fritz Todt, Speer was appointed to replace him. Thereafter the demands of war, and Speer's central preoccupation with it, increasingly interfered with the project but work proceeded, and even late into 1944 Hitler persisted in the belief that it would be realized.

For Hitler this architecture was to be a testament to a new and everlasting order that would end the decline of the West. It was formed in the belief that architecture alone makes the political project reality. Before the declaration of war, in the summer of 1939, Hitler pointed to the crown on the dome. "That has to be changed," he said to Speer. "Instead of the swastika, the eagle is to be perched above the globe. To crown this greatest building in the world, the eagle must stand above the globe."[49]

The man who sought world domination sought also to create the grandest and most permanent symbolic reality in history, a reality that would continue to impose the will of the master race on all the cultures of the earth into an infinite future. To carry his dreams into reality, fate brought to his side

1934

one of the most beautiful and gifted youths of his generation. Within the grip of his master's will Speer never grew up, never discovered himself, never developed an independent character. In all his projects he was merely the scribe to Hitler's vision. On seeing the drawings and the photographs of the models after twenty years in prison,[50] Speer could no longer understand the architecture – it made no sense to him nor did it belong to him. It was as if, he wrote, "the scales have fallen from my eyes." Hitler was the architect. His constructions were conceived as instruments of power and deceit and only the desperate or the foolish could see in them a significance independent from the artifice of the political theater. Only in the presence of a marching uniformed mass would this stage have its play.

3.34
Paul Troost,
Temple of the Eternal Watch,
Königsplatz, Munich, 1934.

Compare Hitler's original drawing for a great hall from 1924 and the dramatic photograph of the Great Hall viewed down the North-South Axis. In what must be a tribute to Schinkel's painting *Triumphbogen*, the photographer frames the dome within the arch [3.35].[51] The dome has swollen to suppress the base; soaring omnipotence overwhelms temporal order. As with the painting the viewer stands in darkness elevated high above the ground and looks toward the ideal. In contrast to Schinkel's gothic dome asymmetrically balanced by a natural landscape, Hitler's desire was for a reality of absolute symmetry, the reassertion of absolute and conservative power in opposition to all the random liberal and liberating tendencies which had undermined Western culture. Fate placed the actual reality of Hitler's Triumphbogen close to the arch of Schinkel's imagination. Out from under the arch, still suspended, there is a rich foreground in the imagination. On the extreme right an octagonal place, a gate to the old city, and an edge of confusion connects absolute certainty with the promiscuous uncertainty of all that had gone before.

3.35
Albert Speer, The Great Hall
viewed through the Triumphal Arch.

In the last months of the war Speer planned to kill Hitler in the bunker beneath the Chancellery garden [3.36]. A colleague used Hitler's own words to crystallize for Speer the extent of the distortion of his governance: "State authority," Hitler had written in *Mein Kampf*, "as an end in itself cannot exist, since in that case every tyranny on this earth would be sacred and unassailable. If a racial entity is being led towards its doom by means of governmental power, then the rebellion of every single member of such a *volk* is not only a right but a duty."[52] Speer planned his attack:

On my walks in the Chancellery garden I had noticed the ventilation shaft for Hitler's bunker.

Camouflaged by a small shrub, level with the ground and covered with a thin grating, was the opening

of the air intake. The air that was drawn in passed through a filter. But no filter worked against our

poison gas 'tabun.'[53]

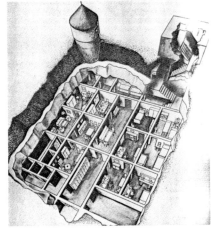

He tried to obtain the gas only to discover that it would only be released by explosion. This could have shattered the walls of the air ducts and made penetration throughout the bunker impossible. The head of munitions production offered to obtain a more traditional type of gas, and the chief engineer for the Chancellery, on Speer's request, removed all the air filters in the system for cleaning. The bunker was unprotected. After a short interval Speer found a pretext to reinspect the shaft:

3.36
Post-war reconstruction of Hitler's bunker in the garden of the Reich Chancellery.

I found a changed picture. Armed SS sentinels were now posted on the roofs of the entire complex,

search lights had been installed, and where the ventilation shaft had previously been at ground level

there now rose a chimney more than ten feet high which put the air intake out of reach. I was stunned.

My first thought was that my plan had been discovered. But actually the whole thing was the

operation of chance.[54]

At the Chancellery very early on a morning in April 1945, Speer had his last meeting with Adolf Hitler:

By now it was about 3 o'clock in the morning. Hitler was awake again. I sent word that I wanted to

bid him goodbye. The day had worn me out, and I was afraid that I would not be able to control

myself at our parting. Trembling, the prematurely aged man stood before me for the last time; the

man to whom I had dedicated my life twelve years before. I was both moved and confused. For his

part, he showed no emotion when we confronted one another. His words were as cold as his hand:

'So, you are leaving? Good. Auf Wiedersehen.' . . . Ten minutes later, with hardly another word spoken to anyone, I left the Chancellor's residence. I wanted to walk once more through the neighboring Chancellery, which I had built. Since the lights were no longer functioning I contented myself with a few farewell minutes in the Court of Honor, whose outlines could scarcely be seen against the night sky [3.37].

I sensed rather than saw the architecture. There was an almost ghostly quiet about everything, like a night in the mountains. The noise of a great city, which in early years had penetrated to here even during the night, had totally ceased. At rather long intervals I heard the detonations of Russian shells.

Such was my last visit to the Chancellery. Years ago I had built it – full of plans, prospects and dreams for the future. Now I was leaving the ruins of my building, and of the most significant years of my life [3.38-41].[55]

3.37
The Court of Honor
of the Reich Chancellery,
May 1945.

1945

MAY

1945

MAY

3.38
The Marble Gallery
of the Reich Chancellery,
May 1945.

1945

MAY

3.39
The Great Reception Room
of the Reich Chancellery,
May 1945.

Speer's memoirs have had the formative influence on the popular perception of Hitler and the Third Reich. His words have softened the memory of the events and sanitized their nature, removing all extremes of obscenity, racism, and torture. He depicts the influence of individuals like Rosenberg and Himmler as aberrant yet uninfluential. He gives the whole play of events a mildly sympathetic and bourgeois character. As the central agent in the public representation of the Reich's ideals he nowhere even hints at the savage, passionate brutality underlying this project for the transformation of the human order.

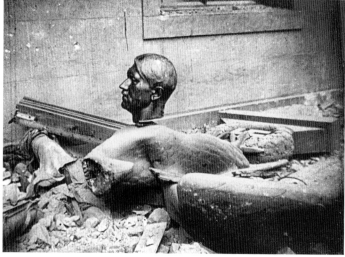

3.40
A bust of Hitler atop the remains
of German eagle, in the courtyard of
the Reich Chancellery, May 1945.

1945

MAY

3.41
The ruins of the Reich Chancellery
from Voss Strasse, Spring 1946.

1946

SPRING

Hitler's project was driven by an overwhelming desire to construct an omnipotent and eternal reordering of the Western world, a new order to be held in place by the stones and forms of architecture. Berlin, rebuilt as the new Rome, would be the great fruit of the war and its architecture would be the primary instrument by which Hitler's presence and power would be maintained into an infinite future. Without the persistent memory of Rome and without Rome's relation to the mythic destiny of the German race, Hitler's play would have remained formless, both physically and politically, and the extremes of destruction and coercion would have been inconceivable.

Hitler's last political statement:

Berlin 29th April 1945, 4 a.m.

My Political Testament

After six years of war which, despite all setbacks, will one day go down in history as the most glorious and heroic manifestation of the struggle for existence of a nation, I cannot abandon the city which is the capital of the Reich. Since our forces are too meager to withstand the enemy's attack and since our resistance is being debased by creatures who are as blind as they are lacking in character, I wish to share my fate with that which millions of others have also taken upon themselves by remaining in this city. Further, I shall not fall into the hands of the enemy who requires a new spectacle, presented by the Jews, for the diversion of the hysterical masses.

I have therefore decided to stay in Berlin and there to choose death voluntarily when I determine that the position of the Führer and the Chancellery itself can no longer be maintained. I die with a joyful heart in the knowledge of the immeasurable deeds and achievements of our peasants and workers and of a contribution unique in the history of our youth which bears my name.[56]

The most sympathetic of Hitler's biographers, Werner Maser, wrote in his collection of *Hitler's Letters and Notes*: ". . . even while he was dictating *Mein Kampf*, writing weighty letters and stilted inscriptions, in his architectural drawings he would try to escape from the onerous present into the 'healthy' past. This may explain why he kept these sketches to the end of his life and preserved them like so many jewels . . . . He always carried them in his wallet or kept them in his desk, together with a four-leafed clover and an invitation to a school dance in Linz." Moser adds in a footnote that "Shortly before he took his life in the bunker, he asked his secretary Christa Schröder to remove the sketches and to take them away with her."[57]

An extract from the deposition prepared by the Russian Secret Service (SMERSH) on the circumstances of Hitler's death:

RE: burying site of the bodies of Adolf Hitler and his wife.

1945, the thirteenth day of May.

We the undersigned, accompanied by the witness Mengeshausen, Harry, investigated on this day the spot where the corpses of the German Chancellor of the Reich, Adolf Hitler and his wife were buried.

1945

MAY

3.42
Box in the courtyard of the
Reich Chancellery allegedly
containing Hitler's corpse, from
the SMERSH report, May 1945.

Witness Mengeshausen, Harry, attested that he, as member of the SS Combat Group Mudtkes, had been detailed from April 20 to 30 to the defense of the Chancellery area and the personal protection of Adolf Hitler.

On April 30, 1945, around noon, he was on guard within the building of the new Chancellery, where it was his duty to cover the hallway passing the Hitler study and continuing to the blue dining room.

On his tour of duty through the above-mentioned hallway Mengeshausen stopped in the blue dining room in front of the farthest window, which is closest to the exit to the garden, and observed what went on in Chancellery Garden. At this moment Sturmbannführer Gunsche and Linge carried the bodies of Adolf Hitler and his wife Ifa Braun (his private secretary) from the emergency exit into the open. This roused his interest and he watched carefully to see how things developed. Hitler's personal adjutant Gunsche poured gasoline over the bodies and ignited them. After half an hour the bodies of Hitler and his wife were consumed; they were taken to a crater at about 1 meter distance from the above mentioned emergency exit, and there buried. Mengeshausen further attested that on April 9 Hitler's dog was also buried in the crater. Distinguishing features: a tall shepherd with long ears, black back, and light flanks. From Paul Phenie, who is in special charge of the dog, Mengeshausen learned that he had been poisoned.

The testament of the witness Mengeshausen is all the more credible since we pulled from the designated crater on May 1945 the corpses of a man and woman disfigured by fire and two poisoned dogs which, as was recognized by other witnesses, belonged to Hitler and his private secretary Ifa Braun.

A diagram of the place where the corpses of Hitler and his wife were discovered, as well as photographs of the place indicated by witness Mengeshausen is appended.

Deposition drawn up in the Chancellery, city of Berlin.

Chief Counter Intelligent Section SMERSH

79th Rifle Core Lieutenant Colonel signed (Klinenko)

[Other signatures deleted] [3.42-43]58

1945
MAY

3.43
Photograph of cremation site (x),
burial site (xx), and Bunker exit (xxx),
from the SMERSH report, May 1945.

The concluding image is a view looking west on Voss Strasse in the spring of 1946. It shows a city destroyed by war. On the left are the remains of the Wertheim Department Store, on the right the great facade of Hitler's Reich Chancellery, and seen over the ruins at the center the long canopy over the roof terrace of Columbus Haus [3.44].

1946

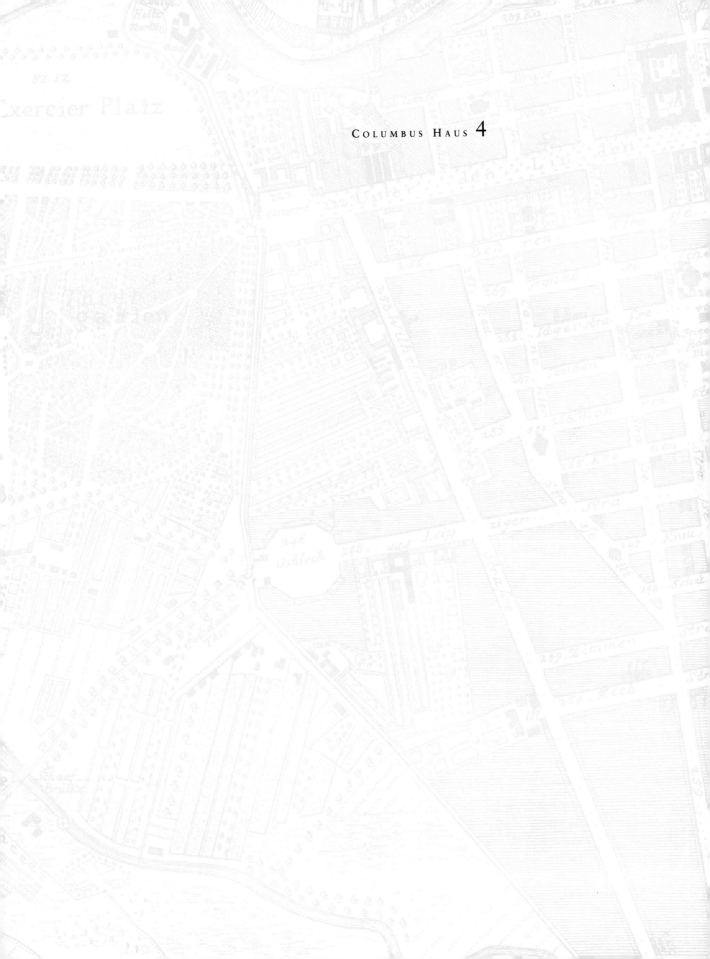

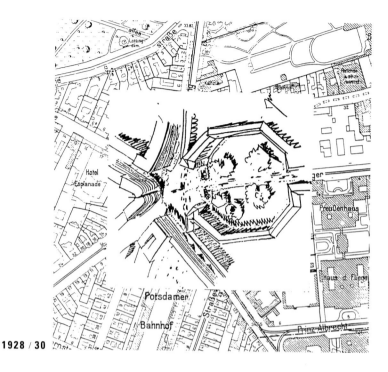

1928 / 30

The dreams of the future would briefly eclipse the dreams of those who would dwell in the past. The illustration is a page from the sketchbook of the Berlin architect Erich Mendelsohn [4.2]. It was drawn in the spring of 1930. The title, "Columbus Haus," is handwritten on the top right corner. Drawings of this kind by architects are quite peculiar. They are descriptions of potential realities seen as a snapshot, seen in life. They are documents of the conversation an architect has with himself. Mendelsohn's drawings are very small; there is a direct relationship between their structure and the muscles of his wrist and hand. They not only seek to express tension, but are created out of it. There is firm concentration in their making. The hand dances an arabesque across the page, leaving forms in the passage of movement, converting the essential power of the words *Columbus Haus* — an allegory in space of the mythical potential of the new world.

Each vignette is intense and deliberate. The impressions in the architect's mind are fleeting, demanding that the drawings be executed quickly. The viewpoint is always the same: set at eye level some distance from the object, the ground in between is undefined, although in the final flourish there is a suggestion of a paved place. They are confident, fluid, effortless productions of a clear intention. There is a direct relationship between the speed and strength of the physical gesture and the symbolism of the image.

Mendelsohn is forty-three years old. He has produced similar drawings for over twenty years. He experiences them in his mind as he experiences music. So habitual has the process become that when an idea is complete or when a drawing satisfies he gives it a final flourish, an arc or a circle, to isolate and enhance it and he signs his initials. It doesn't seem strange to him that he has signed his initials four times on this one small scrap of paper on this morning late in September of 1930. Much of the year has been devoted to completing work on his house. He has controlled its every detail to present a poetic reality he has dreamed of for years. It is the mirror of his soul. He was delighted when Ozenfant called it "the Goethe Haus for this age." He is at the peak of his confidence when he begins work on Columbus Haus. Although the collapse of the economy the previous year unsettled everyone, there is nothing to indicate that this will be his last German building. He is sitting in the small study which adjoins the master bedroom. There are fresh garden flowers in glass vases on the table and on the bookshelf. The wooden Buddha on his desk is an anchor for his contemplation. As his mind drifts through a range of possibilities, he toys with the notion that he resembles the Buddha.

The maid brings coffee. He looks again through the catalogue of the Ozenfant exhibition. Then, as if responding to some internal decision, he takes a small drawing pad from the desk. He likes pencils with medium-soft lead. He writes at the top of the page "Columbus Haus." As he stares idly out of the window trying to focus, images of past projects roll through his imagination. As always, he sifts through these random fragments as they tumble by, reforming and dissolving. He works with an intense critical awareness, a self-conscious concern with matching his feelings about the idea of the future with the forms in his imagination. He is trying to distill the essence, what he would call the *élan vital* of modern desire. He does not disagree with the dogmas of Gropius, but neither does he believe they have much to do with architecture. He views himself as a sensor, finely tuned and unique among men in his ability to distill the form of future reality out of an infinity of possibilities.

He enjoys Potsdamer Platz and Leipziger Platz. They have lively cafes, racy hotels, and, of course, Haus Vaterland. Yet, he has no real concern with the specifics of the place or with its past. What he seeks to begin here is the insertion of a new order for the culture at the very heart of the city. As he begins to draw, it is the intersection of two objects that stimulates his imagination. He begins on the top right-hand corner seeking some vertical inflection within the horizontal plane. He begins with a familiar gesture – a stack of curving plates intersecting a vertical plane. He tries this again. At

4.2
Erich Mendelsohn, studies for
Columbus Haus, 1929-30.

1929 - 30

moments such as this, he feels a sense of elevated consciousness. On to the next drawing, this time with an almost impatient haste.

He views these drawings in different ways. He recognizes that they are physical gestures, their small size determined by the limits of a wrist at rest. They contain for him the character of haiku, the quality of elemental truth. The manner of their execution and their size and spareness is important to their essence.

As he works he plays music on the gramophone. He plays recordings of Bach. He plays certain fugues over and over again. Three problems are at issue: how to be part of the life of the street, how to balance symbolically the horizontal and the vertical, and how to meet the sky. The process is dialectical; when the drawing is done, it becomes an independent entity which he then criticizes. It is a criticism based on a field of continually changing virtues – political, physical, scientific, philosophical, utopian, idealistic, and emotional. Though brief, these rendered gestures distill for him the total phenomenon of architecture. They are moments held in time and space.

They are also subversive. They deny the personification of power and institution that has been the nature of all architecture, past and present. They are gestures of transcendence and revolution which aim beyond modern reason, to explore the fundamental meaning of being and dwelling. In making the transitory permanent, in defeating death, the very idea of architecture must itself be cleansed of the transitory and disassociated from past contexts and histories. All surviving objects of past realities carry representations of promiscuous and deceitful histories and superstitions, and selfish fantasies of imperialism and nationalism. These must be removed to make way for the future. Such a heroic agenda for such slight drawings establishes a reality solely in the horizons of time-ordered space.

Laying aside the studies for Columbus Haus, he thumbs through the small black portfolio in which he keeps the drawings. He selects and ponders his redrawing of Schinkel's engraving of the Potsdam Gate [4.3]. He, like Schinkel, is seeking a synthesis for the future. He is aware of the weakness at the center, but does not share the fractured visions of Grosz or the ominous warnings in Ruttman's ironic "symphony." Whether the great vortex gathering ever more force and speed is destroying or renewing city life is wholly in the hands of those producing the culture. The Schinkel drawing reminds him of how simple and clear the issue of synthesis had been in the past. In the painful and slow movement toward democracy, the quest for a reality defined by the balance between reason and circumstance, between order and freedom, now seems so naive. All the fruits of the new age of science and industry are shaped in uneven and disconnected bursts of energy,

4.3
Erich Mendelsohn, study of Leipziger Platz, 1929. The drawing is a reworking of Schinkel's view of the city wall and the Potsdam Gates.

1929

with no connection to history as they each in their own way compete with the promise of a rational future.

The sound of a car horn brings him out of these reflections. Heavy footsteps cross the yard. He feels suddenly uneasy. It is the insecurity that underlies all experiment. Or is it something more direct, something more deeply wrong? The page of drawings is complete. The process is both reflexive and reflective – he doesn't always remember having completed the design. Looking over the page he is pleased with this brief period of work. He is pleased with his role as the agent and transmitter of forces infinitely greater than he.

Erich Mendelsohn was born in Allanstein, East Prussia (now Poland) in 1887 and raised in an affluent merchant family. He first studied economics at the University of Munich and then, between 1908 and 1910, entered architecture studies at Berlin's Technische Hochschule. He rode a wave of exceptional fortune through all the post-war chaos to become, by the end of the 1920s, Berlin's most successful modernist architect.

He served on the front line in the First World War and from the trenches produced a series of very small and intense drawings conveying his vision for architecture, apocalyptic drawings in the mood of expressionism with the character of living organisms. They were exhibited in Berlin and colleagues of Albert Einstein saw in them a spiritual affinity with their scientific work. In 1919 he was commissioned to design the Einstein Tower in Potsdam, a Prussian state facility for research in astrophysical phenomena arising from Einstein's relativity theory [4.4]. The building was shaped to present a new order to transcend the cultural destruction wrought by the war.

4.4
Erich Mendelsohn, study sketch
for the Einstein Tower, Potsdam,
1920-24.

1920 - 24

In the same year, in a lecture to the Berlin Art Workers, Mendelsohn said:

The simultaneous process of revolutionary political decisions and radical changes in human relationships in economy and science and religion and art give belief in the new form an a priori right to exercise control, and provide a justifiable basis for a rebirth amidst the misery produced by world-historical disasters . . . .

That which seems today to be flowing with viscous slowness will later appear to history as having moved at a breakneck and thrilling speed. We are dealing here with an act of creation!

We are only at the early beginning, but we are already faced with the possibilities of its development.

Before such a future the great achievements of historical times step back of their own accord; the immediacy of the present loses its importance.

What will happen has value only if it comes into being in the intoxication of vision.[1]

Not untouched by Nietzsche, he saw himself as the solitary genius. He is reported on a number of occasions to have told his assistants: "when God created the world he had no associates. So why should I?"[2] Another favorite expression was: "Would you have asked Beethoven for the Seventh Symphony when he was ready to create the Ninth? All I'll say is you'll get a Mendelsohn!"[3]

He rejected any notion of the decline of the West and believed profoundly in the sacred character of the new world and in his role as its prophet. "What today is the vision and faith in a single individual, will one day become the law for all." He sought to project a vision of a glorious and vital future, a vision to be the antithesis of all existing realities.

Lecturing on the "New Architectural Thought" in Amsterdam in 1923, the year in which the German economy was in total collapse, he said:

Rarely, it seems to me, has the order of the world revealed itself so directly, rarely has the logos of existence been further revealed than in this time of supposed chaos. For we have had time to rid ourselves of prejudices and of sated contentedness. As creative people we know how very differently the driving forces and the play of tensions work themselves out in the individual.

It therefore becomes our duty all the more to meet excitement with reflection, exaggeration with simplicity, and uncertainty with the clear law; to discover once more, amidst the wreckage of energy, the elements of new energy and out of these elements to form a new whole.

Seize, hold, construct, and calculate anew the earth! But shape the world that is waiting for you. Shape with the dynamics of your own vision[4] the actual conditions on which reality can be based, elevate these to dynamic transcendence. Simple and sure like the machine, clear and bold like construction. Create art out of the real requirements and inconceivable space out of light and mass. But do not forget that the creation of the individual can only be understood from the entirety of the manifestations of the age. It is as much tied to the relativity of these manifestations as present and future are to the relativity of history.[5]

His confidence was limitless, sustained by the creative bond he felt with Einstein. When he wrote of elevating to "dynamic transcendence" and creating "inconceivable space out of light and mass" within the "relativity of history" he wholly believed that architecture could embody the scientific project. Goethe wrote that "nature has neither core nor surface, nature is everything all at once," and Mendelsohn believed he alone could present its embodiment. "Expressing the power of an age has always been the task for art," he wrote in 1927, and giving physical presence to the relativity of space and time became the mission for his architecture.[6]

Beginning in the mid-1920s, his reputation established, he produced a series of designs for commercial and industrial buildings that epitomized the brilliant surge of energy that had jolted Germany out of cultural stagnation. He had become a public figure whose words and designs aimed to recharge the nation. For the opening of his Schocken department store in Nuremberg in 1927 he delivered a long epic poem. It proclaimed that "to want to deny our [modern] way of life is self-deception, it is pitiful and cowardly."

To want even to hold back its development is

Self-immolation, it is foolish and fruitless.

So be brave, be wise! Seize life by the forelock,

At the point where its heart beats strongest, in the midst

of life in the midst of technique traffic and industry.

Take it straight, as it is, take its tasks as it

presents them, To you, to us all.

For each one demands functionalism, clarity, simplicity.

Each must be functional, for all work is

too valuable to be senselessly wasted.

Clarity, because not only an elite but every

man's reason must understand them.

Simplicity, because the best achievement

is always the simplest.

No great age has ever trusted

another age more than itself.

And so should we architects, all alone, come limping behind,

Wearing wigs, we engineers and master-builders,

who build your house? your cities and the whole visible world?

Do not let yourselves be persuaded.

Only he who cannot forget has no free mind.

Only he who cannot invent is unfruitful.

Only he who does not live dies before his time.

Only he who has no rhythm in his body – don't think of jazz, be serious! –

Fails to understand the metallic rhythm

of the machine, the humming of the propeller, the huge

vitality which thrills us, overjoys us and

makes us creative.[7]

"Only he who cannot forget has no free mind." Mendelsohn's message is to forget the past and to oppose the corruption of reality embodied in the Western city. The city had become a mask of existence, its architecture merely a fancy dress and an empty promise on the sick and aging body of the culture, establishing the authority of autocracy by the resurrection of forms and words from the past – temples, basilicas, and medieval halls, all elaborate deceits in an imperialistic fiction. City life had become imprisoned in a stone mask of transitory desire, polarizing and driving the culture to a breaking point. Only in functionalism, clarity, and simplicity, in harmony with the power of the machine, was the future clear.

Mendelsohn sought to present a vision that would transform a city of selfish acts and deceitful gestures into one whose physical form was unified by natural order and mutual consent, and which recognized the superiority of efficiency and reason tied to the power of machines and new scientific knowledge. Mendelsohn, the liberal democrat, argued in his politics and his architecture against *Übereinander*, the one-on-top-of-the-otherness of the pillars of state, in favor of *Nebeneinander*, the horizontal side-by-sidedness of the individual elements of the race.[8]

The abstraction in Columbus Haus was an expression of Mendelsohn's desire to represent Einsteinian relativity, passages in space in time, but beyond that is a more complex dimension. From its basis in the forms of temporal circumstance, Columbus Haus can be seen as an expression of Hebraic values. Bruno Zevi's essay, "Hebraism and the Concept of Space Time in Art," places Mendelsohn's desire in an ancient tradition and culture:

Hebraism is a concept of time, that while the divinities of other peoples are associated with places and things, the God of Israel is a god of events and that Jewish life, nourished by the book, is permeated with history, that is, with a time-related consciousness of human tasks . . . . Hebraism cannot be reduced from any point of view to the concept of space. At the root core the very Hebraic idea of God denies it.[9]

On the crucial differences between the Jewish and Greek views of man, Zevi writes that "the Greek ideal represents the human being as an absolute, above history, beyond time – the human type, indeed the prototype" whereas for the Jew, man is defined in the dynamics of daily living:

For Hebraism, art is not a catharsis in the mythical guilt-ridden sense. Rather it opposes myths of whatever nature, whether transcendent or immanent, just as does science. On different levels, both Einstein and Freud are desecrators of myths.[10]

Columbus Haus can also be seen as a desecrator of myths. The insecurity of Jewish culture within Western society, its distrust and rejection by Jewish philosophers, must have affected the focus of Mendelsohn's desire. Mendelsohn, Freud, Einstein, and many others, were all readjusting the perception of reality, reacting against the historical constraints on Western thought, and producing works that were both subversive and brilliant complements to Western culture. Mendelsohn's desire was not to reflect the age, but to create it anew, reflecting it only as a mirror of his own invention. In his dream of the rebirth, the new man walks naked into a naked future.

The accumulation of images that follow documents the brief existence of Columbus Haus which, because it has perished, assumes a greater power in the imagination than it ever had in life. While Columbus Haus stands still, great and terrible events in Western culture rage around it. It is a visual essay on space in time.

1930
SPRING

4.5
Erich Mendelsohn, study
drawings for the Galeries
Lafayette, Berlin, 1930.

ERICH MENDELSOHN'S STUDY DRAWINGS FOR THE GALERIES
LAFAYETTE ON POTSDAMER PLATZ

         The first plan for redeveloping
the site of the Grand Hotel Bellevue was for the French department store
Galeries Lafayette. Mendelsohn's drawings have a carefree vigor that almost
conceals the seriousness of the underlying project [4.5].

A TEMPORARY STRUCTURE SCREENS THE SITE OF THE
PROPOSED GALERIES LAFAYETTE

"Architekt Erich Mendelsohn"
shares the advertising with "Lux" washing powder, "for all soft fabrics," and
"Willie's Overlander." Mendelsohn designed the structure to give the owners
advertising revenue while the work was under construction [4.6]. The
ephemera of advertising could be separated from the substance of architecture.

1930
FALL

4.6
Temporary structures
covering the proposed site of
the Galeries Lafayette,
Fall 1930.

These drawings follow the collapse of the Galeries Lafayette project [4.7]. The financial backers, damaged by the world economic crisis of 1929, withdrew in the spring of 1930. With the memory of the department store in his mind Mendelsohn begins to design Columbus Haus. The program is different but the formal problem is the same – to create an architecture of dynamic power to hold the corner of an important public space.

4.7
Erich Mendelsohn,
studies for Columbus Haus,
1930.

1930

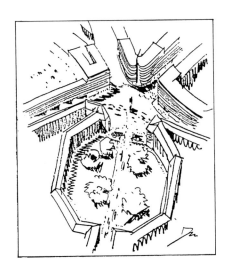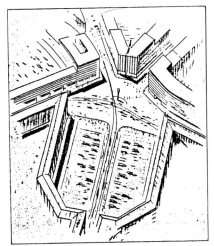

1931

<h3>Studies for the redesign of Leipziger Platz and the Potsdam Gate</h3>

These are graphic illustrations of Mendelsohn's political vision. The future city would be horizontally unified in continuously moving layers of space [4.8]. The first drawing completes Leipziger Platz in a regular form. The second destroys the idea of the Achteck and the Schinkel Gates, transforming rational geometry into dynamic disorder. Mendelsohn, as with all the architects of modernism, rises above the stage of the city. His perspective has become omniscient.

4.8
Erich Mendelsohn,
studies for the reconstruction
of Leipziger Platz and the
Potsdam Gate, 1931.

THE FINAL DRAWINGS FOR COLUMBUS HAUS

Although not the first, Columbus Haus was the equal of all the prototypical commercial buildings of modernism [4.9-11]. "For the first time [in any building] all window mullions," wrote Mendelsohn, "are load-carrying structural members to permit a maximum flexibility and rental value." The architecture is silent in every regard save its free and expansive treatment of space. Its contained energy makes all else in Potsdamer Platz seem fat and tired.

4.9
Erich Mendelsohn,
section and typical floor plan
of Columbus Haus, 1931.

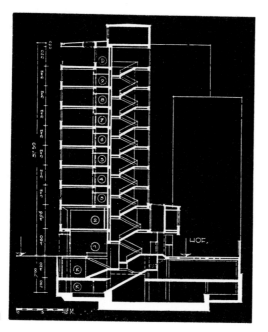

1931

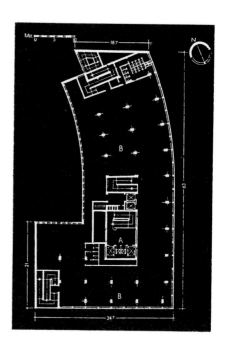

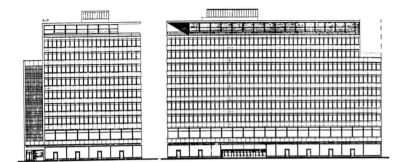

4.10
Erich Mendelsohn,
front and side elevations of
Columbus Haus, 1931.

4.11
Erich Mendelsohn,
perspective drawing of
Columbus Haus, 1931.

1931

4.12
Columbus Haus under
construction, October 1931.

1931

OCTOBER

COLUMBUS HAUS UNDER CONSTRUCTION

Mendelsohn's name has been removed from the billboard along with Galeries Lafayette [4.12]. The elegance of this temporary object has been lost. The advertising is for the movie *Flute Concert of Sans Souci* starring Otto Gebuhr at the Palast Cinema by the Zoo, and for Makedon cigarettes. Next to a cigarette shop on the corner are a series of theatre posters under the banner of "Reinhardt Buhnen" (Reinhardt Productions); these include *Elizabeth of England* at the German Theatre, *The Fairy* at the Kommodie, and the enigmatic *2F79* at the Theatre Abonnement.

4.13
Columbus Haus
with propoganda display for
the re-election of President
Hindenburg, March 13, 1932.

1932

MARCH 13

COLUMBUS HAUS WITH A PROPAGANDA DISPLAY FOR THE
RE-ELECTION OF PRESIDENT HINDENBURG

The text reads "Oppose the
system: the two-fold united choose Hindenburg!" [4.13]. Political slogans
replace cigarette slogans and the first political message to resound from this
symbol of the future is from a man born in 1847. The building presents its
revolutionary character to the square. It is clearly an object in opposition to
all that has gone before, and seems slightly intolerant of its neighbors.
Although it has yet to be named publicly, the developers are actively selling
the space with the myth of American dynamism.

1932

NOVEMBER

COLUMBUS HAUS

      The first major tenant is the F.W. Woolworth Company [4.14]. The sign says "opening in January." Someone has drawn a face on the whitewash of the second floor. Columbus Haus was being acclaimed by critics throughout Europe as the most impressive modern building in the city.

1933

WINTER

POTSDAMER PLATZ WITH COLUMBUS HAUS

Mendelsohn confided his increasing concern with the political situation in a letter from Berlin on February 11, 1933:

The first consequence of the new orthodoxy coming into the open is in my not being invited to take part in the competition for the new Reichsbank building. Thirty German architects, and I am not one of them.

I expected as much, but the task would have stimulated me and would have brought me somewhat more into equilibrium. Meanwhile, yesterday, we heard Hitler outline his program.[11]

Hitler became German Chancellor on January 30, 1933. Shortly thereafter, Mendelsohn left Germany with his family forever.[12]

In the photograph the billboard advertises the movie "The Rebel" with Louis Trenker at the Palast Cinema and Odol toothpaste [4.15]. There is snow on the ground, and the windows of Columbus Haus are all covered up. In the first weeks of March, senior members of the SS negotiate with the owners of Columbus Haus for the use of the top six floors. The Schutzhaft (protective custody) program was put into effect immediately after the proclamation of the emergency decree of February 28, 1933. It led at once to the arrest of the officials and members of the Communist party. It allowed for up to three months police detention under "The Protection of the German People Decree" issued by President Hindenburg on February 4, 1933. By the end of April 1933, more than 25,000 people had been arrested in Prussia, at least 10,000 of whom were Berliners. By the end of April 1933, the SS had established Columbus Haus as its central protective custody prison.

Rudolph Diels, then head of the political division of the Berlin Police Praesidium, reported later on these operations:

In those March days, every SA[13] man was 'on the heels of the enemy,' each knew what he had to do. The Sturm cleaned up the districts. They knew not only where their enemies lived, they had also long ago discovered their hideouts and meeting places . . . . Not only the communists but anybody who had ever expressed himself against Hitler's movement was in danger. . . . The gay victors [the SA] roared along the Kürfurstendamm and the Linden in elegant automobiles. Manufacturers or shopkeepers had presented them with these cars or put them at their disposal in order to assure themselves protection. The cars of Jews and democrats were simply confiscated.

In those March days the concentration camps around Berlin were set up . . . . The 'bunkers' in the Hedemann and Voss Strasse became hellish torture chambers. The SS Columbia prison [Columbus Haus], the worst of these torture chambers, was established.[14]

As with each of the camps, a special SS division with its own insignia was established to run the Columbus Haus prison. By March 1935, the total prison population in the seven camps under SS control was approximately 9,000. Thirty-five hundred were in Dachau. It can be inferred that Columbus Haus held three to four hundred prisoners. Each prisoner would have carried a distinguishing mark, a triangular piece of material sewn on to the uniform, varied in color depending on the category – red for political prisoners, purple for Jehovah's Witnesses, black for anti-socials, green for criminals, pink for homosexuals, blue for immigrants. Jews were made to wear two yellow triangles sewn to form the Star of David.

The choice of Columbus Haus for a prison was essentially a practical matter. It offered the largest amount of free space close to the center of political operations on Voss Strasse. Also, the building's modern planning offered advantages that would not have been present in older buildings. The floors, completely open except for the structural columns, allowed the construction of a facility tailored to the needs of a detention program. The vehicle access at the rear of the building, screened from the street, allowed for the passage of prisoners away from the public eye. The service elevators allowed for access to the detention floors without disturbing the other activities in the building.

4.16
A minute of silence in
Potsdamer Platz on the death
of President Hindenburg,
August 8, 1934.

1934
AUGUST 8

A MINUTE OF SILENCE IN POTSDAMER PLATZ
ON THE DEATH OF PRESIDENT HINDENBURG
                    Columbus Haus and Woolworth's
can be seen at the top of the picture, and the imperial salutes face all directions
[4.16].

1934
SEPTEMBER

POTSDAMER PLATZ WITH COLUMBUS HAUS
                    Unaware of the ways in which
Columbus Haus was being used, the English architectural historian and
biographer of Erich Mendelsohn, Arnold Whittick, wrote: "The best view for
obtaining a notion of the entire design, as both the facades are clearly seen,
is from the opposite side of Potsdamer Platz near the Haus Vaterland [4.17].
Rising to a height of 125 feet with its uncompromising horizontal emphasis,
it has from this point, a grandeur and magnificence which make it for me the
most impressive modern building in Berlin."[15]

THE INTERNATIONALE APOTHEKE IN COLUMBUS HAUS

   The German travel agency on the second floor proudly displays posters for the coming Winter Olympics in 1936 [4.18]. The Apotheke is described in the windows as an "English Dispensary" and as an "American Drugstore." Above, in the midst of a vast city, the SS Columbus Prison was able to operate without interference and, to a large measure, in total secrecy.

1935

FALL

4.18
 The Internationale Apotheke
 in the ground floor of Columbus
 Haus, Fall 1935.

1935

FALL

POTSDAMER PLATZ FROM THE AIR

The new order has arrived [4.19].[16]
The architecture of Columbus Haus would order a future free from words,
free from memory, free from old gods, free to explore the infinite character
of space and time. However, most of the windows are still blocked up.

4.20
Woodcut, untitled,
artist unknown, 1935.

1935

WOODCUT, UNTITLED, ARTIST UNKNOWN

By the beginning of 1934, many
of those who had escaped detention fled to Paris or to Zurich and attempted

to draw international attention to the brutality of the protective custody program and to the emergence of the concentration camps [4.20]. The SS developed regulations in response:

In accordance with the law on revolutionaries, the following offenders, considered as agitators, will be hanged. Anyone who, for the purpose of agitating, does the following in the camp, at work, in the sleeping quarters, in the kitchens and workshops, toilets and places of rest: discusses politics, carries on controversial talks and meetings, forms cliques, loiters around with others; who, for the purpose of supplying the propaganda of the opposition with atrocity stories, collects true or false information about the concentration camp; receives such information, buries it, talks about it to others, smuggles it out of the camp into the hands of foreign visitors or others by clandestine or other means . . . .[17]

In March of 1935, two prisoners were shot in the SS Columbus Prison,[18] allegedly for resisting their captors. Subsequent investigations revealed that many of the general guard regulations developed for Dachau in October 1933 were enforced in Columbus Haus. These included the following:

Anyone who allows a prisoner to escape will be arrested and handed over to the Bavarian Political Police for negligently releasing a prisoner. A prisoner who tries to escape will be shot without warning. Guards who in the execution of their duties shoot a prisoner will not be punished.

If a guard is assaulted by a prisoner the attack will be countered not by physical force but by use of firearms. A guard who fails to observe this regulation may expect to be dismissed immediately . . . .

In case of mutiny or revolt by a detachment of prisoners all guards on duty will open fire. Warning shots are not permitted on principle.[19]

Legal authorities in Berlin were aware of and disturbed by the imposition of such regulations. In the Columbus Haus Prison case, although the SS guards were given token sentences, the Berlin Chief Public Prosecutor declared that "service regulations cannot exonerate the accused." Though most forms of punishment – regular beatings, hard labor, isolation, and the hanging of prisoners from hooks to dislocate arms – were frequently applied in Columbus Haus, one result of the case was that the more severe penalties could not be enforced without the approval of the inspector of concentration camps.

The SS Columbus Prison was disbanded in the spring of 1936 as part of a plan to reorganize the Shutzhaft program. It can be inferred that the facility had become too small and inconvenient for what had become a nationwide program of detention and eradication.

COLUMBUS HAUS

4.21
Columbus Haus, Winter 1936.

Columbus Haus remained in government possession, the lower floors housing various nationalized industries such as steel, bus, and wagon manufacturing. In the photograph, swastikas fly from the roof terrace and in every bay of the lower floor [4.21]. Mendelsohn wrote years later, in one of his few references to Columbus Haus, that in the course of its erection "my client demanded the introduction of horizontal stone bands for neon advertisements. He practically makes a fortune. I lose one – architecturally!"[20] Yet, the agencies of the Nazi government were the only ones ever to advertise from its walls before the war.

1936
WINTER

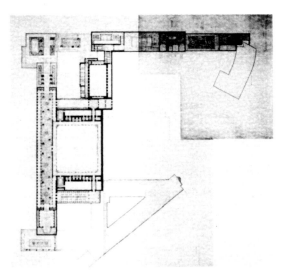

4.22
Albert Speer's study plans
for the Palace of the Reich Marshal,
March 1942. Columbus Haus
was an alien appendage on the
order of the Reich.

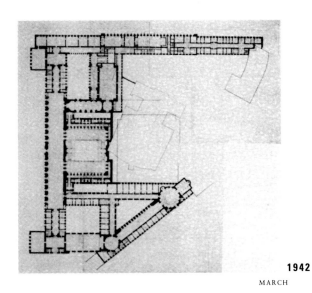

1942

MARCH

THE CENTER OF ALBERT SPEER'S PLAN FOR BERLIN

Though all else on the northwest
of Potsdamer Platz is to be demolished, Columbus Haus is to survive and will
adjoin Speer's Palace for the Reich Marshal [4.22].

Mendelsohn and Hitler represent extreme positions in the struggle for the form of the future between those who see only the future and those who see only the past. The implications go far beyond the surface of buildings.

ORDER

Order for Hitler and the Thousand Year Reich would always remain autocratic, axial, symmetrical, and hierarchical.

For Mendelsohn, order in the potential future would be circumstantial, horizontal, indeterminate, spatial, sensual, transparent, reflective, illusionistic, improvised, and dynamic. It would be jazz in contrast to Hitler's Wagner. It would delight in ambiguous and fluid passages in a continual state of reformation and rediscovery.

TIME

The eruption of eternity into time was at the very base of Hitler's project. He built to create an eternal present and to defy the temporal limits of existence. His were objects of a constant and singular time, utterly predictable in an unchanging future.

For Mendelsohn time was a wave-like force determining the order of things in space. Time existed in his imagination as a fourth dimension of endless ambiguity and freedom. Time was a conceptual force advancing the perceptual condition of reality out of the constraints of Euclidian and Cartesian order. He would construct in irregular times, superimposed times, times without perspective, times of endless potential, and times without memory. His time was in motion and by the time you asked "what time was this place," it had gone.

Hitler wished in reality to stop time; Mendelsohn sought to expand time infinitely into the relativity of space.

MEMORY

Architecture's noblest and highest significance, for Hitler, was in symbolizing the power of the state and the memory of its founder. He sought to form a collective conscience to the memory of German culture by the construction of monuments that time could not change — save to turn the acts commemorated into myths of invincibility and absolute superiority. His was an architecture nurturing mass obedience through the power of its continual remembrance and redemption.

For Mendelsohn, memory was not the concern of the state. Architecture could not speak and should not speak to the memories of individual experience. His was be an architecture without memory that refused to monumentalize anything save the ideals of freedom and potential. Within its walls, memory existed in cycles of ritual in the passage through life. The representation of past architectures could distort the potentiality of the future; reviving ancient and forgotten gods and symbols could interfere dangerously with the soul.

SYMBOL

The dome of Hitler's Great Hall was to stand forever as the ultimate universal symbol. Greater than Hadrian's Pantheon or St. Peter's, Hitler's Great Hall was to be the root of domination. All else in its shadow would be merely a variation in loudness, dialect, and physiology; it would be the egg and the seed, the cycle of life, eternal recurrence, and the perfect oneness, forever unchanging.

For Mendelsohn, such simple roots and concrete forms were too narrow to release the myriad meanings offered in the future. There was also a danger in the recovery of ancient orders and symbols, the danger of resurrecting the tyranny and persecution they represented. Vital symbols for the future would have been present in each unique structure and in the ever-changing plays of circumstance.

PROGRESS

The dictatorship of the state, Hitler believed, would end the degeneration of Western society caused by materialism and the emergence of mass cultures. Architecture would set the stage for the return to order. Only a constant reality could provide the foundations on which world reformation could be built. The proposition that an evolving and changing modern society needed an ambiguous architecture that ignored the past was demonstrably false. The more social structures are in a process of change, the more architecture should remain constant, otherwise all will end in unreality and alienation.

For Mendelsohn, the progression to the new world demanded a new stage and a new beginning. Progress in reality had to take infinitely varied forms to present the multitude of new possibilities and desires. There could be no constants in progress, only differing rates of change. Any attempt at constancy only limited the potential for the future, and all things had to pass.

CULTURE

The culture of place, according to Hitler, could be rooted only in the ancient desires of its people; all else was insignificant. The issue of culture, however, could not be separated from the issue of race,[21] and architecture was a fundamental represen-tation of race.[21] The distinction of Greek architecture was equivalent to the distinction of the German race, each the evolved product of a millennium of significant breeding.

For Mendelsohn, the culture of place was always intimately connected to the culture of knowledge. Modern science and technology made diverse cultures supranational and redefined the nature and order of all things. Architecture was to provide the fluid structure within which the future would be equipped. Only the weak and the foolish would direct society to the recollection of local histories.

Lies

The righteousness of Hitler's cause gave truth to whatever was touched by it. The Great Hall was to be built, not to deceive, but to establish the truth and continue to represent its ideal and order into the infinite future. There was in the ancient language of architecture an autonomous significance that transcended the uses to which it was put, and despite the pettiness of temporal circumstances that language could never lie.

We exist in a reality of endless deception, according to Mendelsohn. The argument that centuries of the careful evolution of classical forms present the highest and most virtuous state of reality, irrespective of use, is a two-thousand-year lie, an absurdity promoted by forces that seek to reestablish an imperialist order. Temples enshrining the power of gods, kings, and manufacturers are mere theatrical disguises. Only in the rejection of past architectures and past realities can the truthful character of the culture and of the time be revealed.

Violence

For Hitler, people and cultures must pass through periods of great violence in the struggle for the highest performance of the human spirit. Architecture, however, must rise above it, maintain a meaningful order, and persist in the representation of the ideal.

For Mendelsohn, the fulfillment of the modern age requires violent change in the order of all things to rip culture from the interference of mythical histories. Only those who seek power over others are condemned to manipulate the dead forms of reality. Architecture must speak only of its own nature to become the deliberate instrument of the manifold plays of the future.

1945

MARCH

4.23

The construction of a
defensive wall on Potsdamer Platz,
March 1945.

BUILDING A TANK BLOCKADE ON POTSDAMER PLATZ

In the last weeks of the war a barricade is
being built between the Schinkel Gates at Potsdamer Platz [4.23]. With scrap
metal from the trolley rails and rubble from the buildings, the work of old
men and boys must withstand the concentrated force of all the approaching
Russian armies. It will be the last defense before Hitler's headquarters in the
Chancellery. In the background, the burned hulk of Columbus Haus shows
little direct bomb damage. The second and the third floors have been put
back into use and reconstruction work continues at the ground floor.

1945

SUMMER

POTSDAMER PLATZ

The war is over and all is lost [4.24].

1946

SPRING

POTSDAMER PLATZ FROM THE POTSDAMER BAHNHOF

The war is over and everything is
united in death [4.25].

POTSDAMER PLATZ

The war is over and the barricade has gone, taking with it most of Schinkel's little gate temple [4.26]. One exquisitely proportioned column survives to lend the scene a spirit of ancient tragedy. The masonry buildings in the background have been deeply penetrated by the aerial bombing, yet Columbus Haus on the right is still a complete presence. There are few people around and everyone carries a bag.

4.26
Potsdamer Platz and
the remains of Schinkel's gates,
March 1946.

1946
MARCH

COLUMBUS HAUS

The unified steel structure of Columbus Haus withstood the aerial bombing. The marks on its facade and damage to the terrace came from Russian shells fired during the occupation of the city and in attacks on the Potsdamer Platz barricade which destroyed the Potsdam Gates. In the photograph it is being reoccupied [4.27]. Hastily built walls of salvaged brick fill in the horizontal bands to accommodate the crude metal windows framing small panes of glass. Large sheets of glass no longer exist. The Wertheim Store has moved from its gothic ruin on Leipziger Platz to occupy the space formerly used by Woolworth's. Next door the Columbus Restaurant has opened for business.

4.27
Columbus Haus,
October 1946.

4.28
Potsdamer Platz,
December 1946.

1946
DECEMBER

POTSDAMER PLATZ

Framed by the ruins of Schinkel's gates, Wertheim's puts up a neon sign and Heinz Gaunitz promotes his business with banners on the upper floor – "Parfum Superbe"[4.28].

1948

MAY

4.29
Russian soldiers on
Potsdamer Platz,
May 1948.

RUSSIAN SOLDIERS ON POTSDAMER PLATZ

Physically, little has changed; there is, however, an increasing awareness of the distinctions between the sectors of occupation. The Russian creation of the communist state of East Germany has isolated the Western sector, now called West Berlin, in a hostile nation. Potsdamer Platz marks the boundary between the British and Russian sectors. It has become the center of an extensive black market trade arising from the disparity between Western and Eastern economies. In the picture, Russian soldiers negotiate with a concealed figure, and in the background Columbus Haus has been crudely restored to the fourth level [4.29].

In June 1948, Russia responded to Western currency reforms intended for West Germany and West Berlin by attempting to impose their own currency reform on all of Berlin. To achieve this, Russia imposed a blockade on West Berlin cutting all ground connections to the West. By the end of the month, the Berlin Airlift had begun. The task for the British and American air forces was to supply West Berlin with the daily necessities of life, above all fuel and food. In November and December, the East Germans cut the energy supply, telephones, and most transportation links to the Western sector. With the persistent demonstration of Western will, Russia backed down and the airlift ended on May 12, 1949. During the eleven months of the airlift, Berlin was kept alive by 272,264 flights.

THE BORDER WITH EAST GERMANY

Workers erect a barricade between the districts of Mitte and Tiergarten, between the Russian sector and the British sector, between East Berlin and West Berlin. By random chance Columbus Haus sits on a triangle of land under the jurisdiction of East Germany that projects into West Berlin. The East Berlin city government moves to socialize all properties under its administration. In the photograph, Wertheim's and all the other retail stores in Columbus Haus have been replaced by the state-run department store H.O. [4.30].

4.30
Potsdamer Platz,
April 10, 1951.

1951

APRIL 10

1951

APRIL

COLUMBUS HAUS/H.O. STORE

The state department store occupies the restored lower floors of Columbus Haus [4.31]. The old name has been removed. The signs on the building now call for peace and advertise meats and vegetables.

1951

AUGUST 17

THE H.O. DEPARTMENT STORE

The H.O. Department Store stands heroically on the border with the imperialist West [4.32]. One large mural proclaims: "We love life, therefore we fight remilitarization." In the mural on the right, the youth of many nations link hands around the globe, reading: "The youth of the world united in Berlin help us to maintain the peace." The foreground carries the last traces of the Hotel Palast. The road appears closed and at this point in the city there is a barricade between the East and West sectors.

4.33
Riots in Potsdamer Platz,
June 17, 1953.

1953

JUNE 17

RIOTS IN POTSDAMER PLATZ

The people of East Berlin, led by construction workers angry with the decision to increase work quotas, riot against the government and against communism. A major confrontation between the rioters and Russian tanks takes place at the Potsdam Gate and many people are hurt in the confusion [4.33]. In the photograph the H.O. Department Store has become the focus of the action because of its symbolic presence at the edge of the Eastern city and it has been set on fire. The figures relaxed and smiling in the foreground are in West Berlin. They are spectators to their brothers' pain.

4.34
Columbus Haus, Autumn 1954.

1954
AUTUMN

NAMELESS BUILDING

The damage from the riots was minor but the city is dying along the division [4.34]. The authorities close the department store and board up the structure.

4.35
Columbus Haus from the West,
April 11, 1956.

1956
APRIL 11

THE FORMER COLUMBUS HAUS FROM THE WEST

East Berlin authorities decide to demolish all buildings on the peninsula of land projecting into West Berlin [4.35]. This decision was the result of a military plan that foresaw the need for a permanent division.

1957

FALL

DEMOLITION ON POTSDAMER PLATZ

The former Columbus Haus is being carefully demolished floor by floor, its materials, especially the steel, salvaged for re-use [4.36]. Potsdamer Platz is now at the edge of both cities, East and West. Trolley cars still pass through, but people seldom go there. The subway entrance in the foreground is still used.

4.36
Demolition of Columbus Haus,
Fall 1957.

1961

OCTOBER

THE BERLIN WALL AT POTSDAMER PLATZ

The first wall, hastily put together, follows the exact boundary line between the Tiergarten and Mitte districts, save for one large triangular piece of land that the authorities choose not to enclose for practical reasons. In the fenced area on the left once stood Columbus Haus [4.37]. The subway entrance in the foreground is now closed.

4.37
The Berlin Wall at Potsdamer Platz,
October 1961.

NOWHERE

          A spur in the Wall indicates that this is the territory of the GDR and the chain-link fence maintains the memory of its authority. This place, the exact site of Columbus Haus, is now nowhere and the land is returning to wilderness [4.38].

4.38
Potsdamer Platz, August 1981.

1981

AUGUST

In 1929 Mendelsohn produced a book of pictures he had taken the previous year in Russia and America. It was titled *Russland Europa Amerika Ein Architecktonischer Ouerschnitt*. In the conclusion he wrote two short poems. In the first, he reviewed the oppositions in character and will between Russia and America:

The hope of the new world has as its signal beacon a magnificent

combination:

Russia's power of sacrifice,

Vehemence of emotion -

the intuitive,

the impulsively religious element in its nature -

combined with America's unproblematic activeness and energy,

applied at America's high technological level!

Russia and America,

the collective and the individual,

America and Russia,

the earthly and the divine.

This is the problem of the new world architecture:

The finiteness of mechanics

plus the infiniteness of life.[22]

In the second he displayed an intense existentialism:

Only the active hand, the active mind has a right to life.

Symbol of the machine, the aeroplane, the splitting of the atom.

God lives only in the deed,

not in faith,

not in reflection.

Art creates only reality.

Art is the highest expression of life,

is life itself.[23]

There is no record of Mendelsohn's reaction to the use of the airplane and the split atom in the world war that followed. How, if "God lived only in the deed," could Mendelsohn become reconciled to such a willful and destructive God? He never commented publicly on the tragic part played by Columbus Haus in its failure to reach a synthesis between America in "the finiteness of mechanics" and Russia in "the infiniteness of life." He died of lung cancer in America in 1952.

Architecture participates in life more than any other art, and much of it is inevitably changed and destroyed in its use. The ideas that inform architecture are rarely related to those uses to which it is often put. Yet, as it does represent the formative ideas of a culture it is appropriate to consider how such ideas are received, and to examine whether the built forms in any measure shape the flow of events.

For all its force Columbus Haus can be viewed, not as a unique product of modernism, but merely as the simple negation and antithesis of the much more ambiguous products of modern commercialism – Wertheim's, Haus Vaterland, Pschorr Haus, and the Hotel Der Fürstenhof. Where they concealed structure, Columbus Haus revealed it. Where they took style from history, it found style in the removal of history. Where they sought individuality, it sought neutrality. Where they sought compromise with the culture, it wished to do battle. Those children of the Wilhelmine bourgeoisie, like Mendelsohn, who promoted the modern vision that equated the liberation of architectural forms with cultural freedom, failed to reflect that they were merely reacting against the values of their parents. They failed to anticipate that the removal of the rich and subtle accretions of culture from architecture also meant the removal of their censuring and constraining influence. They failed to ask what sort of past this architecture would have in the future, when the present always dwelt in the promise of the future.

In opting for neutrality and in removing the authority of historical form, Mendelsohn's project could be seen to compliment and support extremes of action in all directions. A reality empty of meaning would be free to carry any meaning. What may have begun as a liberal and liberating vision resulted in a projection and imposition by a detached elite of a new, universal order no less constraining and conservative than the projects of absolute kings and dictators.

The architect's desire as represented in the object is, in a sense, unknowable, and its influence on subsequent ages cannot be anticipated. It is too early to judge whether the idealists of modernism were right or wrong in believing that architecture could clarify the future in an age still in the midst of profoundly disordered change, or in believing that there could be a beneficial relation between their simple structures and the multiple forces released by the revolutions in the order of all knowledge.

Architecture, thus, may be seen as a mask, a temporal illusion reaching for a deeper reality that is suspected to exist, yet never fully perceived or realized. Its virtue is in briefly concealing the uncertainty of its own task and in interfering briefly with the inevitability of death. Art can become the antithesis of reality.

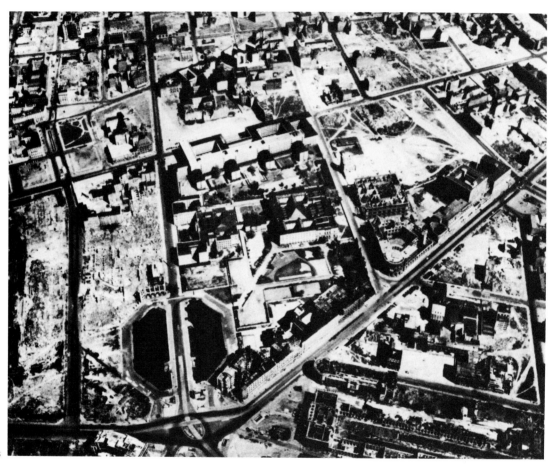

1950s

5.1

Aerial view of central Berlin from
the mid-1950s. At the bottom
left is the roof of Columbus Haus,
and everything north of Leipziger
Platz has been demolished,
except the ruin of Wertheim's.
The Prussian House and Goering's
Air Force Headquarters have been
fully re-roofed and put back into
use. The Hotel Der Fürstenhof
remains dead and unattended as
it has for the last ten years.

On the first of April, 1945, the 3rd division of the Russian Garde
Panzerarmee invaded the city from the south through the suburbs of
Lichterrade and Marienfelde. For the first time the Russian heavy artillery
could concentrate on the center of Berlin. To the west, on the 23rd of April,
the Russian 28th Army took the suburb of Rudow, and by the 26th it had
formed a line from Tiergarten across to Alexander Platz linking with the
2nd division of the Russian Garde Panzerarmee, the 3rd and 5th Russian
Stossarmee, and the 8th Russian Gardearmee to encircle the city and place a

stranglehold around Hitler's crumbling center of power, the Chancellery.

A moment of truth:

At the end the whole of Berlin seemed to be pounding with high explosives and roaring with flames. On May Day the bombardment rose to a crescendo, which only sank when the commander of the city surrendered Berlin the next morning. We had long ago become used to the debris and desolation, since the great raids of the R.A.F., but after two weeks of Russian seige it seemed that we were living in a ghastly inferno. Not only ruins everywhere, and entire blocks gutted and smoking, but everywhere craters in the streets, half-hearted trenches and pits for guns and tanks: bodies, ammunition, civilian cars smashed to scrap iron, trams torn and riddled, walls cracked and blackened, the crash of falling masonry mingled with the whine and burst of mortars and 'Katyushas,' the moan of rocket guns, the sharp defiant note of rifles, or the abrupt drilling noise of a Spandau from heaps of wreckage where it seemed impossible for any man to be. It was not just the end of the war, it was the end of war as we knew it, the ultimate reduction to ghastly absurdity. The civilians did not know what to do; in any case they could do nothing. They locked themselves into houses and cellars, and waited for the next explosion and the hurrying footsteps of the advancing Russians.[1]

At four a.m. on the morning of April 29, Hitler married Eva Braun, wrote a will, and dictated his last political statement. Soon thereafter he and his new wife took their lives, she with poison, he with a pistol shot. Their bodies were removed from the bunker and burned in the Chancellery garden. Later that morning, Russian tanks entered Potsdamer Platz and the following day the Red Army took the Reichstag and the Ministry of the Interior. On the evening of May 1, the Chancellery fell. On May 2, the remains of the Berlin Army, numbering around 60,000 soldiers, surrendered. During this final offensive some 250,000 of Hitler's last defense force, soldiers and auxiliaries, many of them children, were reported killed, captured, or missing.

As the remnants of the German armies were rounded up, obscene materials were found among the papers of both officers and foot soldiers. From the Eastern front came photographs of the victims of torture, hanging, and flogging, some of them children. Conquest did not appease the Russian wrath. In this city, above all others, the killing of twenty million of their countrymen and the leveling of their cities would be avenged. The combined Russian forces, numbering hundreds of thousands of men, divided the city between them, and moving neighborhood by neighborhood, street by street, and house by house, entered every private place to smash, defile, and gut every living thing, possession, and surface in a blind and frenzied fury. This state of random violence persisted until the American, British, and French forces moved into the city after the first of July, 1945.

1946

SPRING

"The days in Germany were like the days in no other country, there to be breathed into being as one might breath into the lips and nostrils of the dead. The hours of them seem suspended, perhaps brought to a halt by the monumental rubble, but halted so long ago that it could no longer be recalled in what month, or year, or even in what lifetime their sequence had reached this pause," said one observer.[2] Another, the poet W.H. Auden, walking through the destruction in the summer of 1945, said it caused the same straining of the imagination he had felt in the Roman Forum, the persistent and intensely painful presence in the imagination of what was against what remained. The ruined city had a soul and gravity it never had in life [5.2].

All the buildings look alike and the smell of destruction catches every breath. The odor is in the dust, an earthy chemical smell, and some-

5.2

Leipziger Platz from the roof of Columbus Haus in the Spring of 1946. At left are the remains of the Palast Hotel. The street in front of it has collapsed through to the subway tunnel. Hand pushed carts on rails carry rubble from the mountains of crushed stone. The north wall of Leipziger Platz is completely destroyed, and the remains of the Wertheim Department Store on the north-east corner have become a gothic ruin. On the southwest corner stands the burnt-out shell of Hotel Der Fürstenhof, behind which sits the exposed structure of the dome of Haus Vaterland. Only the portico of Schinkel's south temple gate still stands; on the north only a single column and the rear wall remain. The central park has been leveled and plowed and planted with vegetables; on the south it remains a dangerous field of craters and unexploded bombs. On Leipzigerstrasse the trolley cars roll by as if nothing had happened, and a great many market stalls lend a festive air to the scene.

where barely perceptible is the scent of rot. Every object, large and small, has been mutilated. Yet the mind continues to force a wholeness on everything, the way it at first refuses to acknowledge the loss of a limb; it is as a veil shaped from memory, bright and sharp, not of what was but of what will come. It excites the imagination into a sense of terrible freedom, and even as months stretch into years, moods continue to swing from euphoria into choking terror. It is the terror of the unknown. The destruction removes not only memories but ancient and comforting symbols whose accumulation in the texture of a city had given meaning to life. The loss of the past means the loss of the future.

The winter of 1945-46 was less severe than predicted, yet it took its toll on the will and health of the survivors. The Russians had desecrated every building and the Berliners – only the old and the young, women and children – moved back into the ruins. To get through the winter they combed the streets of rubble and sifted through the parks, taking the possessions of neighbors and strangers, anything that could be eaten or would burn. The ruined city evolved into a crude labyrinth of caves and passages, places of refuge tunneled out of the rubble and insulated against the cold with whatever could be found. With no gas or electricity and a meager food supply from the conquerors, the Berliners were reduced to hunting and gathering for survival.

Places familiar from childhood, deeply imprinted in memory, were now present only in traces beneath the rubble. Thresholds survived, thresholds of mosaic and tile and words now meaningless. However, it was not the surviving fragments that upset the imagination, but a new reality created in the clearing of the rubble. In their harsh and primitive shelters they felt the loss of a thousand years of culture.

Throughout the ruins, at every corner, door, and gate, and on the surviving walls of shops and bars, thousands and thousands of messages appeared. Scrawled and scratched in chalk or paint, on paper or cards nailed to doors or forced into cracks, were thousands of notes through which people sought their mothers, brothers, sisters, children, and friends. It was the first act of reconstruction, an intense and tragic correspondence that persisted throughout the first year until hope or memory faded.

However, it was the act of clearing the rubble, of removing the past, that rekindled a sense of the future. The awareness that hands working in concert could literally move mountains eased the agony and relieved the sense of helplessness. Disciplined brigades of tens of thousands of women systematically, hand over hand, stone by stone, and brick by brick, recreated a new and elementary order out of the fragments. Opening passages, clearing the subway tunnels, and making the roads whole again was more significant to the renewal of life than the resurrection of walls.

The building magazine *Baukunst Und Werkform* carried a message from the heart of the survivors in 1947:

1948

5.3
Leipziger Platz from
Potsdamer Platz, 1948.

1947 A Post War Appeal: Fundamental demands. The collapse has destroyed the visible world that constituted our life and our work. When it took place we believed, with a sense of liberation, that now we should be able to return to work. Today, two years later, we realize how much the visible breakdown is merely the expression of a spiritual devastation and we are tempted to sink into despair. We have been reduced to fundamentals and the task must be tackled afresh from this point.

All the peoples of the earth are faced with this task; for our people it is a case of to be or not to be. Upon the conscience of us, the creative, lies the obligation to build the new visible world that makes up our life and our work.[3]

It was signed by some of the leading architects who had returned to Berlin, including Lilly Reich, lover and colleague of the architect Mies van der Rohe, and Albert Speer's teacher, Heinrich Tessenow.[4]

The city had been divided into four zones of occupation, with the Russian sector, by far the largest, in the east and those of France, Britain, and the U.S. in the west. Each sector was under the legal and administrative control of its army of occupation.[5] In basic terms, the division was a political opposition between East and West, between Marxist-Leninism and liberal capitalism. Below this, the real culture of the city had been critically wounded but was not dead. By the spring of 1946 the occupying armies began, each in their own way and according to their own ideals, to construct the temporary illusion of a new reality. Like side shows on a carnival midway, temporary shops and banners established with ease a new and colorful stage in the midst of ruin. A photograph of Leipziger Platz in 1948 shows that strange moment in which two illusions of the future meet along the edge of the divided city [5.3]. The West fosters commercial activity around objects of extreme luxury – watches, jewelry, and porcelain – which are sold from kiosks on the corner of Potsdamer Platz. The East responds with murals of heroic proportion representing to the West their ideal of a healthy and vigorous life free from the corruption of materialism.

The Russians, however, sought from the very beginning to make a much deeper and more permanent mark on the city. Within weeks of the surrender, in the midst of the ruins, the Soviet army began to construct a monument to their victory [5.4]. The symbolism was explicit. Within a hundred yards of the Reichstag, in a field still strewn with the detritus of war, a monolith of white marble was erected to support the figure of a Soviet soldier. It had the theatrical presence of a spike through the heart of an evil state [5.5].[6]

The Stalinist reconstruction of East Berlin and East Germany began with the removal of every usable asset, from hand

5.5
The Soviet War Memorial and the
remains of the Reichstag, from
the Tiergarten, 1945.

tools to power stations, as reparation to Russia for German aggression and destruction. Russia, while reducing East Germany to raw poverty, promised through its rigid and loyal Communist administration a great future under socialism.[7] The new Soviet Embassy [5.6], visible across the ruins north from Potsdamer Platz, was the major mark of the communist conquest of the city.[8] It was a project in which Stalin took a personal interest. In 1938 he had written that the artist who understands the "totality of social relationships" comes forth as the engineer of the human soul,[9] and, like Hitler, he saw himself as the supreme artist of the state. The site immediately to the east of the Brandenburg Gate had been occupied by the Russian Embassy since the nineteenth century and was now at the very edge of the Soviet sector, at the very edge of a new nation. Western allies had refused to recognize East Germany as a separate and independent nation with Berlin as its capital, so for Stalin the new embassy had to be a compelling, powerful, and permanent symbol of the Russian presence and the idea of East Germany.

1945

1951

It was the design of the Moscow architectural collective Stryshewski, Lebedinskij, Sichert, and Skujin, and it emerged as an object of calm self-possession formed in the style of French neo-classicism. At its center, placed above the massive cubic hall, is a small temple with stone figures at each corner standing in eternal mourning to the memory of the war dead. As evidence of the simple yet ironic character of the language of architecture, the temple in its form and expression closely resembles the Temple of the Eternal Watch on Königsplatz in Munich where Hitler, in his will of 1938, asked to be buried. Begun in 1950, the embassy and its temple were all but finished with Stalin's death in 1953.

5.6
Stryshewski, Lebedinskij, Sichert, and Skujin, The Soviet Embassy, East Berlin, 1951.

DIALECTICS IN REALITY

Lenin, in a footnote to *Materialism and Empirio-Criticism*, gives a definition of the operational power of dialectics:

The identity of opposites is the recognition of the contradictory, mutually exclusive, opposite tendencies in all phenomena and processes of nature (including mind and society). The condition for the knowledge of all processes of the world in their self-movement, in their spontaneous development, in their real life, is the knowledge of them as a unity of opposites. Development is the struggle of opposites.[10]

Here is the essence of the philosophical motivation that underlay all Soviet action in the restructuring of Germany and Berlin. In 1948, Stalin forced the division of Germany when he reformed the Soviet area of occupation into a new autonomous nation, the German Democratic Republic. The remainder of Germany under U.S., French, and British occupation was reconstructed as the Federal Republic of Germany.[11] Berlin, one hundred and twenty miles inside the Soviet sector, remained divided among the four armies of occupation with East Germany claiming Berlin as its capital. The Russians immediately moved to establish socialist control over all aspects of city life in the Eastern sector and to make explicit the struggle of opposites by isolating West Berlin and exaggerating the capitalist response. All attempts at projecting the future were in some measure beyond control and made the evolution of reality blind.

How do a people and a culture restore order and reality to a city after such complete destruction? The question was taken much more seriously in the East than in the West. Ernst Hoffman wrote in 1952 in the first issue of *Deutsche Architektur*, a building magazine for East Germany, that the principal architectural task to be confronted was the theoretical development of a new, intrinsically German architecture imbued with worker's realism. The great difficulty to be overcome, he argued, was "the ideological murkiness of the architect." He attacked the prevailing fashions in architectural theory:

Formalism, which includes the modernist schools of Constructivism and Functionalism attached to the Bauhaus style, reflects the declining imperialist world with American finance capital at its head. Its worst fault is to propose an architecture independent of the social structure, a development equally at home in New York and Moscow.

Functionalism satisfies only material needs, spiritual needs are discarded and the working man finds his house a living machine and he himself degraded to a functional appendage.

Constructivism sees construction as the first principle relegating other considerations to second place. Arbitrarily selected geometrical pictures substitute for apartments, cultural and government buildings.[12]

In rejecting the schools attached to the Bauhaus he was rejecting the most significant contribution of Germany to architecture and design after the First World War.[13] He was led to this position by the adoption of post-Lenin Soviet artistic theory. After Lenin's death, the dismissal of all modernist experimentation in the arts as bourgeois indulgence had, with Stalin's encouragement, produced years of theorizing to define the appropriate architecure for the Russian Soviet. What emerged was the adoption of classical architecture as the most appropriate and highest expression of social realism. The masters of the new German Soviet would impose this classicism on the future order of Berlin. The Soviet Embassy had been the first sign.

Hoffman's argument for "realism" was brief and echoed much of Hitler's thinking:

Both Functionalism and Constructivism turn buildings into spiritless boxes, but Realism builds upon the classical German heritage and the Soviet experience, it mirrors democracy, peace, and socialism. It blends pragmatic needs with artistic discipline; it serves the material needs of society, and the spiritual aesthetic needs of man by bringing a historically determined ideo-content to expression![14]

In *Deutsche Architektur 3* the following year, the architect G. Minerwin, in his essay "Lenin's Theory of Reflection and the Question of the Theory of Social Realism," continued to struggle to establish a German dimension to the debate. He repeated the attacks on modern formalism:

Formalist tendencies were already unmasked and eliminated in the 1930s. Some, however, remain and unfortunately show themselves in the handling of form as an artistic expression, or in the revelation of pure function, or in the expression of constructive technology, or when single buildings are dressed with the architectural forms mechanically borrowed from the past.[15]

But his main concern was to place aesthetics on a truly scientific basis. He argued that the theory of cognition had always played an important part in Lenin's philosophy. His text was Lenin's *Materialism and Empirio-Criticism*, in which Lenin had defended Marxism against its critics. Of particular interest to Minerwin were those aspects of Lenin's argument that addressed our experience of reality and his theory that material objects must be wholly independent of subjective sensation:

Things exist outside of us. Our perceptions and conceptions are their images, . . . essentially [Lenin's] interpretation of Marx is the independence of the object of reality from sensation. In this he is countering the old mechanistic view that sensation is the source of existence with a dialectical view which holds that matter is the source of existence and it is independent of sensation.[16]

Hence the subjectivism of expressionist works of modernism could in no way be authentic documents of the reality of mass culture:

Subjectivism and agnosticism show themselves in the theory according to which the symbol becomes the primary means of artistic expression. Poelzig, Mendelsohn, and Taut are examples of this line of thought. To subject architecture to the symbol means to distort the nature of architecture and the apprehension of artistic form – to break the ties between art and real life. So it is understandable why the bourgeois aesthetic strives to prove that each art is symbolic according to its own nature.[17]

Minerwin was unable to offer a specific redefinition of architecture except for his argument that it was above all an objective social phenomenon, but he presented what he called "incorrect viewpoints" *vis a vis* architecture:

In capitalistic society architecture loses its organic character in that it is called upon to express no great social idea. New building types and the general development of technology do not lead to the creation of a true architecture. Functional, technical, and artistic aspects of architecture are split apart. Different formalistic tendencies arise which ultimately destroy the architecture by robbing it of its inner content . . . [what was] an artistic form, rich with the reflected content of material reality, is exchanged for the play of abstract forms.[18]

It was a sincere struggle to form an authentic architecture with which to represent and enhance the promise of proletarian culture. Modernism in all its forms was the product of bourgeois intellectualism. Classical architecture alone would build upon German heritage, would mirror democracy from its roots in ancient Greece, and would mirror socialism by providing unambiguous symbols of equal meaning to all. The classical alone could express the inner content of the great social ideal, yet remain rich in the material, spiritual, and aesthetic reality of two and a half thousand years of philosophical ideo-content. The classical alone would satisfy Lenin's definition of "typical appearance":

The universal, the lawful in artistic form comes to the fore in the particular as "typical appearance." Such unity between the particular and the universal is the dialectic order which reflects the alternating relationships between the particular and the universal in the objective world. As Lenin says: "the universal exists only in the particular, through the particular."[19]

Along with such careful theorizing, the profession was reorganized into collectives of architects who were re-educated to suppress their individual creative impulses to the will of the state – a process of continual discussion in meetings amidst the ruins to prepare for the construction of this vision for the future.[20] Late in 1952, a great project for the creation of a social realist East Berlin was presented to the public. Even in 1952 the Soviets considered no reality beyond the edge of their sector; West Berlin had already ceased to exist [5.7].

The plan is as nationalistic and imperialistic as the project of Hitler. It reflects a deep convergence of the right and left in the ideology of nationalism. It is a proposition of extreme conservatism whose order would be based entirely in the past [5.8]. Gone are the dense inner courts where the urban poor labored in the nineteenth-century city, but continually present are the great monuments of past emperors and religions, all subjects of the new autocracy. It would be a city without promises or ambiguity, concealed in the forms and authority of past totalitarian states.

5.7
Model for the project to rebuild the Soviet sector of Berlin, view down Unter den Linden, 1953.

1953

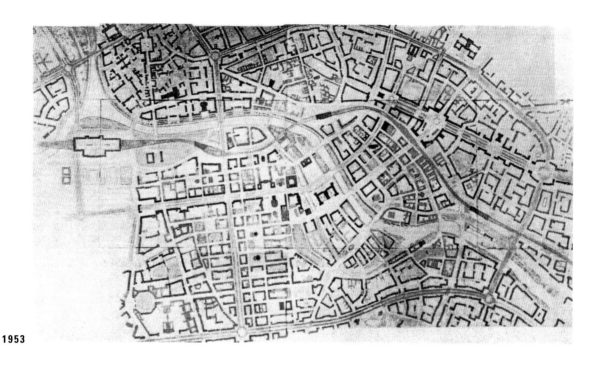

1953

5.8
Plan for the rebuilding of the
Soviet Sector of Berlin, 1953.

5.9
The headquarters of the German
National Democratic Party seen
from the corner of Mohrenstrasse
and Friedrichstrasse.

The major result of the plan was the construction between 1952 and 1958 of Stalin Allee, later changed to Karl Marx Allee when Stalin fell into disfavor. It is a boulevard of epic character formed from the walls of apartments whose facades are dressed thinly in an Oriental classicism. They are urban palaces for the proletariat. With the passing of time their critical position has in many ways been validated; they convey a civic bravura, and a strange charm and sincerity, although they have suffered from being poorly built. However, they have more of an affinity with the projects of Albert Speer than with the thoughts of Lenin, and the struggle of opposites is nowhere in evidence.[21] The building of Stalin Allee was to be the only major reconstruction in East Berlin until the physical division of the city in 1961, and then only one building within the spirit of the plan was built in the central city just to the north of Leipziger Platz [5.9].

As a curious coda to this search for a national architecture, the ministries of the Socialist Unity Party, until recently the ruling communist party of the GDR, have been housed from the foundation of the nation in Goering's former Air Force Ministry, close to Leipziger Platz on Leipzigerstrasse at the very edge of the Russian sector [5.10]. Though it stood in the center of the heaviest bombardment, by some strange operation of chance it survived the war virtually undamaged [5.11].[22] The inexorable forces in a culture are often stronger than the structures of political rhetoric.

5.10
Leipzigerstrasse looking
toward Leipziger Platz, 1938.
The headquarters of the
Luftwaffe is on the left.

1938

5.11
Leipzigerstrasse looking
toward the Wall, 1986.
The House of the Ministries
of the GDR, formerly the
Luftwaffe Headquarters,
is on the left.

1986

How do a people and a city and a culture reestablish order and reality after such complete destruction? In West Berlin it has been with deep uncertainty. Ten years after the war the devastation at the center remained unattended until economic and political confidence among Western powers led to the promotion of an international design competition – Berlin, Capital City. Organized in 1957 by the government of the Federal Republic of Germany and the Senate of Berlin, it covered twenty-four thousand acres and stretched from the Tiergarten in the west to Alexander Platz in the east, and from Oranienburger Tor in the north to Mehringh Platz in the south. The competitors were allowed to consider the area a clean slate, with the exception of a few buildings of historic significance and the incorporation of a new highway plan.[23] However, much of it was in the Russian sector at the center of the capital of the German Democratic Republic, an area containing all the major monuments of historic Berlin. It was a blatant act of political provocation, but the explicit objective was to recreate a symbolic center for the capital of a unified Germany.[24]

In contrast to the anonymity of the Eastern collectives, the Western architects understood their role only as an indulgence in personality. Of the many submissions from across the world, three have particular significance: the unplaced project by Le Corbusier, the second place entry by Hans Scharoun and Wils Ebert, and the winning project of the team led by Friedrich Spengelin. All the architects were in many ways as bound by untested ideologies as their Eastern counterparts, many were equally committed to socialism, and all of them had been intimately familiar with the city before it was destroyed. Berlin had been the stage for the formative years of their professional lives, when the walk from Friedrichstrasse to Potsdamer Platz was the most exciting in any German city. They had been intimate with this place – lunches at Aschingers' or at the Cafe Krantzler; visits to the Panopticon with its bizarre tableaus and wax representations of everything from sexual freaks to the famous; evenings at the Apollo Theater indulging in the wonderfully wicked circle bar; and coffee afterwards in the Vienna style at the Victoria on the corner of Friedrichstrasse and Unter den Linden.

All this, and much that was more personal, they had known when they worked in the pre-war city. Yet, in contrast to their Soviet-inspired colleagues, these architects desired places in which all traces of the past were removed or made insignificant, places in which their own memories of Berlin life were blanked out. For each the war was an appropriately dreadful event. Yet, for each it seems that the horror and degradation of its destruction represented a necessary catharsis, necessary to erase the past to make way for the modern world. The war had been an act of liberation. In these ravaged streets the dark jungle of the nineteenth-century city had been cleared to make way for the clean and rational garden of modernism.

Although the post-war governments in Western Europe were free from the ideological burden of Marxist-Leninism, they were as strongly committed to the politics of rational modernism and as open to philosophical instruction as the Soviets. The Swiss-French architect Le Corbusier had, from the late-1920s, held the position of international propagandist for the cause of the modern city and the new architecture.[25] His moral defense for the modern city was spelled out in a manifesto entitled *Athens Charter*, which had a wide influence after the war.[26] The themes are many, but underlying all is the project of scientific Marxism:

The [urban] situation reveals the incessant accretion of private interests ever since the beginning of the machine age. The ruthless violence of private interests provokes a disastrous upset in the balance between the thrust of economic forces on the one hand and the weakness of administrative control and the powerlessness of social solidarity on the other . . . .

To accomplish this great task it is essential to utilize the resources of modern techniques which, through the collaboration of its specialists, will support the art of building with all the dependability that science can provide and enrich it with the inventions and resources of the age . . . .

Private interest will be subordinated to the collective interest.[27]

Le Corbusier's polemics were aided and often concealed behind the brilliant drawings of his vision for the future. Yet, in contradiction to his socialism he believed in the salvation of the culture through singular genius, through his self-image as the architect-superman:

. . . who possesses a complete awareness of man, who has abandoned illusionary designs, and who, judiciously adapting the means to the desired ends, will create an order that bears within it a poetry of its own? The answer is, the architect![28]

At the war's end he was utterly convinced that he alone had the vision to reform the European city from its ashes and he waited more than ten years for the perfect opportunity to demonstrate this – the rebuilding of Berlin.[29] The project for Haupstadt Berlin was perhaps the most challenging of his career. It called for the complete restructuring of one of Europe's greatest cities, not only to establish a new order or to heal the terrible wounds of war, but to address the increasing division between East and West. Here, a vision was demanded that would reconcile the opposing realities of the divided soul of Western culture, a project of such compelling physical virtue that it would transcend all petty circumstance.

The aerial projection of Le Corbusier's plan [5.12] reveals the characters of his social and political imagination. He littered the stage of his new world order with many of the objects and types that he had been developing over the years – an architectural menagerie.[30] Yet, apart from the restoration of the octagon to Leipziger Platz, his projections sought a new beginning. The new city would have been scientifically determined to produce, with the utmost precision, the rational reordering of society. The city in his imagination was an organism. "Remember," he wrote, "that organic life in the course of the evolution of the species leaves the primary stage of the concentric shell to follow an axis, to take a direction, to fix a goal for itself."[31] He saw in the transmutation from medieval city to enlightenment city to rational city the inevitability of natural selection. His faith in the virtue of his vision never wavered and he saw metaphysical significance in the ease with which his urban machinery, developed for Paris thirty years before, could fit exactly into the place and structure of the devastated Berlin.

Optimal relations would be established between each room of each unit, between the units themselves, between the clusters of units, and between the paths and roads linking the units – in four orders of speed – to the places of work and pleasure. It was an order consciously in opposition to nature, a rational order virtuous and intrinsically complete, a reality offering passages through time without ambiguity, paradox, struggle, mystery, or privacy. The antithesis of the labyrinth, it denied history, memory, opportunity, and change [5.13]. This obsessive and rational God was stifling the sensuality in Le Corbusier's imagination.

In place of Hitler's funeral pyre Le Corbusier would have built a free-standing school in an open landscape, removing all memory of what had gone before. Potsdamer Platz would disappear beneath the path of a new divided highway; and if he was aware of the destruction of Columbus Haus, or of the fate of the triangle of land projecting into the West from the Russian sector, the drawing does not record it. All the surviving monuments of history, the great churches and palaces and museums, float fragmented in his unwilling-ness to weave a city fabric capable of incorporating past order.

The great symbol for his city would have been the House of Bureaucracy. Here, it dominates the upper left of the drawing. Sixty-five-stories tall, it would have faced and overwhelmed the most politically sensitive structure in the central city, the new Soviet Embassy. The House of Bureaucracy would be the cathedral for the new city and the home of the scientific managers, the priests and aristocracy of the new order. The people in the drawing trail ant-like towards its 700-foot prow, behind which two low buildings consume the entrance. This, then, was the promise of the greatest utopian of the century – one nation under new management. If only Josephine Baker could have danced across his vision.

All competitors had to address one explicit problem: should the restructured city consolidate the Russian sector, or by emphasizing connections between the East and the West make a physical bridge between the increas-

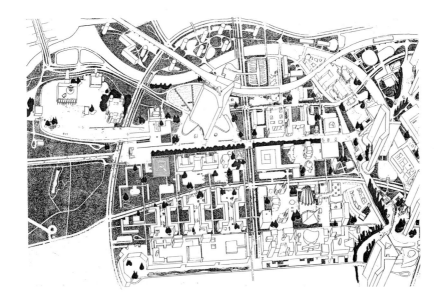

5.12
5.13
Le Corbusier,
Haupstadt Berlin, 1957.

1957

ingly antagonistic powers? Le Corbusier could not have been unaware of the symbolic implications of the plan, yet he chose to turn Friedrichstrasse into a great divided highway, destroying the walls of the buildings and explicitly consoli-dating the power of the Soviet sector.

In a witty gesture recognizing the presence of French taste in the making of Berlin, Le Corbusier would have restored the octagon on Leipziger Platz [5.14]. Perhaps he hoped to recapture, as he wrote of Place Vendome in 1947, a place where "the streams of architecture and town planning have joined to form a lake of repose in the bristling town."[32] But Le Corbusier's plan, whether shaped by ignorance or irony, would close to the West what had once been the glorious gate to the city from Sans Souci.

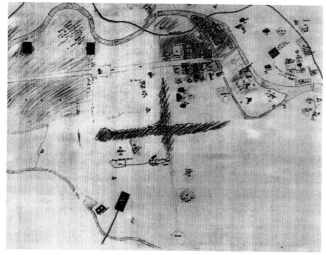

1957

5.14
Le Corbusier, study sketch for Hapustadt Berlin, 1957.

Le Corbusier's project was unplaced. He was extremely angry at being rejected by the jury. He wrote of the events:

There had been no hesitation: no need to pull down master-works of the past in order to rebuild. The demolition had been performed by airplanes and nothing was left standing in the center of Berlin. The German government had invited Le Corbusier to participate in the competition. In Berlin Le Corbusier found himself faced with the problems which he had already studied for the center of Paris 40 years earlier.

In Berlin it was not practicable to take the city on a ride into the countryside or the forests of Brandenburg. The program had been very well prepared by the authorities. The planning study was made in the Atelier at 35 Rue de Sevres with extreme care, a total realism. The time had come to take advantage of forty years of study and experimentation in architecture and planning.

But the feat of planning in three dimensions was considered a crime. Of 86 projects thirteen were retained; the thirteenth was that of Le Corbusier. It was eliminated.

The report of the Jury declared that the project had completely resolved the problem of circulation in large cities such as Berlin, but that a certain building, which was quite high, hid a municipal administration building located on the other bank of the Spree. Before the bombardment and the destruction, this latter building was, as all of the buildings of this height, visible only from its immediately adjacent surroundings. The excellent design conforming with the principles advocated by

CIAM [International Congress of Modern Architecture] *for 30 years (1928-1958), a modern exercise in three dimensional planning, was rejected. Walter Gropius was to have been a member of the Jury and it was for this reason that Le Corbusier agreed to participate. Walter Gropius remained in America because of his health. However, also on the jury was Alvar Aalto, [Cornelis] Van Eestern, and Pierre Vago!*[33]

The "certain building which was quite high" was Le Corbusier's House of Bureaucracy.

The entry by the "wonder-children" of English architecture, Allison and Peter Smithson, which took third place, offers a glimpse of the disturbing influence that Le Corbusier's work had on the generation that followed. The perspective drawing included with their submission is a view from a bridge across a transformed Leipziger Platz [5.15]. That gifted men and women at a time and place of deep political and social uncertainty would thoughtfully endorse such a brutal vision of the future reveals the poignant instability of Western ambitions. Given that many sites in the new Berlin closely resemble the Smithson ideal suggests that there is a profound danger in making permanent the transient dreams of a minority. A society gets the reality it asks for and much of that reality depends on how it asks and who it asks to provide it.

5.15
Allison and Peter Smithson, sketch of the redesign of Leipziger Platz, Haupstadt Berlin, 1957.

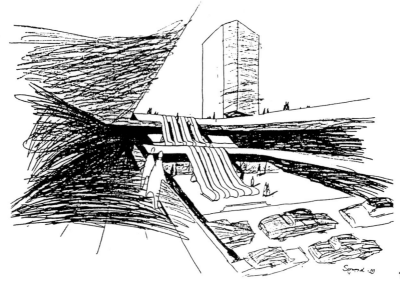

1957

1957

The contrast between the winning submission and the second place entry reveals the ability of architecture to carry significant political thought. The winning project was designed by the Berlin architects Spengelin and Pempelfort. Their drawings represent, as do the winners of many competitions, a series of elegant but uninspired compromises [5.16]. Its order emphasizes both east/west and north/south passages, with a bias perhaps on the east and west, but without political clarity. It respects and provides new settings for most of the surviving fragments of the old city, though Leipziger Platz is removed without a trace. There is a mild dialectic in the relation between the natural order of the dwellings hidden in the forest of an expanded Tiergarten and the new center of government which sits asymmetrically in a natural landscape. Friedrichstrasse would have become the exemplar of the new commercial street where, above a continuous deck of shops and cafes, the offices of the new business culture would arise. Much to the jury's pleasure, Unter den Linden would be restored to the scale and character of the past [5.17]. Some on the jury complained that it was a project without passion, without a grand idea, but for many this was its virtue. It was the very model of bourgeois respectability in modern dress.

The ideology in the second place entry by Hans Scharoun and Wils Ebert is explicit [5.18]. Friedrichstrasse is totally removed in a deliberate violation of the structured eighteenth-century city. The reasons are obvious: only by removing the interference of the north/south axis could a powerful bridge be made between East and West, across Unter den Linden and across Leipzigerstrasse. The Nazis had classified Scharoun a "cultural Bolshevist."

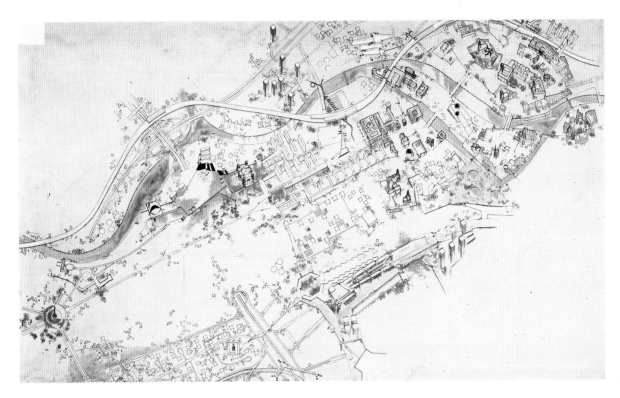

1957

Throughout the existence of the Third Reich he survived on a few modest private commissions.[34] His decision to remain in Germany when all his colleagues had gone was due to an intense belief that his work was rooted in the spirit of German culture and, in his own words, "would not be understood elsewhere." He believed he could act only in relation to German culture, and at the war's end he was the only major modernist architect left in Berlin.[35] He, above all, understood in the fullest sense the need for reconciliation. In this devastated city his vision alone had the power of salvation.

In his notes for the competition Scharoun called for a new order. He compared the dislocation in the new city with cities of the past in which content and form were identical. He saw the imposition of road networks causing "indecisiveness and confusion, instead of differentiation and clarity." He sought to provide places in which "the individual, and great groups of individuals, have the same fundamental chance." His new society and his new city had to be formed from the combination of "freedom and connection." He wrote that his plan would "only be successful when in the hands of all, or one organization committed to the good of all."[36]

5.19

Hans Scharoun and Wils Ebert,
plan, Haupstadt Berlin, 1957.

His disagreement with Le Corbusier had long been public and bitter. At the foundation of the International Congress of Modern Architecture in 1928 most of the architects shared a social agenda, but were profoundly divided on the nature of the city. The critical opposition was between Le Corbusier and Gropius on one side and Der Ring, the Berlin group led by Scharoun and the architect Hugo Häring, on the other. The issue was simple; Scharoun and Häring believed that form should grow in response to circumstance rather than be a product of the imposed geometrical order advocated by Le Corbusier. Häring wrote in 1932:

In nature, form is the result of the organization of many distinct parts in space in such a way that life can unfold, fulfilling all its effects both in terms of the single part and in terms of the integrated whole; whereas in the geometrical cultures form is derived from the laws of geometry. . . . We should not try to express our own individuality, but rather the individuality of things . . . .[37]

This is the underlying spirit of Scharoun's vision for the city. The isometric drawing is delicate and tentative. It seeks to establish a reality tied

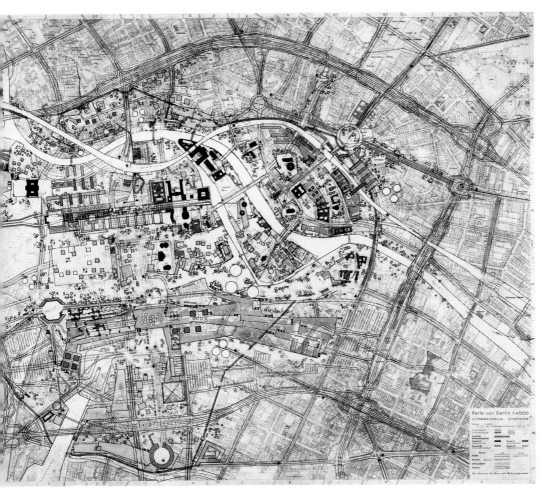

closely to nature, informal, organic, and random, with room for free associations and for opposition. Scharoun presents a reality in which all potential permutations between order and disorder, between man and nature, become possible. The imposition of rational and autocratic order since the Enlightenment had led to the abuse of power. The memory of this past and the memory of Hitler's obsession with a dominant order would be deliberately replaced by its antithesis – an order of fragmentation and decentralization. The new city is dissolved back into nature, reformed in the memories of medieval landscapes and villages and in the images of life among the fields and forests. Within this informal order he drives the two powerful passages between East and West, bridges across the ideological gulf [5.19]. The vision and the instruction came from the philosopher Martin Heidegger:

The bridge gathers to itself in its own way earth and sky, divinities and mortals. Gathering or assembly, by an ancient word of our language, is called 'thing.' The bridge is a thing and, indeed, it is such as the gathering of the fourfold which we have described.[38]

The drawing seeks to express a place of many different times, people, places, rhythms, potentials, pasts, and futures. The disorder of reality, the inevitability of fragmentation, and the collapse of imposed and coherent external worlds is the price of freedom. Scharoun presents the antithesis of all past architecture, an architecture which would be self-effacing, nihilistic, demythified, and detached from the personality of architects in favor of the infinite personalities of the culture. He reestablishes the octagon on Leipziger Platz to become, not simply a gate to the Tiergarten, but the magnification of the passage between East and West.

HAUPSTADT BERLIN (EAST)

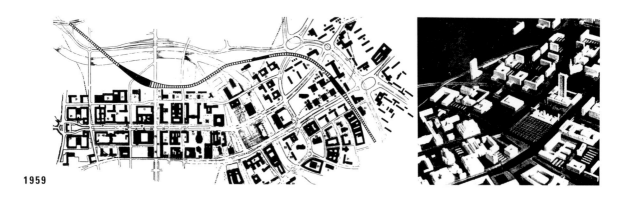

1959

5.20
Georg Kröber, plan and model for the rebuilding of the Soviet Sector of central Berlin, Haupstadt GDR, 1959 (from *Deutsche Architektur*, September 9, 1959).

The West Berlin competition was much publicized in the general press and in the professional journals. In reaction, the Social Unity Party of the GDR held a series of architectural and planning competitions for central Berlin beginning in 1958. They were contained, however, within the Russian zone of occupation and were limited to Eastern block architects. These projects offer direct evidence of the struggle to construct a socialist Berlin and to detach it from the reality of the Western city. No first place prize was awarded in the initial phase of competitions, but the project of an East German team lead by the architect Georg Kröber typifies the character of the entries [5.20].[39] The project's major concern was the creation of a "Forum" in celebration of socialism to be built on Marx-Engels Platz. Even at the project's symbolic center (at the right of the plan and the center of the photograph) the vision for the architecture is purely circumstantial and practical. Unter den Linden becomes a fast-moving divided highway rushing to the West, following the same transportation plan applied to the international competition of 1957 – through the Brandenburg Gate, which is surrounded by new building, suggesting that Kröber and his associates were unaware of the impending physical separation of the city. Although it maintains the conservatism of the great plan of 1952 in the piece by piece reestablishment of the historic city, the character of the architecture has moved from the classical forms of Soviet social realism back to Bauhaus modernism, back to an order rooted in German culture, thus demonstrating the emerging confidence of the new nation.

Revised plans for the rebuilding of Berlin appeared in *Deutsche Architektur* in August 1961, the month the city was divided. The three submissions published exemplify the socialist vision for the city just before its detachment from the West.[40] Kröber, with a different team, revised his project of 1959 with a new plan that withdrew from both the western and the southern edges of the Russian sector. The Brandenburg Gate and the House of the Ministries of the GDR would survive at the edge of a forest, into which the West and (in the lower left quadrant of the drawing) Leipziger Platz would disappear. Similarly Leipzigerstrasse, reformed in continuous walls of housing on the north, runs into the same forest edge, its two-lane highway disappearing into an area of uncertainty. In reality this would happen. The only significant mark at the Russian edge is what appears to be an ornamental lake close to the site of the former Reich Chancellery.

5.21
The Schweitzer Proposal for the rebuilding of the Soviet Sector of central Berlin, Haupstadt GDR, 1960.

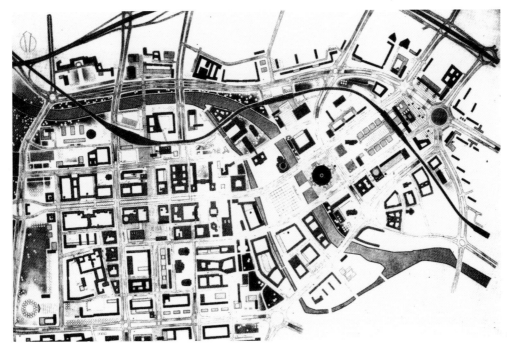

1960

The winning project from a competition in April of 1960 was prepared by a collective under the direction of architect Peter Schweitzer [5.21]. Here again the fabric of the Russian sector pulls back from the West. The architecture is conservative; a reweaving of the material of the old city will establish the form of the future, and the combination and opposition of highways and new public monuments will shift the scale and establish German social realism. Although Leipziger Platz has disappeared, a circular grove of trees would be placed between the north wall of the octagon and the main facade of Hitler's Reich Chancellery.

Published after the Berlin Wall was in place, the Schweitzer project was further developed in the spring of 1961 to become the basis for a five-year construction program [5.22]. The symbolic center of the renewed city would be to the east in Marx-Engels Platz, and the five-year plan would give priority to the rebuilding of Unter den Linden, visible from the West through the arches of the Brandenburg Gate. The exposed and painfully sensitive national border between East Germany and West Berlin running along the south edge of Leipzigerstrasse would remain unattended for some time to come.

5.22
The Schweitzer Proposal
for the rebuilding of the
Soviet Sector of central Berlin,
Haupstadt GDR, 1961.

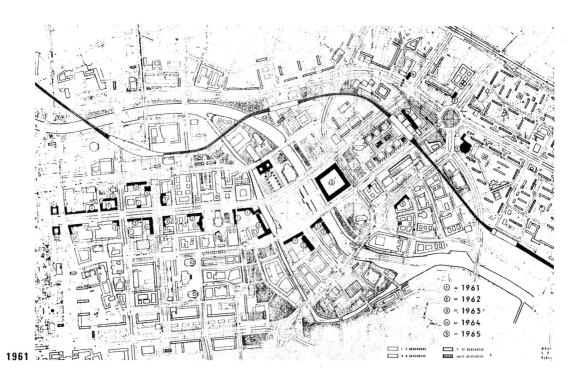

In contrast to the cults of personality that reigned in the West, the drawings and symbols of the Eastern collectives became increasingly depersonalized as they surrendered all sensual judgement to the authority of what was seen as a rational order. However, the German projects on both sides reveal that, as the aftershock of the war passed and the two new German nations emerged from the burden of occupation, they began to display a converging vision for the future in the rational modernism of the Bauhaus.

With the exception of Le Corbusier, what now seems strange about these visions of the future is the way they sought to depersonalize the order of reality. The poetic essence of the significant objects of Western art and architecture has rested in the figure of the male body. Within the great medieval theocracies the clothed figure of Christ was embedded in the plan and in the presence of the cathedral. Christ's love and pain was celebrated in anthropomorphic spaces stretched between heavenly desire and earthly sensuality. The Renaissance explicitly made the idealized figure of man the measure of all things, allowing the emperors and princes and kings of the subsequent autocracies to be enshrined in architecture as heroes or self-made gods. Such was the task faced by Gilly in shaping the tomb for Frederick. And in the midst of conceiving this monument deifying and embodying the memory of a hero, he contemplated its complete inversion, a negation not of the structure of history but of the presence of the body. Schinkel's dialectical struggle can be seen more explicitly as lying between the material and the immaterial, between the ethereal body in the presence of the cathedral and its negation in the absolute geometries of a universal state. This universal state, rational and depersonalized, becomes the structure of reality for both the liberal and socialist visions of the future, visions complicated by the manipulative sensuality of industrial capitalism. The pre-war architecture of Hitler and Stalin can be seen as equal reflections of absolutist empires in which the leaders saw themselves monumentalized as heroes and gods. Marx and Lenin as prophets and gods have complicated and subjectivized the formulation of Russian revolutionary symbolism in a way that separates it entirely from the visions of Western modernism. In a direct sense, the removal of the personification of power in an idealized body seems to have had the effect of removing the presence of the body from the significant symbols of the culture. More deliberately, the liberal and socialist majority, in seeking to negate the power of an autocracy, unwittingly removed the body from the structuring vision of the culture, moving an idealized order of things into the mind and into abstraction.

What begins in a divided post-war Berlin as a "struggle of opposites" converges with the waning of Soviet influence into the shared negation of the past. This is not an abstraction that would cleanse from the culture the pollution of industrial materialism. This is the persistent cry of liberalism, heard for more than a hundred years on both sides of the divide, to negate the memory of centuries of feudal rule and to reject the distortions of history.

The history of this century is a violent catalogue of aberrant and erroneous behavior by national and ideological interests; nowhere is this more evident than in the history of Berlin. In all of the confused events of the post-war period the act of destruction must be seen as conceptually bound to the act of construction; and in the brutal aftershock of the war those on all fronts of restoration could not avoid the desire for a physical reality shaped in the negation of all pasts, the desire to place the trust of the future in reason, and the desire to deny the body and the personification of power. Thus arises the paradox of an architecture seeking order and permanence in the temporary disorder of a traumatized culture.

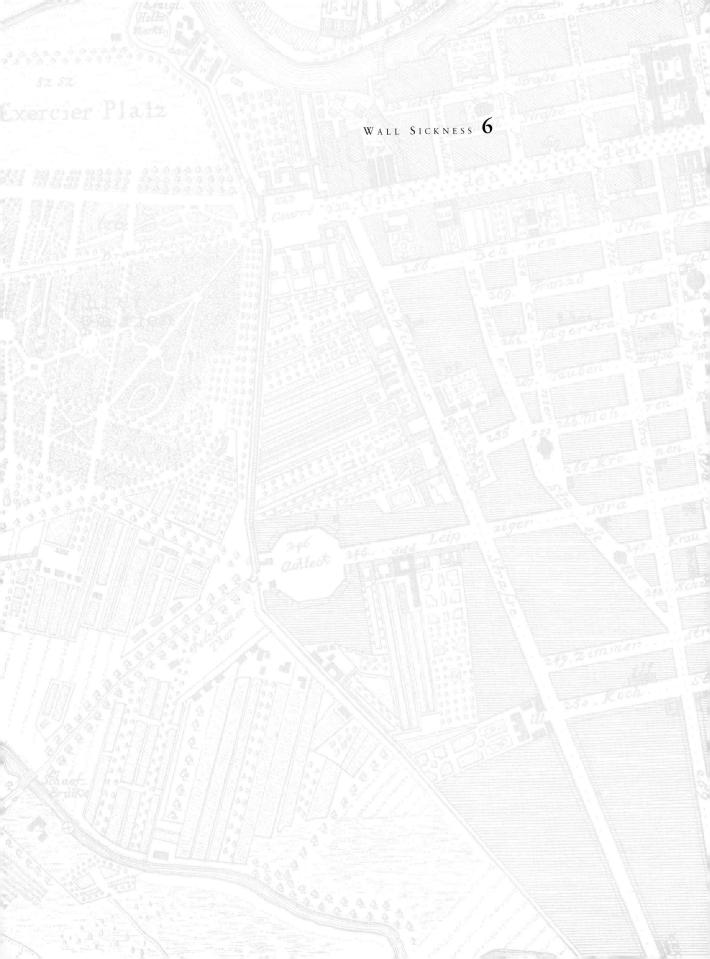

The enclave of West Berlin, one hundred and twenty miles inside the German Democratic Republic, remains a zone of Western military occupation. France, Britain, and the United States maintain military bases there, and air access to the city was, until recently, restricted to the national airlines of the armies of occupation. The Russians never accepted the existence of West Berlin. In 1955, partly as a reaction to the West German alliance with NATO, the USSR granted full sovereignty to the GDR and allowed its entry into the Warsaw Pact group of nations. In 1958 Khrushchev demanded that West Berlin become a city free from the armies of occupation. He gave the allies six months to leave after which Russia's rights and powers in the city would be handed over to the GDR. The NATO powers responded by reasserting that their rights of occupation stemmed directly from the surrender of the Third Reich. The Soviets backed off. Because of the division of the nation at the end of the war, no peace treaty had been signed with Germany as a whole and in 1961 Khrushchev, moving on what he saw as a young and inexperienced American president, demanded one. He believed that such a treaty would end the right of Western occupation. The West refused to move and in response on August 13, 1961, the Russians completely sealed off the Western sectors of the city and began to build the Wall. In June of 1963, John F. Kennedy, facing the Wall a few hundred yards north of Potsdamer Platz at the Brandenburg Gate, proclaimed "All free men wherever they may live, are citizens of this city of West Berlin and therefore, as a free man I am proud to be able to say that 'Ich bin ein Berliner.'"

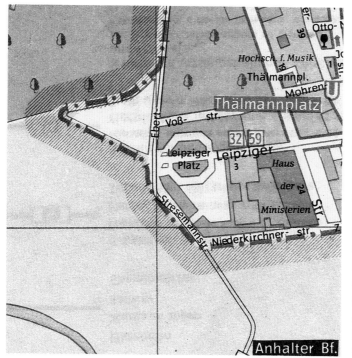

1984

6.1
The official tourist map of
East Berlin from 1984.

HAUPTSTADT GDR STADTPLAN, VEB TOURIST VERLAG

In the tourist map of East Berlin the West exists only as a trace of the major roads and the line of the city rail system [6.1]. In a testament to the presence of the place, Leipziger Platz persists in name even though it has no substantial reality. The dotted line marks not the actual physical line of the Wall but the territory officially under Eastern control. The black lines defining the inner and outer lines of the Wall do not appear on any official map.

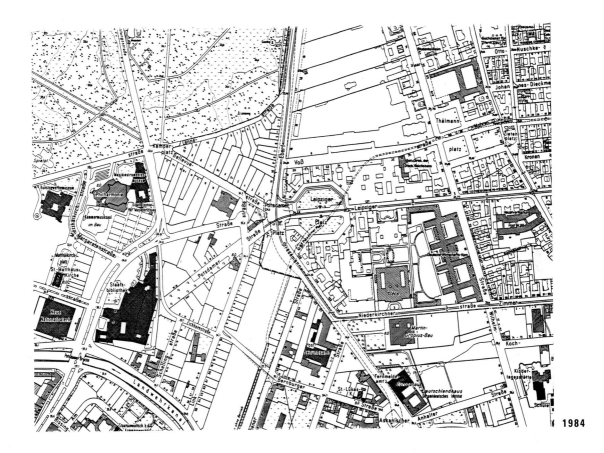

1984

KARTE VON BERLIN, DER SENATOR FÜR BAU-UND
WOHNUNGSWESEN V

The official Senate map of the
city of West Berlin is, in many particulars, a complete fiction [6.2]. It shows
the line that separates the districts of Berlin but refuses to acknowledge the
existence of the Wall or the division of the city. In the triangle where
Columbus Haus once stood and throughout the eastern city, the map records
the precise outline of every building that existed there before the war and
before the division. It is understandable that within Western capitalism,
property rights, no matter how abstract, must continue to exist. Among these
ghostly traces are chilling representations of past realities. The Chancellery is
present, its grand court precisely marked, and Wertheim's still holds the
corner with all the other buildings in a Leipziger Platz whose physical reality
is now almost traceless. It does not recognize the existence of the Wall. In
the official view trolley cars still run through Potsdamer Platz and within the
octagon there remains a charming garden where nothing really exists.

6.3
The division of East and West at
Potsdamer Platz in 1948.

1948

SECTOR EDGE

The process by which a city is divided begins
with a man painting a line on the ground [6.3]. This first step is being made
under British Army supervision. The line starts at the sidewalk on the west
side of Potsdamerstrasse.

6.4
The Reich Chancellery, April 1949.

1949
APRIL

REICH CHANCELLERY

In the distance behind the line, the Reich Chancellery is demolished under a Russian directive [6.4]. A political act, the demolished stone will be used in the construction of the great Russian War Memorial in the eastern city. They will attempt to remove all traces of this former center of world power and all memory of Hitler's presence in East Berlin, but they will not succeed.

6.5
Leipziger Platz from Potsdamer
Platz, April 1951.

1951
APRIL

LEIPZIGER PLATZ

A rather gentle forewarning of what is to come, the photograph shows the construction of a message board by the Berlin Free Press to carry the Western news in lights to the East, answered on the other side by a similar construction promoting the state department store, H.O., residing in Columbus Haus [6.5]. Most of the Wertheim Department Store survives in the background.

1953

6.6
Riots in Leipziger Platz,
June 17, 1953.

Leipziger platz

The people of East Berlin rise up against the government led by construction workers angry with a decision to increase work quotas [6.6]:

Heavy rain was falling . . . when at about 8:30, the first great column of marchers turned into Leipzigerstrasse from Friedrichstrasse, filling the whole width of the street. Truck loads of Peoples' Police arrived and cordoned off the area in front of the Ministry . . . shortly before 9 o'clock the first Russian vehicles were to be seen in the streets of the Eastern sector . . . in the main streets of East Berlin speaking choruses were heard: 'Ulbricht, Pieck and Grotewohl we have got our belly full.' 'We demand free elections.' 'We are not bums, we don't need guns.' 'We refuse to be slaves.' 'Down with billy goats!'[1]

They are joined by white collar workers, housewives, and even members of the Peoples' Police, all demonstrating against the division of Berlin, the division of Germany, the food situation, the political interference in their lives, and against the Russians. Cobblestones are hurled at the Russian tanks, crowbars jammed into the tracks, exhaust pipes plugged up; but such an unequal struggle cannot last and there are dead and wounded and thousands are arrested. There is never fulfillment in reality, only the tempering of desire.

1956

AUGUST

LEIPZIGERSTRASSE FROM LEIPZIGER PLATZ

The eastern sector is closed to traffic [6.7]. The ruins of the Wertheim building are supported by temporary shoring, dramatically reinforcing the barricade across the square. One column of Schinkel's northern gate still stands.

1957

SEPTEMBER 24

6.8
Leipziger Platz,
September 24, 1957.

LEIPZIGER PLATZ

Leipziger Platz, some twelve years after the great destruction, is still fading but very slowly [6.8]. Wertheim's has just been reduced to rubble, but the ruin of Schinkel's little temple still remains and a man leans against the rail. The advertisement is for the beauty salon run by Mitropa, the East German Railway.

1960

AUGUST

6.9
Leipziger Platz,
August 1960.

LEIPZIGER PLATZ

Is it the same man leaning on the rail [6.9]? Perhaps he comes here every day. Perhaps he has a reason. The gardens of Leipziger Platz are now tended by the state and, in addition to the modest planters and other signs of civic concern, the place carries the thoughts of the new Ministry of Propaganda. The panel in the middle of Leipziger Platz reads "We demand general and total disarmament." The park's south fence carries extensive calls for peace and a free Berlin. The panel on the left welcomes all "Freedom Fighters." The remains of Schinkel's pavilion have been removed.

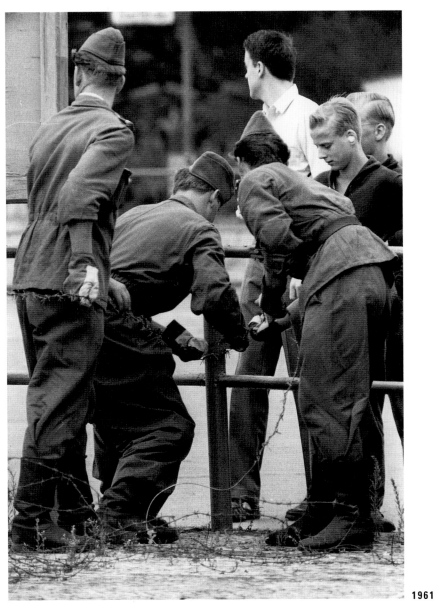

1961

AUGUST 13

AT THE EDGE

Under Russian supervision young
soldiers weave a net of barbed wire through the railings on Potsdamer Platz
[6.10].

1961

AUGUST 14

THE LINE IS DRAWN

The morning after the separation is made the inner-barrier of barbed wire crosses the east end of Leipziger Platz [6.11]. In the foreground, East German soldiers maintain surveillance. On the sidewalks people gather and stare in disbelief. A woman marches with determination towards the barrier, refusing to put up with the nonsense. Drivers in automobiles heading towards Leipziger Platz from the east stop and get out of their cars in disbelief. There is shock but no great surprise. The Wall has been building for fifteen years. Leipzigerstrasse – half in ruins, half patched-up and put back to use – will be entirely demolished and remade to represent the new socialist order of things.

6.12
View toward Haus Vaterland,
August 15, 1961.

1961

AUGUST 15

VIEW OF THE DIVISION

        In the south, toward Haus Vaterland,
West Berliners gather to watch with fascination and horror the walling off of
the central city [6.12].

6.13
Potsdamer Platz,
August 19, 1961.

1961

AUGUST 19

POTSDAMER PLATZ

        It is six days after the division and a
temporary wall is in place [6.13]. It follows the exact line of the district
boundary. The concrete posts and barbed wire in the middle distance are
planted on the site of the Hotel Palast. Behind them is the former garden of
the Reich Chancellery.

6.14
Potsdamer Platz Stadt Bahnhof,
August 1961.

1961
AUGUST

POTSDAMER PLATZ STADT BAHNHOF

The station is closed, but the trains still run [6.14].

6.15
Potsdamer Platz,
August 23, 1966.

1966
AUGUST 23

POTSDAMER PLATZ

A new wall has been built of angled steel buried deep in the ground, slotted together with concrete blocks, and topped with concrete pipe [6.15]. Itself a boundary, it knows no boundaries, crossing cobbles, trolley rails, sidewalks, and foundations. The sign reads: "Wer die Staatsgrenze mit Gewalt einrenen will, wer an der Mauer provoiert, macht alles nur schlimmer!" – "Whoever threatens by force this authorized National Border, Whoever commits acts of provocation at the Wall, will only make matters worse!"

1967
SPRING

POTSDAMER PLATZ AND LEIPZIGER PLATZ

As a helicopter rises at West
Berlin's edge, Potsdamer Platz displays a palimpsest of conflicting orders
[6.16]: Schinkel's circle, the lines of the trolley cars, a frame of concrete
blocks and soft sand holding little mines designed to blow off human legs,
and a range of tank barriers. The sign reads: "Vorteil für West Berlin [tear]
beziehungen mit der DDR" – "Advantage for West Berlin [tear] in this
respect with the GDR."

6.17
Potsdamer Platz and Leipziger Platz, Spring 1967.

1967

SPRING

POTSDAMER PLATZ AND LEIPZIGER PLATZ

The Achteck – an eighteenth-century illusion of reason in urban form. In 1797, Gilly stood on this ground [6.17] and imagined the exact outline of his monument to Frederick the Great. Walking this land in 1815, Schinkel's imagination soared with the desire for a great cathedral to symbolize the liberation of the will, an object like flames in the forest.

A trace of Leipzigerstrasse still bisects the octagon, flanked as it nears the Wall by the memory of the gates to the city. They are marked now by concrete slabs sealing the entrances to the Leipziger Platz U-Bahn. Below ground the trains still run. The once-noble north facade of Leipziger Platz is now occupied by a terrace of kennels for attack dogs. The Free Berliner Press still cries from its high sign to an ever-receding East.

6.18
Potsdamer Platz, 1969.

1969

POTSDAMER PLATZ

The Wall is unchanged, the Bahnhof forgotten [6.18]. The great swathe of land cleared in the divide has been graded and seeded. The mound on the right covers the remains of Hitler's bunker.

1976

APRIL 28

POTSDAMER PLATZ

The Wall is reconstructed [6.19]. The photograph shows the exact form of the new structure and displays the necessary indifference of the East German worker to life at the edge of reality. Before they are allowed into the zone, an outer barrier is built by the very few who can be trusted not to escape. Life at the edge makes them painfully aware of their imprisonment. In his book, *The Wall Jumper*, Peter Schneider wrote:

The border between the two German states, and especially between the two halves of Berlin, is considered the world's most closely guarded and the most difficult to cross. The ring around West Berlin is 102.5 miles in length. Of this, 65.8 miles consist of concrete slabs topped with pipe; another 34 miles is constructed of stamped metal fencing. Two hundred and sixty watchtowers stand along the border ring, manned day and night by twice that many border guards. The towers are linked by a tarred military road, which runs within the border strip. To the right and the left of the road, a carefully raked stretch of sand conceals trip wires; flares go off if anything touches them. Should this happen, jeeps stand ready for the border troops, and dogs are stationed at 267 dog runs along the way. Access to the strip from the east is further prevented by an inner wall, which runs parallel to the outer Wall at an irregular distance. Nail-studded boards randomly scattered at the foot of the inner wall can literally nail a jumper to ground, spiking him on the five-inch prongs. It is true that long stretches of the inner wall still consist of the facades of houses situated along the border, but their doors and windows have been bricked up. Underground in the sewers, the border is secured by electrified fences, which grant free passage only to the excretions of both parts of the city.[2]

6.20
The Wall south of
Leipziger Platz, 1986.

1986

SOUTH OF LEIPZIGER PLATZ

        Embedded in the Wall is a pregnant woman,
cast in plaster, struggling to escape [6.20].

1986

THE WALL FROM POSTSDAMER PLATZ

The Wall now carries the message [6.21]:

Sarah Pryor, wherever you are we love you · Age 9 missing Oct. 1985 Whalen, MA · God loves you

1980s

POSTCARD: BERLIN POTSDAMER PLATZ

The photograph was taken from the viewing platform on Potsdamer Platz at the corner where Columbus Haus once stood [6.22]. It was the most popular place for viewing the Wall and the Eastern Sector from the West. The view embodies the conflict between seeing and understanding. From the platform there was little to see – a clear space with grass, an access road, a cobbled street with rails, and a triangle of land whose vegetation was returning to the primordial forest. With the Wall gone what reality would bridge the divide? What structure could restore the separate states of the culture? Toward the second millenium, the burden of shaping the future becomes increasingly heavy.

It is not the history of this place that matters but the experience. Loss of perspective makes it difficult to grasp. There is all around a dreadful confusion of pasts. In East Berlin the walk back to Checkpoint Charlie down Charlottenstrasse and across Werderstrasse to Gendarmemarkt is through what is still called Stadtmitte, or the city center. For thirty years after the war, this place held the most romantic and tragic ruins in all of Europe, two great Baroque churches and Schinkel's Schauspiel Haus, standing as the bombs and fire had left them, softened over the years by nature, sprouting trees from high parapets and gently redressed in moss and ivy. Now, in a massive program of restoration, the government has begun to resurrect their eighteenth-century image.

On down Mohrenstrasse is the entrance to the Thalmann Platz U-Bahn station, once remade to serve the Chancellery. Here, on an empty platform, is a complete survivor of Hitler's order and style for the city. The wall panels, the color of congealed blood, would have matched the marble from the Great Hall of the Chancellery. Throughout this area the street names have been changed to honor the heroes of the socialist revolution. Yet the name Voss Strasse, despite its association with Hitler and the Reich Chancellery, remains. Reality runs out as it approaches the border, and much of the street, with the foundations of the Chancellery, now lies between the walls. Fifty years ago this was a center of world power; now, in the twilight, there is a sense of standing at the edge of existence.

At the edge of what was once Leipziger Platz is the first structure of many that form the Wall, a metal fence behind which soldiers move casually toward anyone approaching. There is no other life. Something that had been so comfortable, real, complete, and ordered survives only as a trace of curbstones and cobbles, most of it imprisoned between the walls.

Down Leipzigerstrasse a few small shops survive on this once-great street, an industrial supply house and a grimy beauty parlor among them. On the corner of Leipzigerstrasse and Leipziger Platz, close to the inner wall as it cuts across the octagon, is the site of Wertheim's, now the end of the line for the mid-town bus service. Opposite it is Preussen Haus, an epic survivor from the nineteenth century, grey and defiant and unrepentant. To the west is nothing, and to the east is the illusion of a modern city – East Berlin – with its blank repetitions of walls and apartment buildings down the length of Leipzigerstrasse.

In the middle of the strange, yet powerful space between the two cities at Checkpoint Charlie there existed, until recently, a control building.[3] Although little more than a shed, it was a critical instrument of communist order. Yet, the walls were covered in floral-patterned paper, the windows draped in net curtains, and half-dead geraniums sat on the radiators. Its architecture, that of the real, surpassed in its proletarian domesticity that of the ideal. A new gatehouse preserves the curtains.

In the West, along Nieder Kirchnerstrasse, are the backs of Prussian and Nazi buildings now occupied by the GDR. Goering's former Air Force Ministry is here, seemingly untouched by the war. On its south side are the crumbling apartments of a once-petit bourgeois, untouched since the war's end with the marks of shells and bullets still visible. The streets are as deserted as in the East, and it is equally cold and damp. Somehow, because the Wall can be touched, there is less of a menace. Yet it is a real edge, charged with disturbing power.

The city is a palimpsest of lost order. Each layer, though compromised, represents the limits of knowledge and the consensus of the reality of each age. Defensive and circumstantial, rational and democratic, imperial and universal – there is a grain and texture to each, and where they intersect or collide the strongest order survives. The Wall alone defies interpretation. Below its primitive reality lies the order of modern desire, an order detached from reality – selfish, brutal, fast, and sleek. Its floodlit passages were more coherent than anything else at the center of either city, a brilliant illumination of the negation of reality and a total abstraction.

In the minds of its engineers it was merely the means by which the socialist state was reinforced and defended. All circumstantial implications were irrelevant. It was a paradox of order, an imposed order that opposed all past orders, erected in total disregard for human law yet supremely lawful. Its making disrupted and denied history. Its nature rewrote history. In dividing a city and a nation, it became necessary to eradicate all past existence and to destroy any attempt at reconnection. For Jung it symbolized the divided soul of Western man.

GDR TIME

The great barricade, in reordering the city, allowed revolutionary culture to operate according to its own enforced sense of time. The revolution, in preparation for a rational and scientific future, demanded an existence in time. It had one clock, the West had many. It had one rhythm, the West had many. Progress on all fronts was continuously measured in time. The five-year plan was, and to some extent still is, the basic building block. All else being equal, the party would have abandoned the Christian calendar for its own revolutionary calendar starting, one presumes, with the death or birth of Lenin or Marx. Time was and is the essence of socialist control, and it was against Western time that the Wall was built. It allowed the revolution all the time in its world. While the West merely consumed time, passed time, and spent time, the revolution would use and control time.

Consider the past, present, and future of time and order in Leipzigerstrasse:

6.23
Karl Friedrich Schinkel,
perspective study for a
proposed reconstruction of
Leipzigerstrasse, 1820.

1820

LEIPZIGERSTRASSE

This was the street of aristocrats
drawn so perfectly by Schinkel [6.23]. His meticulous perspective reconstruction of Leipzigerstrasse is a view from Leipziger Platz, made while preparing
his designs for the Potsdam Gates. In the foreground, marked by stone posts
and a sentry box, is the point at which the road can be closed.

6.24
Leipzigerstrasse, 1901.

1901

LEIPZIGERSTRASSE

From the Baedeker Guide: "It is
perhaps the chief artery of traffic in Berlin, and excels even Friedrichstrasse
in a number of its handsome commercial buildings, most of which are in
renaissance style. The visitor is advised to inspect the street in the evening
when the shop windows are brilliantly lighted." [6.24]

1986

LEIPZIGERSTRASSE

In 1969, East Berlin began to rebuild Leipzigerstrasse as a dramatic symbol to reinforce the Wall. It had to screen East Berlin from the West and block the view of the Axel Springer lightboard flashing Western propaganda across the divide. It had to project to West Berlin, and particularly to the overcrowded slums along the Wall in the center city, a symbol of the strength and superiority of the socialist path. It had to be the tangible fruit of the division, the visible new reality of German socialism. Freed from the polemics of Russian neo-classicism, Leipzigerstrasse and the German Democratic Republic moved back into the abstractions of Bauhaus modernism.

The architect of the socialist state argues that the removal of the gratuitous, the irrelevant, and the pseudo-mystical from the material experience of life will lead to greater self-knowledge. But life in the apartments and public places of Leipzigerstrasse has been persistently harsh. Its occupants live in a groundless vision [6.25], a promise of the future consisting of denatured emotions and relationships. The reconstruction was an absurd production of bourgeois metaphysics, conforming the lives of simple people into constructions of naive Platonism. The Soviet warnings of the dangers of Bauhaus modernism had come true. The esential agenda of this architecture, though masked by a veneer of reason, was the imposition on the culture of the moralizing order of an intellecutal elite whose dreams stemmed from a different struggle, a different revolution. Increasingly the role and nature of architecture was losing its place. There arose, it would seem, a close relationship between the fading significance of architecture and its inability to shed the desire to control the future.

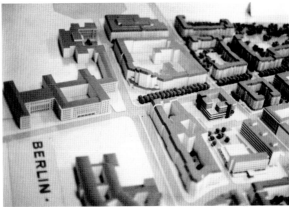

1986

In the summer of 1986, in preparation for the 750th anniversary of the founding of the city, the East Berlin Planning Office presented its program for the final reconstruction of Berlin Mitte (Berlin Center), presenting to the Western world the order and character of socialist reality for the twenty-first century [6.26-27]. By 1987, the anniversary year, the work was rough but complete.

The revolution changed the nature of public order and, in reaction to modernism, produced a synthesis surprising in its modesty and compromise with the past. Architecture moved beyond mental abstraction and returned to a respect for circumstance. These were to be simple and familiar places seeking a unity with tradition and past experience. Here and elsewhere in Berlin energy and money was spent on filling the many gaps in the streets and public squares that the detached visions of modernism couldn't fill, gaps that were a continual reminder of the war and of the unresolved order of the future.

The revolution matured and revealed the true nature of its objective – to return to the people of East Berlin the comfort and style of the petit bourgeoisie. The new socialist city confidently reestablished the streets and buildings of the nineteenth-century city, and those more equal than others had the pleasure of moving from the crumbling abstractions of the "old" modern apartments to the new post-modern townhouses. The revolutionary dimension remained only in the means of production. This re-creation of the nineteenth-century city was mass produced in concrete.

6.26
Model of the East German reconstruction plan for East Berlin, 1986. The Wall is absent where it passes through the ever-present outline of Leipziger Platz in the foreground.

6.27
Model of the East German reconstruction plan for East Berlin, 1986.

The corner of Friedrichstrasse and
Leipzigerstrasse looking west.

Stand at the corner of Friedrichstrasse and Leipzigerstrasse and
look west [6.28]. The new apartment buildings on the left blend imperceptibly
with the pre-war survivors on the corner of Friedrichstrasse. The war-shaped
wall on the right continues to mark the old road of Leipzigerstrasse. All one
can see between the shabby lumps of buildings is the Wall, and behind it in
the West the vague outline of large disconnected objects.

6.29

The corner of Friedrichstrasse and
Leipzigerstrasse looking east.

Stand at the corner of Friedrichstrasse and Leipzigerstrasse and
look east [6.29], to the metamorphosis of Leipzigerstrasse from a broken and
patched-up survivor of war to a ruthless political abstraction in the image of
the old city. The old street and the old order will host these new places that
enclose courtyards in the rear, re-creating the public, private, and intimate
layers in the life of the city so hated by the modernists.

Stand at the corner of Friedrichstrasse and Leipzigerstrasse and look south [6.30]. Beyond the new construction, beyond Checkpoint Charlie, across the Wall and just out of sight is a strange monument to bourgeois intellectualism and the increasingly desperate attempts to radicalize reality. It is an apartment house by the American architect Peter Eisenman. In East Berlin, architecture has become quiet and acquiescent; it no longer has anything new to say. In West Berlin, architecture is becoming increasingly noisy.

6.30
The corner of Friedrichstrasse and
Leipzigerstrasse looking south.

Stand at the corner of Freidrichstrasse and Leipzigerstrasse and look north and west [6.31-32], to the recently completed Grand Hotel, named in the memory of the Grand Palast Hotel which stood close by on Leipziger Platz. The sign says that this GDR Interhotel is a product of VE AHB Limex Bau-Export-Import, the Japan GDR Project Co. Ltd., and Kajima Corporation of Tokyo, Japan, architects and general contractors. The title board proudly declares this a Japanese import, its facade a veneer of effeminate classicism, its interior the most meretricious kind of genteel indulgence, its thin classical style precast in concrete, happily coexisting with the surviving nineteenth-century office building it adjoins. Here is post-modernism, in a much more significant social sense than is present in the West. Is this simply the revolutionary state continuing to whore for hard currency, or is it a portent of a more complex revolution? The diverse vigor of Western capitalism is undirected, the collective power of socialism is unmotivated, and even at the front lines of the ideological battle both retreat before the energy and productivity of Japan.

Further west the path of Voss Strasse still bends at the same point it did when fronting the Chancellery, before disappearing into the Wall. Now it is rebuilt into a street of townhouses behind which, in place of the Chancellery garden, children play in the shadow of the Wall oblivious to the past.

6.31
The Grand Hotel,
Friedrichstrasse north
of Leipzigerstrasse.

6.32
The corner of Friedrichstrasse and
Leipzigerstrasse looking north.

The revolution abandoned the ideological promises of architecture and architecture has abandoned ideology. The surfaces of the newly reformed Berlin Center reveal a culture in the midst of a traumatic shift in the recognition of self, almost physiological in character, as if a spell had been broken and society were allowed to rediscover its place. It has eased the transition through timid representations of the body drawn from the figures of history, through modest objects defined by circumstance. The power of the Wall has vitiated the epic project of modernism.

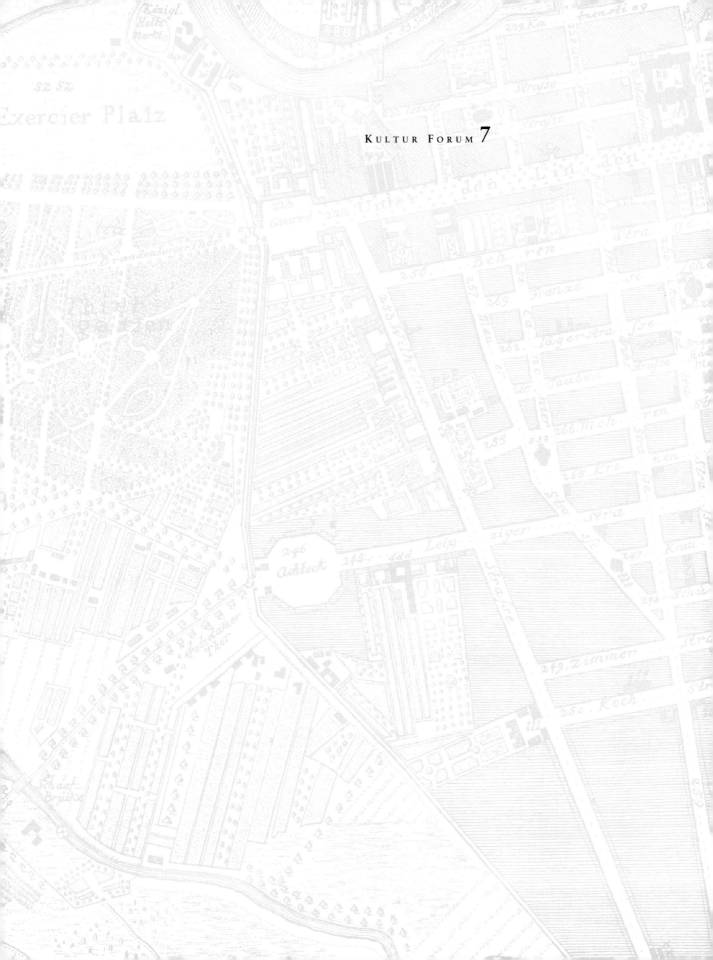

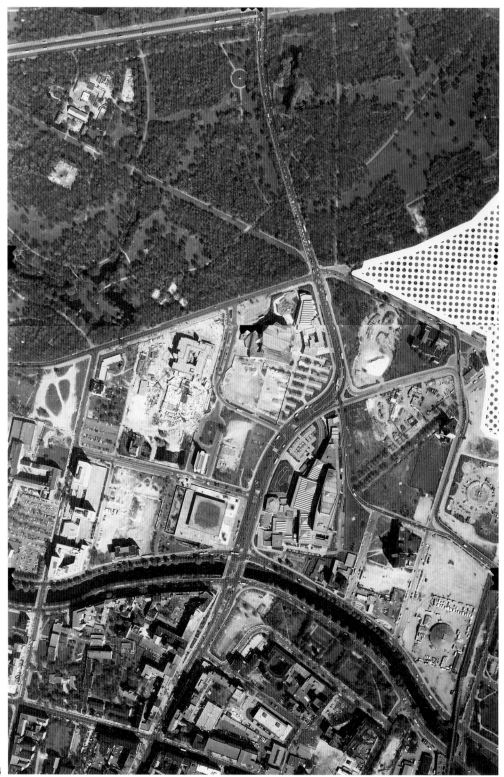

1984

These frames from an aerial survey made by the Berlin City Planning Department in 1984 reveal a fragmented reality, a scattering of cultural bones thrown by architect-metaphysicians hoping to discern the future of the Western world [7.1]. In the 1970s the West Berlin authorities named this place, created by the destruction of the war, Kultur Forum. This area, more than any other in Berlin, represents the greatest rupture in the division of Western civilization and culture. Though a hard and fast dividing line running from the Baltic Sea to the Black Sea marked the boundaries of the Iron Curtain, it was, for the most part, anonymous; neither its presence nor its effect registers on the imagination. Only here, at the center of Berlin, is the wound of a severed Europe still apparent, at a point one hundred and twenty miles inside East Germany with three hundred thousand Russian troops positioned between it and the West. Here and only here has the West constructed objects in symbolic opposition to the East.

With the division of the city all the major public and historic buildings, with the exception of the Reichstag, remained in East Berlin. West Berlin, recentered around the commercial street Kurfürstendamm, was left without a cultural or political heart. While East Berlin moved its cultural and symbolic center away from the Wall and neutralized the character of the division, the West responded by attempting to construct a "forum" for the divided culture at the very border of its existence.

Since the Enlightenment, the architects of this place have viewed themselves as cultural metaphysicians, divining through their architecture the essential order of reality. However, as the nature of such essences and orders became increasingly elusive and ambiguous, architects began to reflect on a chaotic cosmos and on the indefinite nature of all things – a task, for some, antithetical to the nature of architecture.

All the great works of architecture that were built to establish Kultur Forum have been shaped in the presence of the Wall. All have been conscious of their place at the heart of a global ideological schism. Hans Scharoun's Berlin Philharmonic Hall of 1960-63, Mies van der Rohe's National Gallery of 1965-67, James Stirling's Berlin Science Center of 1979, Peter Eisenman's "Checkpoint Charlie" Apartment House of 1980-87, and Hans Hollein's Kultur Forum Project of 1984 – all of these buildings reflect not only the shifting reaction of the West toward a world divided, but also an increasing uncertainty in the politics of all order.

7.1
Two frames from an aerial survey of West Berlin, 1984. Kultur Forum is the area contained by the Tiergarten to the north, the remains of Potsdamerstrasse to the east, and the Landwehr Canal to the south. East German territory is identified by a superimposed dot pattern.

1961
AUGUST

7.2
The Berlin Philharmonic Hall
under construction, August 1961.
In the distance are the remains
of the House of Tourism, the only
building completed in Speer's
North-South Axis plan.

HANS SCHAROUN AND THE BERLIN PHILHARMONIC HALL

Late in 1960, the ground was cleared by the West Berlin authorities for the construction of a new Philharmonic Hall [7.2-9]. In July of that year, in a speech to the students of the Berlin Academy of Art, Scharoun declared the epic agenda for his architecture:

Now that the collective of the people has replaced the prince, there is a need to find a way to serve and impact on the collective effort; to facilitate cooperation – remember and work to put the arts at the peak of this effort in partnership with other areas of public life. This is hard to do. No place with the character of a 'Weltstadt' [world city] exists. The 'genius loci' of the 1920's Berlin does not exist.

Our duty is to determine and make known the task of art. The task, after the question posed by M. Heidegger, is to consider the meaning or significance for art in our space/area [in] the middle, between east and west, between north and south.[1]

Berlin was the "space/area" in the middle and the Philharmonic would be the epicenter. The task for art in this place was to carry a burden of heroic proportions – to invest this symbolic home of German music with the power to renew life and order at the center of devastation, to renew and yet reject the past history of this place. Here, amidst a culture debased in the eyes of the world and increasingly divided against itself, an object of compelling honesty and originality was needed. The words of Heidegger gave substance to Scharoun's acts and dreams.[2] "Poetically man dwells," he wrote,

. . . poetry, as the authentic gauging of the dimension of dwelling, is the primal form of building.

Poetry first of all admits man's dwelling into its very nature, its presencing being. Poetry is the original

admission of dwelling.[3]

The poetics of the Philharmonic are an intense blend of socialism and naturalism. "Music was the focal point of the whole composition," Scharoun wrote in the program notes for the opening in 1963. "This was the key note from the very beginning. This dominating thought not only gave shape to the auditorium of Berlin's new Hall but also insured its undisputed priority within the entire building scheme." After that, however, the space would be formed from an explicit socialist order:

1964

7.3
Hans Scharoun,
The Berlin Philharmonic Hall,
1964.

The orchestra and conductor stand spatially and optically in the very middle, and if this is not the

mathematical center, nonetheless they are completely enveloped by their audience. Here you will find

no segregation of 'producers' and 'consumers,' but rather a community of listeners grouped around an

orchestra in the most natural of all seating arrangements. Thus, despite its size, the auditorium has

retained a certain intimacy, enabling a direct and co-creative share in the production of music. Here

the creation and the experience of music occur in a hall not motivated by formal aesthetics, but whose

design was inspired by the very purpose it serves. Man, music and space – here they meet in a new

relationship.[4]

With no segregation of "producers" and "consumers" but rather a collective joined in a co-creative experience, the Hall embodied a one-to-oneness between orchestra and audience which was carried even further by the subdivision of the hall into parts, each the size of an orchestra, so the performer and audience become, in a sense, interchangeable. What now seems a strongly subjective and eccentric work (it is called by some "expressionistic") Scharoun believed was the product of a wholly depersonalized

7.4
Hans Scharoun,
The Berlin Philharmonic Hall,
plans, 1961-63.

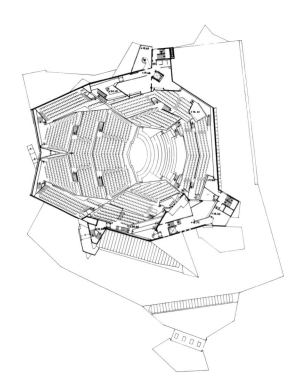

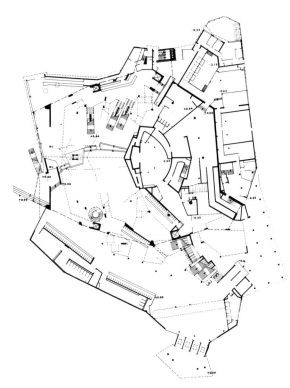

1961 - 63

process in no sense "motivated by formal aesthetics." He saw himself, not as the subjective artist but as the objective servant of a culture seeking to reveal its nature in the essence of experience. "Hugo Häring posed this task," he wrote in the speech to the students of the Berlin Academy:

in his treatise on the secrecy of form, which includes the form of political man – all events occur in

accord with genetic processes. The work of the artist is to search and extract the truth from essences.

To use elements of logic not as rigid forms of thought but as a method of operating on given

situations. So personal expression will be a reality that is not subjective.[5]

He viewed the single building as he did the city: it should replicate nature, not simply as a romantic emulation of organic form, but by being shaped from a multitude of human actions. It was a vision of nature that vividly clarified his orchestration of the auditorium:

The construction follows the pattern of a landscape, with the auditorium seen as a valley, and there at

its bottom is the orchestra surrounded by a sprawling vineyard climbing the sides of its neighboring

hills. The ceiling, resembling a tent, encounters this 'landscape' like a 'skyscape.' Convex in character,

the tent-like ceiling is very much linked with the acoustics, with the desire to obtain the maximum

diffusion of music via the convex surfaces. Here the sound is not reflected from the narrow side of a

hall, but rises from the depth and center, moving towards all sides, descending and spreading evenly

among the listeners below.

7.5
Hans Scharoun,
The Berlin Philharmonic Hall,
section, 1961-63.

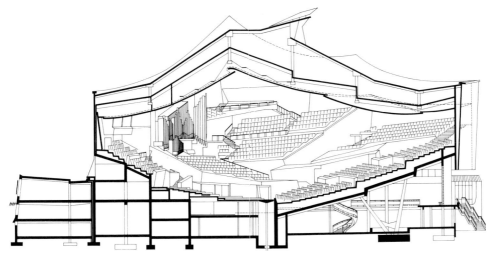

1961 - 63

1961 - 63

The power of the music is reflected in the faces of the listeners as the sun on the landscape, all under a billowing, cloud-like roof. Although its form arises from nature, the auditorium is raised above the ground creating below it, in and around the foyer, a state of ordered disorder unprecedented in the history of architecture:

Every room had ample opportunity for the free development of its own particular function. Even the complex of stairways seems to play about the foyer, yet rhythmically adopting its lively form to the demands of the auditorium . . . The ancillary space stands in a dynamic and tense relationship to the festive calm of the auditorium, which is truly the jewel in the Philharmonic crown.[6]

The foyer produces a confusion of people and activities, eating and drinking, robing and disrobing, and browsing and laughing, in total contrast to the community that would develop in the presence of the music.

This concentration of forces radiating outward from the performance of the music produces continually changing and ambiguous public facades, reflecting only the building's internal order. It is a place that would escape history and speak only of the peculiar circumstances of its own nature in its own present. In the midst of a ruined city the Philharmonic had to be devoid of sentiment, nostalgia, and regret. It promised nothing but its absolute self. It was silent and this, to a people crying out for the comfort of easy promises, was and is its virtue. It has never been comfortable in its context. At a point and place in time crying out for rhetoric and empty gesture, it says nothing but that which relates to itself, and nothing at all to the future of Berlin or to the division of Europe.

In his mind, Scharoun was creating a physical realization and validation of Heidegger's existentialism, an object shaped from the direct description of immediately experienced phenomena, an object to renew and purify physical reality in its isolation from all external realities. Yet, in its every dimension, it is wholly the product of this place and of the horrific events of its history. It is a supreme object of negation whose every line is defined by the past. Its extreme introversion can be seen as the absolute antithesis – a complete implosion – of Hitler's Great Hall, a reality stripped of everything but the essential elements, as in the collapse of a star. Each extreme could not exist without the other.

7.7
Hans Scharoun,
The Berlin Philharmonic Hall,
1961-63.

1961 - 63

It is all in the words. The words describe every element, every space, every surface in the syntax of ancient realms. Yet the Philharmonic has moved outside the limits of known words. When there are no words to describe what is present, what will be the basis of future understanding? There seems little control over the forces that undermine reality. Consider what might have resulted if Scharoun had committed his vision to East Germany rather than the West. Could the intense dialectical character of his theory and his method – revealing contradictions in the suborder of things to give a unique vitality and significance to the whole – have clarified and empowered socialist reality?[7]

The Philharmonic continues to disturb the shaping of Kultur Forum with the paradox of its existence. Is it a sign of a new synthesis in reality, the constraining of simplistic geometrical order by the random events of circumstance, or is it merely a fragment of a shattered vortex, an object that no longer tolerates the dialectical struggle? Though formed from human action, it remains a disembodied abstraction, dense and paradoxical at the still-torn edge of the city, its epic cast diminished somewhat by a coat of gold aluminum. It remains a man-made mountain.

7.8
Hans Scharoun, foyer of
The Berlin Philharmonic Hall.

1961 - 63

1961 - 63

1945

MIES VAN DER ROHE AND THE NATIONAL GALLERY
OF ART

With the completion of the Philharmonic,
planning began on a new National Gallery of Art to be built four hundred
yards to the south. It would sit close to the foundations of the House of
German Tourism, the only part of Speer's North-South Axis to be
constructed [7.10-12]. The great hulk of its ruin had remained unattended
since the war's end.[8] The architect was to be the German-American Ludwig
Mies van der Rohe, former director of the Bauhaus and considered then, as
now, one of the four great masters of twentieth-century architecture.[9]
Scharoun, in contrast, was never widely regarded outside Germany.

Mies had a long and involved relationship to many of the struggles
that surrounded the site. His project for a city crown of 1919 would have
been visible from there, and during the 1920s he lived close by, across the
Landwehr Canal on Am Karlsbad.[10] In 1926 he was commissioned to design
the Liebknecht and Luxemburg Monument; the construction, now destroyed,
was his most political and expressive work. Liebknecht had known Mies by
reputation before the First World War, and reminiscent of Goethe speaking

of Schinkel, had said to the philosopher Hugo Perls: "your architect seems a most capable man. When the Independent Socialists take over the government, we will keep him busy."[11] In 1919 Liebknecht's body, with that of Rosa Luxemburg, was found floating in the canal within view of the National Gallery site, martyrs of the Spartacist uprising.

It is argued by Mies' biographers that his concern with the absolute and the timeless detached him from the temporal-political issues of the day. When his attempt to reestablish the Bauhaus in 1933 was forcefully opposed by Hitler's new government he was confronted with the brutal character of national socialism. Yet, in the same years he prepared designs for Hitler's Reichsbank and in 1934 made tentative studies, garnished with uneasy swastikas, for the German Pavilion at the International Exposition in Brussels. Slowly, because of his uncertain political commitments, Mies was starved of building commissions, and his ties to the textile industry, a supportive client, were publicly usurped by Nazi Party favorite Ernst Sagebiel, the architect of Goering's Air Force Ministry and Mendelsohn's assistant on Columbus Haus.

7.11
Matthaikirch Platz with
St. Matthaus-Kirche, March 1939.
Designed by Friedrich August
Stuler, the church was built from
1844 to 1946.

1939

By the late 1930s Mies van der Rohe was forced to leave Germany. And so in 1964, after thirty years of exile and half his professional life, a world master of modern architecture was invited back to a beleaguered capital city in the nation of his birth to create a great national museum that would reaffirm the virtues of Western culture at the very edge of its existence.

7.12
St. Matthaus-Kirche seen
from the plaza of Mies' National
Gallery of Art, July 1969.

1969

It must be said from the outset that the evolution of the National Gallery is a tale of the absurd. It begins in Santiago, Cuba, where Mies was commissioned to design the corporate headquarters for Bacardi Rum in 1957 [7.13]. The design which emerged in 1958 – a vast floating roof plane, unsupported at the corners, covering a glass-enclosed volume – is in every element save one the prototype for the National Gallery. The project for Bacardi would have been cast in concrete instead of steel. The great overhanging roof was explicitly to give shelter from the Cuban sun. The project was thrown out of Cuba along with the client in the revolution of 1959, and thus Fidel Castro inadvertently became the agent by which this symbol of Western culture came to Berlin.

In 1961 Mies was commissioned by George Schaefer (his grandson's father-in-law) to build a museum in the city of Schweinfurt to house his collection of nineteenth-century German art, and the design proposed was the Bacardi Headquarters building, this time made in black-painted steel. The commission for the National Gallery came while the Schaefer project was well underway and for a period both projects developed simultaneously. However, Mies became convinced that the Bacardi Headquarters form was best suited to the needs of a great national museum. Schaefer withdrew his commission, claiming nineteenth-century art would not fit in a modern steel box, leaving Mies free to project his ideal space on Berlin.

1959

7.13

Ludwig Mies van der Rohe, model for the Bacardi Rum Headquarters in Santiago, Cuba, 1959.

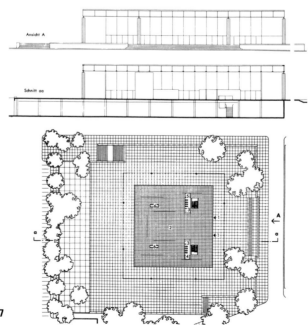

7.14

Ludwig Mies van der Rohe, plan, section, and elevation of the National Gallery of Art. 1962-67.

1962 - 67

1962 - 67

The design [7.14-17] is an abstraction of reality more extreme than any previously seen around Leipziger Platz. Yet, the nature of its violation of natural experience and the political implications of its order remain concealed behind its absolute conviction. The architect sought to create an object embodying the absolute and truthful essence of his age. His spiritual guide lay in the teachings of Saint Thomas Aquinas. Thomistic thought, a blending of Aristotelian philosophy and Christianity, holds that the spirit is higher than matter, the soul greater than the body, and theology truer than philosophy. "Truth," said Aquinas,

. . . is principally in the intellect, and secondarily in things as they are related to the intellect as their

principle . . . . For this reason truth is defined by the conformity of the intellect and thing and hence to

know this conformity is to know truth.[12]

In 1960, the American Institute of Architects awarded Mies its Gold Medal for distinguished service to the profession. "I have learned that architecture must stem from the sustaining and driving forces of civilization," he wrote in his acceptance speech:

. . . and that it can be, at its best, an expression of the innermost structure of its time.

The structure of civilization is not simple, being in part the past, in part the present,

and in part the future. It is difficult to define and to understand. Nothing of the past can be changed

by its very nature. The present has to be accepted and should be mastered. But the future is open —

open for creative thought and action.

225

This is the structure from which architecture emerges. It follows, then, that architecture should be related only to the most significant forces in the civilization. Only a relationship which touches the essence of the time can be real. This relation I like to call a truth relation. Truth in the sense of Thomas Aquinas: As the Adequatio Intellectus et Rei. Or as a modern philosopher expresses it in the language of the day: Truth is the significance of facts.

Only such a relation is able to embrace the complex nature of civilization. Only so, will architecture be involved in the evolution of civilization. And only so, will it express the slow unfolding of its form.[13]

7.16
Ludwig Mies van der Rohe,
National Gallery of Art, 1962-67.

1962 - 67

This was an epic agenda and it made no difference to Mies whether it was enacted in Cuba or Berlin. Architecture in its highest form must be "an expression of the innermost structure of its time . . . related to the most significant forces in civilization," and only through such a revealing order could there be truthful reality. In a splendid speech to his students at IIT in 1950 he said:

It is true that architecture depends on facts,

but its real field of activity is in the realm of significance.

I hope you will understand that architecture

has nothing to do with the inventions of forms.

It is not a playground for children, young or old.

Architecture is the real battleground of the spirit.

Architecture wrote the history of the epochs

and gave them their names.

Architecture depends on its time.

It is the crystallization of its inner structure,

the slow unfolding of its form.[14]

There is evidence that from his formative years Mies had seen himself as "the great architect," alone able to produce works in which "the very soul of his time speaks." He was deeply impressed by Spengler's *The Decline of the West* and its fatalistic project: "we cannot help it if we are born as men of the early winter. Everything depends on our seeing our own position, or destiny, clearly, or our realizing that though we may lie to ourselves about it, we cannot evade it."[15] In this time of profound uncertainty the dialectical character of the Thomistic argument had a particular significance. The synthesis of Platonic and Augustinian thought; the reconciliation of classical and Christian cosmologies; the exquisite distinctions between nature and supernature, reason and philosophy, and faith and theology; and the relationship between the idea of being and the objective reality of architecture, between essence and existence, all must be somewhere present in the National Gallery. It was to be the "battle-ground of the spirit" of the age and offer "the crystallization of its inner structure." It would present a universal and absolute essence.[16]

The National Gallery is a projection of faith on material reality as heartfelt as in any cathedral. It is intended as an object of reformation. It is ordered absolutely because all around it is in disorder. It sees no virtue in random circumstance when the destiny of Western civilization is at stake.

With ruthless clarity it attempts to will the survival of the future, and to demonstrate man's ability to rise above the body and advance an ideal order.

Yet, it is a desolate place and nothing in its twenty years of existence has made it comfortable. It is absolutely intolerant of random circumstance and its myths are limited by its ideals. It is a dreadful mix of the pagan and the Christian. Denying the sensual and the bodily, it negates all pasts and all circumstance and conveys a spirituality more intense, more alienated, and more tragic than the future needs. In its obsessive autonomy it diminishes all the art and the people placed within its area of influence.

In its silence the National Gallery is matched by the Philharmonic –

1962 - 67

two dinosaurs from the extinct modern age. A blunt reading of their contradictory characters pits Marxist existentialism against Platonic fascism. Where Scharoun avoids all pre-established ideas of order Mies tolerates nothing else. They are brilliantly matched opposites within the narrow frame of modern abstraction, one of the supernatural, one of circumstance; one of Aquinas, the other, of Heidegger; and one ontological, the other phenomenological. They may be the last heroic works of the Age of Reason. The force of their essential and opposing truths, exquisitely balanced, seems to suck the very energy from the air around them and inhibit all future growth.

For ten years after the opening of the National Gallery in 1968 this undefined place, now called Kultur Forum, continued its uncertain existence between ruin and renewal until the creation of the Internationale Bauausstellung Berlin (the Berlin International Building Exhibition), or IBA, in the late 1970s. The IBA program sponsored numerous international competitions for designs addressing many different sites and problems in Berlin. They were first planned for completion in 1984 but were subsequently held until 1987, conveniently tying them to the celebration of the 750th birthday of the city.[17]

The IBA program was as political as it was architectural. It was one of many programs and events that, since the division of the city, sought to keep the idea of West Berlin alive in the Western mind, investing it with significant experiments in "western reality" to ease insecurity about its eventual fate. It also brought to this part of the city, for the first time in two hundred years, the work of foreign architects.

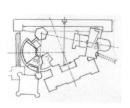

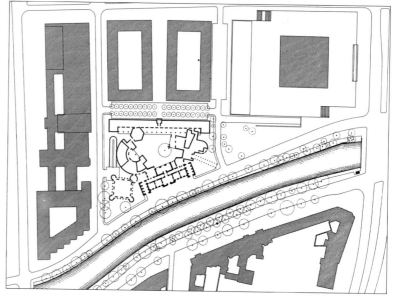

1979

7.18
James Stirling,
Berlin Science Center,
sketch and plan, 1979.

JAMES STIRLING'S BERLIN SCIENCE CENTER

The Berlin Science Center [7.18-21] is a think tank for the study of environmental and sociological issues. It lies between Shell House, a heroic survivor of the 1930s, to the west and the National Gallery to the east. The new buildings cluster around the great stone pile of the former Teltow Law Courts. Stirling's report describes the program:

The primary need of the Science Center is for a great multitude of small offices . . . . A special concern is how to find an architectural and environmental solution from a program mainly composed of repetitive offices. The rational office solution usually produces banal boxlike buildings. Much of what is wrong with post-war urban redevelopment lies in the uniformity of these rationally produced office blocks and they may be the biggest single factor contributing to the visual destruction of our cities in the postwar period.[18]

Stirling is a foreigner. Born in Scotland, he practices in London and is considered one of the so-called third generation of modern masters. It is the first time in two hundred years that projects conceived outside of German society have been designed for this place. Stirling could not know this city as a German would, nor could he be expected to feel about this place and its destruction the way a German would. Yet, Stirling is concerned with making a German object. In the drawings his debt to Schinkel is explicit. Here the barges from Schinkel's drawings for the Altes Museum have found their way onto the Landwehr Canal. The work is an elegant and knowing reference to the character of early-nineteenth-century thought. Such an assembly could well have been projected by Schinkel, though in a less haphazard manner. The pleasure pavilions around the Roman baths in Sans Souci are just such a fusion of histories, conceived by Schinkel to explore the intersections of classical and romantic realities. The restraint of Stirling's elevations, and the repetition and the staccato rhythms of the windows, are not far removed from the buildings that formed the center of Berlin in the nineteenth century. But this is a very different time and place. Stirling wrote:

7.19
James Stirling,
Berlin Science Center,
sections, 1979.

I made an early decision that, whatever, we would break away from the office block stereotype and I said to those working on it: 'make a cluster of buildings – take for instance a long bar, a cruciform, a half-circle and a square, and juggle them together with the old building.

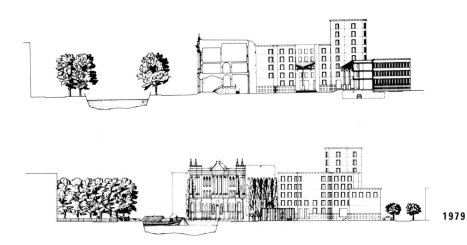

1979

231

What began as geometry evolved as it moved into history. In the mind of its creator it is a simple collection of Western realities. The long bar represents a Greek stoa, the half-circle a Roman amphitheater, the cruciform an early Christian church, the tower a medieval fortress, and the plaza a Renaissance campanile, all scattered around the old Court House which is itself the image of a baroque palace. These elements cluster together in Stirling's imagination not just as fragments of a city but as a city itself – paradoxically, a disordered medieval city. Here in the wasteland of the aftermath of war, culture is reestablished through the illusion of past archetypes and the outline of the objective reality of past ideals. Stirling was quite explicit: "In this place of devastation we hoped to create a microcosm – 'the fragments of a city.'"[19]

Stirling's new reality neither knew nor cared about Potsdamerstrasse or Leipziger Platz. His additions are without ritual and represent only the masks of memory and myth. The architect, asked to redefine reality, has only a vague knowledge and little interest in what has gone before. Although the courtyard is full of charm and security, it presents to the outer world a complex defensive wall. Yet, to view it as an object of alienation assumes more content than the work possesses. There is brilliant invention here but no great lessons; this is a project for no future but it own. It implies universals but does not declare them with any faith.

In contrast to Scharoun, who wished to give human events and activities a pure circumstance free from the distortions of history, Stirling uses the distortions of architectural history to give the illusion of meaning to dull circumstance. In contrast to the work of Mies, this is not a project of ideology. No unforgiving god inhabits these desires. Though it shares the street front with the National Gallery, it shows no concern for the search for the innermost structure of time. Its presence claims no relation to the "significant forces in the civilization." It is an event of local significance reflecting only the imagination of its creator, the object of an English sensibility.

Moving from the astringent yet exhilarating reality of Scharoun, through the ascetic universalism of Mies, and on to Stirling, the project of architecture regresses into a subjective world of wit and pretentious gesture. Stirling's project casts off the moral imperative of modernism. It offers a future without conviction, yet a future confident that conviction about significance is irrelevant. The real world has changed and architecture need no longer signify. It should be honest but with nothing to say. In the history of this place it connects, not to Schinkel's Berlin, but to Kempinski's Haus Vaterland. Reality rests only in the assorted dreams of individuals.

7.20
James Stirling,
Berlin Science Center,
elevation, 1979.

7.21
James Stirling,
Berlin Science Center,
model, 1979.

7.22
Checkpoint Charlie at the
corner of Friedrichstrasse and
Kochstrasse, 1980.

PETER EISENMAN AT THE "CORNER OF THE WEST"

Just at the outer edge of Kultur Forum, Friedrichstrasse is closed by Checkpoint Charlie, the foreigner's gate to East Berlin [7.22]. Here on any given day, East German soldiers would stand just behind a line painted across the sidewalk and stare impassively at the dumbfounded tourists. The interval between East and West is about one hundred meters wide at this point. Immediately south of the gate on the northeast corner of Kochstrasse is an apartment building designed by the American architect Peter Eisenman [7.23-27]. It is on the same block as the Wall Museum, a sensationalistic commercial venture advertised throughout West Berlin.

In all the previous chapters in this history of alternate realities, architecture served merely as a background against which to consider the changing desires of a culture; it was wholly a product of forces outside itself. In these latest acts of building, however, architecture moves into a baseless foreground and becomes limited by the notion of the autonomy of objects, becoming placeless, meaningless, and cultureless.

Peter Eisenman deserves his reputation as the foremost Western architect-intellectual. The Institute for Architecture and Urban Studies which he founded in 1967 became a world forum for the critical examination of architecture. The periodical he founded, *Oppositions,* was singular among journals in the English-speaking world, dealing seriously with the complex shifts in the definition of architecture. In considering the problems of modernism in 1979, he wrote of the displacement of man from the center of his world:

He is no longer viewed as an originating agent. Objects are seen as ideas independent of man. In this context, man is a discursive function among complex and already formed systems of language, which he witnesses but does not constitute . . . . It is this condition of displacement which gives rise to design in which authorship can no longer either account for a linear development that has a 'beginning' and an 'end,' – hence the rise of the atemporal – or account for the invention of form – hence the abstract as a mediation between pre-existent sign systems.[20]

Eisenman proposed a new theoretical base which would change the simple humanistic balance between forms and function to a dialectical relationship within the evolution of form itself:

The dialectic can best be described as the potential co-existence within any form of two non-corroborating and non-sequential tendencies. One tendency is to presume architectural form to be a recognizable transformation from some pre-existent geometric or platonic solid . . . . This tendency is certainly a relic of humanist theory.

However, to this is added a second tendency that sees architectural form in an atemporal, decompositional mode, as something simplified from some pre-existent set of non-specific spatial entities. Here, form is understood as a series of fragments – signs without meaning dependent upon, and without reference to, a more basic condition . . . .

Both tendencies, however, when taken together, constitute the essence of this new, modern dialectic. They begin to define the inherent nature of the object in and of itself and its capacity to be represented.[21]

By an act of chance the tendencies he identifies are clearly represented in the work of Mies van der Rohe and Scharoun, and it is to confront their opposing natures that Eisenman steps in, proposing an architecture of deliberate internal contradiction so that the integrity of each tendency is visible yet compromised. The "new modern dialectic" would manifest itself in the interaction between pre-existing geometrical order, often idealized, and the fragmentary order of circumstance. At the severely strained corner near Checkpoint Charlie it would be realized. Eisenman's initial proposal to IBA in 1980 was conceived as a monument:

The competition project in a sense was a useless design. It was a monument . . . . When the competition was over even though our project won a special first prize we were told that it was not

1980 - 87

what Berlin wanted on that site and that we must build social housing. The requirement for housing

on the site had been stipulated in the competition program, but we chose to ignore it. The thought of

putting a housing project there was abhorrent to me; when I first saw this site next to the Berlin Wall I

said that I would never want to raise a child there . . . .

But to return to the architecture, we are now working on a building on the corner of

Friedrichstrasse. The organizers of the IBA wanted us to close the corner and make a contextual

building. The question is, what is a contextual building here – what does closing the corner mean?

First, it means covering up walls that have the scars of Berlin's history, of the bombings of World War

II, that history and archaeology that are so incredible in Berlin. I told myself that I would never close

that corner in order to restore Berlin to what it was. So this building is a deliberate gesture against the

contextualism that would restore Berlin to its nineteenth-century image, erasing the history of two

world wars and, of course, the Berlin Wall. Second there is the symbolism of the building itself. We

cannot be optimistic today about the future; we live in a futureless present in which buildings have

lost their traditional meaning. The meaning of this building stems from its own internal process.[22]

Some critics said that the agonizing of the bourgeois metaphysician was never more dangerous, and Berliners were slightly disturbed to be told by an American that the scars of war should never be covered up because they represented an "incredible archaeology," or to be advised by the architect chosen to mark the most famous Western gate to the communist world that we live in a "futureless present." However, in relation to the more complex dialectical conditions in the struggle of opposites between East and West, his argument was rich with significance. In contrast to many of his professional colleagues, he would not make an object that erased the history of this place, neither would he produce an illusion of comforting order; rather, he would seek in the application of his dialectical strategy – which must have seemed particularly appropriate to this place and time – to reveal an autonomous symbol of paradox, new meanings and new possibilities in reality. Eisenman explained:

Our original competition site plan had to do with an excavation, an artificial excavation of walls that in some way simulated the history of Berlin. This project takes the trace of the excavation from the site plan and projects it onto the vertical plane. That is, parts of the excavation are propped up to become buildings. Thus an internal dialogue is set up between the vertical plane and the horizontal plane. It is not intended to have any meaning or significance outside of the internal logic of the project; there are no external references, unlike in traditional objects. The analogy may be made to mathematical formulas. Some are elegant, some are not. The only judgment that one can make of them is whether the internal logic is coherent.[23]

1980 - 87

Is the internal logic coherent? Alas, there is not much to it other than the puzzling conflict of simple geometrical orders. His reference to Mercator's grid is surely one of the "external references" he denies having made. The patterns in conflict are skin deep, and the result is a mask of oppositions screening a very conventional reality. Eisenman, in defending the work, said: "This project is about the investigation of making an architecture outside of program, outside of use, outside of context, outside of culture, outside of symbolism."[24] This can only refer to the facade, for all else in the project is a product of program, use, context, and in a negative sense, culture. Though the symbolism of the opposing grids and the detachment of the screen wall are simple and obvious, it is symbolism nonetheless. Eisenman continues:

I don't believe that words can contain the same mythology and meaning that they did in the classical period because in the present, which I see as having no future, all we can do is make empty words. Let others fill them up with their own meanings – nostalgia for the past, hope for the future. All I am saying is that if it is possible to make words empty of meaning, I'd like to try.[25]

These intentions are evident in Scharoun's Philharmonic. However, Eisenman's little apartment building is such a thin demonstration of intent that the words carry much more potency than the object. The critical stance is stronger than the architectural execution.

In fairness to Eisenman, the IBA competition was organized to encourage experimentation that was often in conflict with the needs of the developers who were responsible for the construction. As it was finally built a great deal was lost from its elegant conceptual state. The plane that represents the ideal, aligned along the world-dividing Mercator grid, angles across the corner onto Kochstrasse and is held in a crude patchwork aluminum grid. Although the experience is contrived and without significant presence, it is not entirely silent. It makes a noisy mess on this symbolic corner, like a work of slapstick. It is not "outside of context" and not "outside of symbolism," but it does seem to be "outside of culture." Why then does it play in Berlin? Is it an act of deliberate subversion or merely a fashionable mask of intellectual disfigurement on an already-disfigured city?

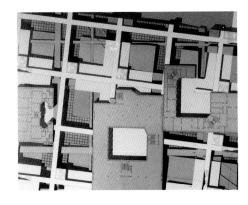

7.25
Peter Eisenman, Apartment House South Friedrichstadt, plan, 1980-87.

7.26
Peter Eisenman, Apartment House South Friedrichstadt, axonometric, 1980-87.

1980 - 87

For all its frailty it is a critical mark in a desperate struggle. It sits in Berlin as the extraordinary and absurd child of Scharoun's existentialism and Mies' absolutism. Even as it becomes apparent that the present is futureless only in terms of the modernist desire for the universal and the rational reconstruction of civilization, Eisenman, at Checkpoint Charlie, continues to struggle with its epic burden. He obeys Mies' command to shape an object "related to the significant forces in the civilization," and to reveal in it "the innermost structure of time." He will not surrender the future to fancy dresses or dead gods. He stands united with Gilly, Mendelsohn, and Scharoun in defending the freedom to explore the infinite possibilities in the order of things. His project is difficult and profound. His inability to reconcile the oppositions within the dialectical tendencies may lead not to the deconstruction of architecture, but to its self-consumption.

In its completed form the Eisenman building on Friedrichstrasse connects to the wall of the neighboring building and is quickly transformed into the facade of a nineteenth-century apartment building, just like those being reconstructed in the eastern city, and it is this comparison with its counterparts in the East that is the most interesting aspect of the work at this time. Social realism in the GDR evolved into an architecture of modest

7.27
Peter Eisenman, Apartment House South Friedrichstadt, 1980-87.

1980 - 87

promises and self-effacement in unity with the past, an architecture without inner struggle or abstraction, devoid of revolutionary significance. The polemical voice of architecture had been silenced, not in any intellectual sense, but simply in recognition that it was no longer relevant. However, Eisenman's self-conscious exaggeration of opposing tendencies in the modern order produced deliberate, though innocuous, disunity and confusion. On such slender evidence it is unwise to extrapolate too grandly. Yet, it is tempting to see two profoundly differing cosmologies emerging – the East, fragmented and distraught behind the illusion of comfort and unity, and the West, increasingly docile behind the illusion of agony and fragmentation.

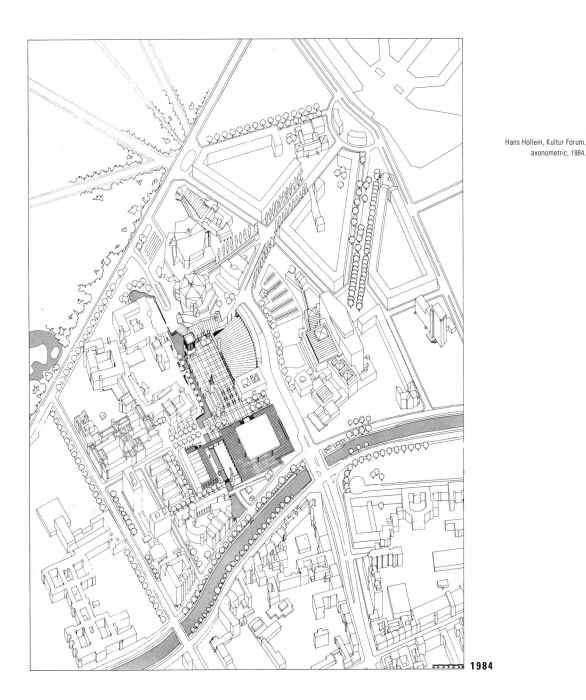

7.28
Hans Hollein, Kultur Forum,
axonometric, 1984.

1984

HANS HOLLEIN IN KULTUR FORUM

As the Austrian critic Friederick
Achleitner observed, Viennese culture since the baroque period – with the
Hapsburg's suppression of literature – has favored the ambivalence of music
and architecture for the staging of semblances of reality. The city has had a
tradition of aestheticizing and equalizing realities, a kind of perceptual
repression through reassembly and collage.[26] Only in the artifice of Viennese

Hans Hollein, Kultur Forum,
plan, 1984.

reality could a sensibility be nurtured, sufficiently amoral, theatrical, sensual, and pragmatic, to tackle this reconciliation of the ideological opposites in Kultur Forum. The sensibility arrived in the person of Hans Hollein. His competition design for the central area of Kultur Forum, bridging the Philharmonic and the National Gallery, was judged most successful by the IBA jury [7.28-31].

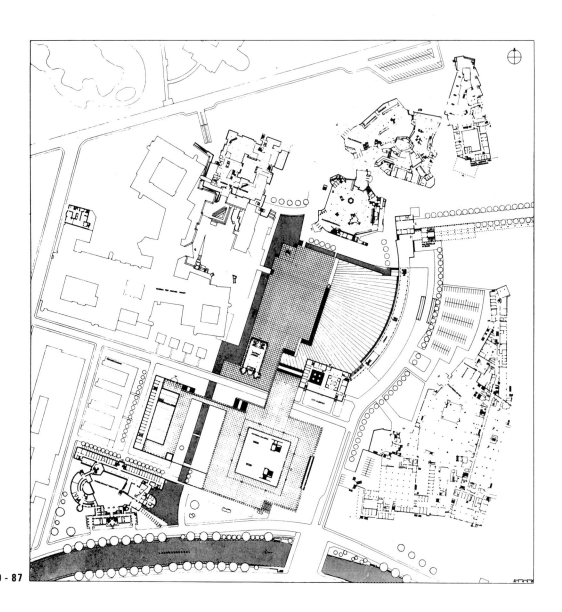

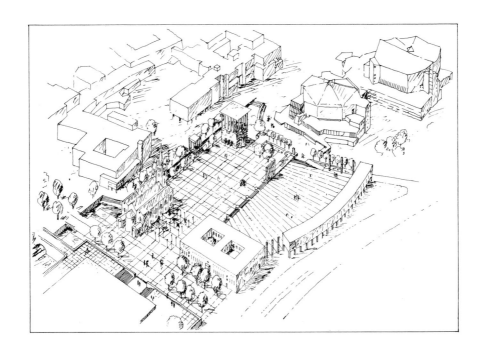

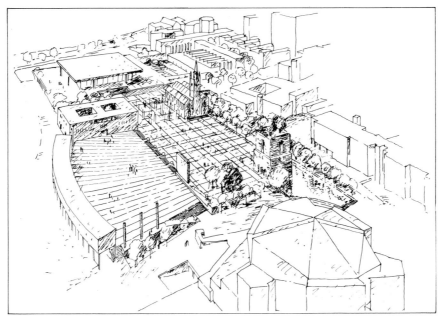

1980 - 87

Hollein's project has the character of a formal garden with pavilions. It is asymmetrical, closed by a canal on the west. On the east, a grand arcade would quite deliberately block the view of the the Prussian State Library, whose lumbering disorder much disturbed Hollein's sensibilities. On the south, a broad bridge connects with and obeys the order of symmetry in the National Gallery, while on the north neither decorative pavilions nor steps and terraces seem to be able to make a connection with the Philharmonic. Its overall nature is one of artifice, soft and charming, without exaggeration and without thunder. Here, where Hitler would have built the great Hall of the Soldier, is both the modest antithesis to Eisenman's pessimism and the reason for it. It is a picturesque assembly that would create, among other things, a center for the study of religion. It addresses the compositional problems of unifying disparate realities. Unconcerned with any socio-political ideals internal or external to itself, it is wholly freed from the moral burden of modernism. Nowhere is the past of this place either symbolized or remembered. Architecture – having been forced to aspire beyond its ability, to carry the desires of a disturbed age – has settled down once again to offer a charming and civilized stage in the hope that the play will be just as good. But nothing is forgotten in Berlin and to a people who take pride in a tough, unsparing acceptance of life Hollein's vision appeared as a confection, as bunting stretched between two opposing machines of war, and as an attempt to stage a fête in the midst of a silent battlefield.

Beginning with the publication of the drawings in 1986, slowly and unexpectedly there grew a passionate resistance to the erosion of Scharoun's vision by Hollein's synthetic reality. A Scharoun Society was created and pamphlets were circulated in public places (the Philharmonic was awash with them). Not since the war had there been such a show of public concern about the symbolic nature of West Berlin culture. It appeared that some essential power was manifest there. In 1987 the IBA and the City of Berlin allowed only the trace of the design to be constructed in scaffolding.

7.31
Hans Hollein,
Kultur Forum, model, 1984.

1980 - 87

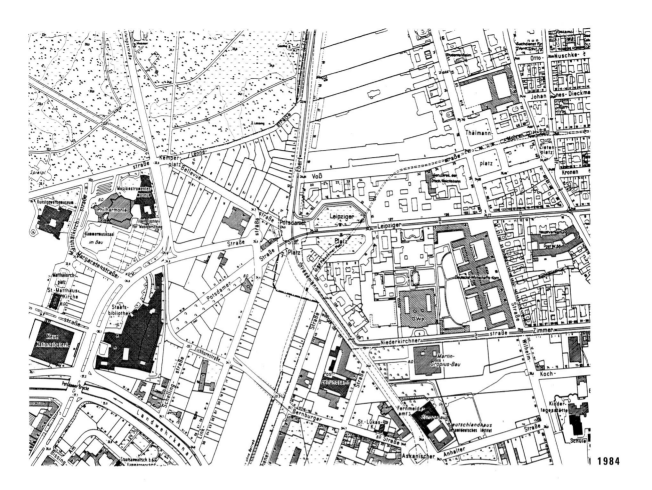

7.32
The official West German Senate
map of Berlin in 1984 displaying the
property lines of 1939.

It may not be possible to create a center at the edge, to impose coherent order on a culture that rejects it. The tolerance for opposing tendencies has reduced the architectural project to fragments. In the longer view of history it is the inevitable by-product of the dialectic struggle. For over a quarter of a millennium Berlin has housed a succession of symbolic projects, increasingly framed in opposition to one another, creating a spiraling polarization which could only end in the destruction and division of the culture. The division of the city has neutralized the struggle of authentic opposites, leaving Kultur Forum at the abandoned edge in an accumulation of disordered residue.

The official map of the city as defined by the Senate of West Berlin in 1989 [7.32] displays the Eastern city in the plots and property lines of 1939, ghostly traces which record not only unresolved legal disputes but also, though unintended, the lost idea of a city. In contrast to the nineteenth-century order of the East, it defines Kultur Forum as a collision of roads, buildings, and property lines – the fragments of opposing ideals. It maps with confidence the destruction of a central authority. It maps with confidence the progression from unified patterns of order to a confusion of orders and ideals. It records the incoherent residue from all the utopias that have shaped the visions for the twentieth century – conservative, socialist, liberal – and the failure or disinterest within the pursuit of freedom to find synthesis between opposing ideologies. In political terms, the charming and indulgent speculations of Stirling, Eisenman, and Hollein can be seen, above all, as the fruits of nineteenth-century liberalism.

At the threshold of the third Christian millennium, after two hundred and fifty years of speculation, the desire to use architecture to control the moral order of the future has faded. The reason, some argue, is an increasing contentment with the immediate material world. Utopian dreams, after all, are only the reflection of a dissatisfaction with the present order of things, and architecture the most convenient means of dramatizing the promise of reformation.

Now, relieved of the burdens and the uniforms of ideologies, architecture has been freed to represent and enhance the myriad mysteries of existence. Yet, a new struggle arises as the significant record of the culture is moving into motion, into multiple images of a self-centered, self-generated experience in which the idea of permanence is an interference. Architecture must learn to coexist with the ambiguity and fertile chaos of a richer illusion.

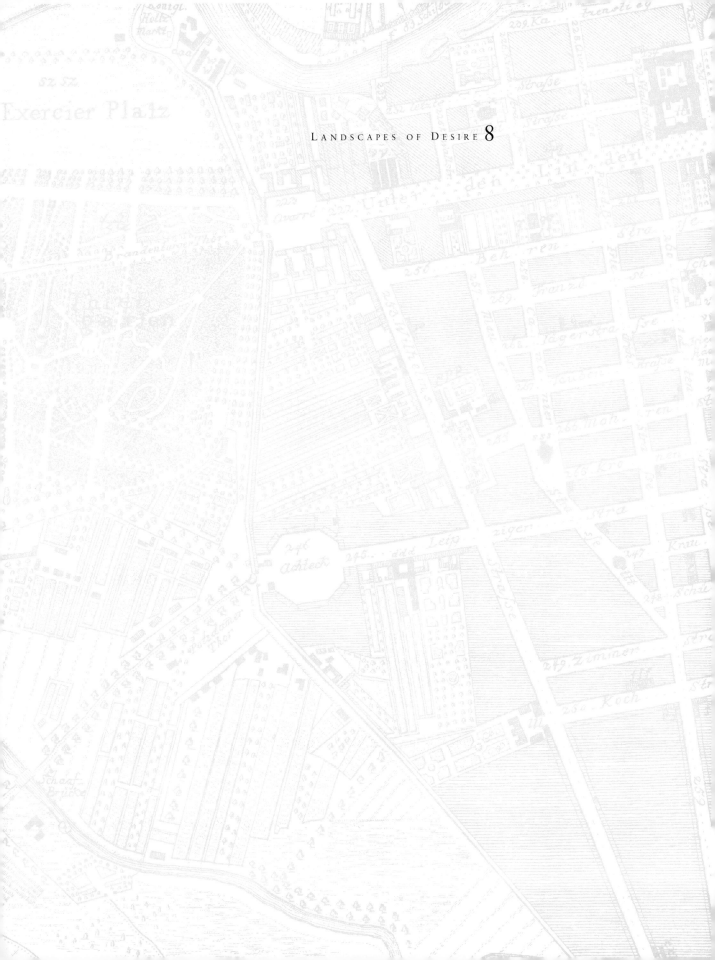

East Berlin, November 12 [1989] – With a shower of sparks and the creak of cranes in the darkness, East German workers today pierced the Berlin wall at what had once been the city's core, and the Mayors of East and West Berlin were among the first to meet at the new opening.

"This is where the old heart of Berlin used to beat, and it will beat again," declared Mayor Walter Momper of West Berlin as he walked through the new crossing at the Potsdamer Platz, took a few steps to the eastern side of the wall and clasped hands with his eastern counterpart, Erhard Krach.

Soon hundreds of thousands of East Berliners were streaming across a trail of cobblestones and tram rails that alone remained of a square once known as the busiest on the continent – a place where chic Berliners used to gather in the Cafe Kranzler or the Cafe Josty to watch the world go by, and where Germany's first traffic signal was lighted in 1924, at what then seemed the crossroads of the world.

The old remember much

There was a special poignancy for the elderly who walked through. The square, reduced to rubble by the war, had been the site of one of the biggest black markets in its aftermath and some of the bloodiest clashes in the East German rebellion in June 1953. The raising of the wall through the square in 1961 left a 100-yard-wide swath of no man's land.

Now, for the first time in 28 years, Potsdamer Platz again resounded with the patter of feet on cobblestones. In all, 800,000 East Berliners had flowed into West Berlin by evening through all the crossings in the city, bringing to 2 million the number of eastern visitors since the border was opened on Thursday and continuing the unparalleled celebration that has swirled through Berlin day and night. THE NEW YORK TIMES, MONDAY, NOVEMBER 13, 1989

The events leading up to these momentous acts began on October 8, 1989, during the celebration of East Germany's fortieth anniversary. The ceremonies were attended by Mikhail Gorbachev, whose presence served as a catalyst for a few small groups of protesters. What began with small crowds of demonstrators chanting "Gorby! Gorby!" and "Freedom! Freedom!" that day led by nightfall to clashes with police involving several thousand demonstrators, revealing the depth of the popular dissatisfaction with the East German government. The dramatic change in direction toward liberalization, both by the Communist Party and by the public, appeared from the beginning to have had the tacit support of Gorbachev.

During September, political changes elsewhere in Eastern Europe led to the opening of borders to the West. Suddenly, for the first time in forty years, East Germans could travel through Czechoslovakia which had opened its borders with the West. On October 3, the East German government responded by closing its borders with Czechoslovakia.

On October 9, the East German government, in response to demonstrations in Leipzig, constrained the police and allowed open public protest. On November 2, East Germany bowed to public pressure and lifted its travel ban to Czechoslovakia. Within hours, more than 8,000 East Germans crossed the border and flocked to the West German embassy in Prague.

On November 4, the same day as the largest public demonstration in East Germany's history, the government agreed to allow its citizens free passage to West Germany, a decision that in essence removed the idea of the Wall. The demonstration, organized by the Union of Actors, brought together a mass, estimated by some to be close to a million people, calling for free speech, free elections, and an end to the "leading role" of the Communist Party.

By November 8, two hundred thousand East Germans had migrated to West Germany, draining skilled labor from the East and straining the capacities of the West German economy. That day, West German Chancellor Helmut Kohl announced that Bonn would be ready to provide comprehensive aid to East Germany if it allowed free elections and made fundamental changes in the state-dominated economy. He stated that "the precondition for reunification in freedom is the free exercise of the right of self-determination of all Germans."

On November 9, East Germany lifted all restrictions on travel to the West. Within hours, tens of thousands of Berliners from the East and the West swarmed across the many miles and layers of the Berlin Wall, concentrating on the long-closed entrances to the old city at the Brandenburg Gate and at Potsdamer Platz. Drinking and singing and kissing and hugging, they remained throughout the days and nights that followed, unwilling to leave the border in the midst of its metaphysical transformation. Many came armed with hammers and began to fracture the Wall, chip by chip.

"This is what we have dreamed of since we were tiny children," said a twenty-three year old East Berliner, moments after he crossed the Wall at Checkpoint Charlie. He asked to be identified as Knobi. "We heard the news at 11:30 PM, then when we heard they were letting people through, well here we are."

"Of course we are going back home," he said. "That's where we live and we want to see what happens now. After this there can be no turning back. This is the turning point everyone has been talking about. THE NEW YORK TIMES, FRIDAY, NOVEMBER 10, 1989

In the days that followed the euphoria continued unabated, day and night, as East German construction crews disconnected the elaborate security systems and devices and began to remove the slabs of concrete that had formed the Wall.

On November 12, an estimated half a million East Berliners streamed into West Berlin:

For the third night a vast throng of people gazed at the bright lights of Kurfürstendamm, West Berlin's celebrated shopping street. Most stores stayed open long past the usual Saturday closing time of 2 PM, and many offered discounts and gifts to the East Berliners.

Thousands more East Germans packed the Olympic stadium for a soccer game while others explored a West they had known only from television. Young men swarmed through the BMW showroom, gazing at models whose twelve-cylinder engines seemed light years beyond their own antiquated little 2-cylinder Trabant. A few slipped into the luxurious Kempinski Hotel to grab a "Do Not Disturb" sign as a souvenir. THE NEW YORK TIMES, SUNDAY, NOVEMBER 12, 1989

Throughout that night, not far from the site of Kempinski's Haus Vaterland, East German cranes worked in the no-man's land that had been Leipziger Platz, laying a path of paving blocks reaching up to the gap cut in the Wall at Potsdamer Platz. Watching passively was a detachment of the East German army.

That day, the Mayors of East and West Berlin met on this newly-created path a few yards from the spot where Schinkel's gates once heralded the entrance into the royal city.

8.1
An East German border guard hands out pieces of barbed wire clipped from the Berlin Wall, November 14, 1989

1989

NOVEMBER 14

Consider an assembly of all the ideals that have shaped this great and ancient city. Its fabric becomes invisible beneath the cumulative dreams of its creators. Their ideals lie inseparable in layers within the land they transformed, the clarity of their presence directly related to the degree to which their projects survive, as traces, shells, and memories. Increasingly, the persistence of the past produces a compound disorder, incoherent conventions of form and content, masks upon masks upon masks.

The reality produced by architecture is always the projection of fictions from the imagination on circumstance. Often that reality becomes no more than the residue of ephemeral desire. The presence of the past persistently interferes with the promise of the future. There are no dreams in isolation; all are in reflection and reaction, in a swirling confusion of past existence. This accumulation, on the land and in the mind, causes irreconcilable confusion in the order of things. In the progression of realities the physical presence of so many pasts denies the operation of any simple struggle of opposites, and all attempts at synthesis seem to increase the fragmentation.

It is by the chance events of world history that this place, Leipziger Platz, has carried the projection of so many opposing ideals. Its origin was, in itself, unexceptional – scrubby forest cut by marshy creeks flowing through clay soil. Its physical nature had nothing to do with the ideas that have been projected on it. As with all ideas about reality, these have been formed out of imagination and desire: desire for power, desire for order, desire for disorder, and desire for illusions to clarify the nature of existence.

Landscapes of desire, landscapes of moral strength, landscapes of power, landscapes of myths – the shapers of reality strain their imaginations to conjure new definitions of existence, comforting, affirming, inspiring, coercing, destroying – all forming and reforming in the fleeting images of the mind's eye. Some sought the immediate and others the unattainable; some wished to end history, other to recover it; some to deny the body, others to deify it; some to reveal the future, others to destroy it.

Leipziger Platz is a palimpsest of past desires. The remains in the ground and in the memory of the earth mimic the record of an ancient parchment, written over many times and in which the previous texts, despite the scraping of the surface, are held forever in the fibers of the sheepskin, persistently reemerging to contradict new texts placed on the page. The compounding of such landscapes of desire is more a palimpsest in the mind than in the earth. There are many such landscapes embedded in and around Leipziger Platz, and the formation of the new order or multiple orders that must be established to heal the wound of division will unavoidably carry their trace.

The first landscape is shaped in the desire to displace the order of God with a field of reason, of autocratic order through which to control the future.

The second carries the resurrection of ancient gods and ancient powers in the desire to deify the memory of the warrior, the god-king, the hero, and the recreator of the nation, conserving and representing his vision into an eternal future. Imagine gently undulating Elysian fields, meadows and streams cut by clumps of cyprus and flowering vine, and in the distance, above stepped layers of rock, stands the temple. It subjects all nature to its presence, bathed in a purifying light against the azure plains of heaven. Yet, all its dense wisdom cannot stave off the dream of a more essential order in the abstraction of reality from all pasts, free from ancient gods and orders, existing only in the mathematics of the mind.

The third landscape is shaped by the desire for a new order of liberalism, a new reality reflecting and enhancing the place of everyman. The dream is to shape a coherent structure from the will of the masses, its authority arising from within. The desire is for an order and a reality that is not eternal, that is not independent of human experience, that does not legislate blindly in its own rhythms but, ebbing and flowing, continually adjusts to the strengths and desires of the people. Reacting against tyranny, coercion, and imposed authority, the imagination can conceive of no other action than the fusion of past orders. It shapes with clarity and caution the fragments of temples, Tuscan farms, and gothic cathedrals, all held in a web of abstracted space against a white sky. Yet, all past orders fail to satisfy the shape of freedom. The imagination fails to find a balance and acknowledges that imbalance may reside in the very nature of freedom itself.

The fourth is a landscape of denial driven by the failure to create the illusion of liberty for all. In the failure to satisfy the desire for freedom, the mind's eye sees in the forms and orders of the past the persistence of the power of those who would deny it. Those willing the liberation of the future see only in revolution and destruction the means by which a new order might be established. The landscape of their desire is formed in the destruction of the structures of their oppression. Onto this disturbed landscape roll the ubiquitous machines of industry that reason brought forth and which drive passages of unreason, utility, and the ruthless disdain for all past orders through the city. The empirical order imposed by the machines overrides all idealized order; the benefits to the people of mobility and a burgeoning flow of products offer ambiguous accommodation to a diversity of free wills. To the dreamers of revolution, these machines are reploughing the fields of an atrophied existence and the significance of their utility is in justifying a disorder inconceivable within any past political structure.

Landscapes of desire form and evolve over many years before the real world is changed by them. The fifth state has two faces: to some it seems as ego and alter ego, to others as positive and negative. The positive is shaped in the image of the god-king, the negative in the dreamless realities of the proletariat. A landscape of internal contradiction exists between the desire for power in the hands of all and power solely in the hands of a sovereign. In the landscape of the masses there are no illusions to relieve the crippling burden of filth and exploitation in the homes and the machine shops. Only in an equal and opposite reality formed through the order of socialism can the king and the exploiters be displaced. In the beginning, the desires of socialism are not for physical things and have no clear form in objective reality. There is nothing to desire in the physical world save escape from the servitude of mercantile feudalism, and nothing from the past gives form to the dream. Those who see in the struggle of opposites mere thesis and antithesis read only the surface of political rhetoric; in reality, the wills in opposition are as water to stone. Those who dream of socialism want to negate the coercive power of historical reality in an order of anarchy. Those who dream of the divine king seek to maintain his power in structures of political instrumentality. But they are both merely masks on a deeper, more essential landscape of negation. In this state of conflict and negation are sown the seeds of a division that would grow to split the culture.

The sixth landscape emerges in dense confusion in the aftermath of the Great War. Though the structures of the physical world survived intact, the order that gave them meaning has totally collapsed. The competing desires to place a new order on the face of all things – dominated by the search for the landscape of freedom – widens the deep divisions persisting in the structures of the state. This landscape encompasses many desires – the singular unity of the imperial state, the instrumentality of the past, visions of mathematical structures, and visions of natural order in *harmony with the emotions and the seasons. The laboring masses have never been encouraged to dream of the future, but forced to live in the dreams of others. Their desires can find no landscapes of trust, no historic reality free from pain and servitude. Those who dream for them see only an inversion of the world they inherited. The chiliastic dreamers are the most passionate, but theirs are the visions of the disaffected privileged class. Their rejection of the material world is the affectation of an elite taught to seek antithesis, taught to seek clarification through negation; but the masses have no stomach for it. It is the growth of the factories and mass-production that breaks the singular authority of architecture over reality, allowing all to indulge for the first time in the construction of personal dreams and fantasies. Then, in a culture unstable and confused by the experiments of a powerful intelligentsia, the conservative masses seek stability through the order of national socialism, creating a god-king of the people and a superman of the German everyman, a mass that will march to the order of Roman imperialism. The new order both physically and metaphysically polarizes the culture and induces a catastrophe in which every thing, every thought, and every desire is fractured.*

The seventh landscape, begun in the desire for world domination, overwhelms itself and in total collapse crushes all in its path. The liberal survivors, preserving their dream for a future free from the corruption of the past, now have a clear field on which to work. The communist proletariat, under Russian guidance, sustain the desire to find social realism through the memory of Rome. But they are both shapes of madness, moving to the extreme and breaking along the unresolved border between the order of the few and the order of the masses. Fragments of the past continue to float around the severed tissue, turning past realities into complex myths. Petrarch, wandering through the ruins of the Roman Forum, saw a landscape in which the strange undulations and the protruding bones of the ancient city were as acts of nature. Feeling his way through the village of tunnels and caves imbedded in the arches of the Coliseum, he forced his imagination to reconstruct and represent the former life of the place. It produced a sense of poignant pain and perplexing nostalgia. The fragments were simply insufficient to establish the ancient order, and in compensation his imagination created a new, potential reality unrelated to the old.

The eighth landscape, as the confusion of floating fragments settles, emerges as two halves inextricably linked and absolutely divided. In the West, the convention of liberal capitalism entertains the culture with its version of Western desire: personal speculations on the transformation of orders and architectures past. There appear to be no larger truths available to command the reformulation of reality and an unintended gift from the liberal cause may be the freedom from the presumption of architecture. The shared landscapes of the Western order have evolved into multiple realities offered by the producers of a consumer culture. In the East the persistence of totalitarianism, inherited by state socialism from the Prussian kings, produces entertaining transformations of reality from the orders and architectures of the past. There appear to be no larger truths available to command the reformulation of reality, and though all else is controlled through insecurity and anxiety, an unintended gift of the socialist state may be freedom from the polemics of architecture. The shared landscape of the Eastern order has an intense desire to move toward the multiple realities offered by the Western consumer culture, realities dangerous to the revolution in their ability to speak to the multiple desires of individuals, thereby threatening the project of the state.

The destruction of the Wall reforms all past landscapes. The Wall was the culmination of two-hundred years of German culture. No other structure succeeded in slowing the passage of time. No other structure succeeded in destroying the passage of space. It was an absolute architecture, and it was the absolute contradiction of architecture – the purest monument to the divided soul of Western man. A machine that drove a passage through history, it divided a city, a nation, and a culture.

The Wall was the abstraction of reality from existence. It was built on the shoulders and imaginations of Goethe, Schiller, Kant, Hegel, and Marx. It was autonomous and rhetorical, and the most outrageous construction of Western civilization. Its simplicity had magnificence. It was the great barricade, the supreme testament to the power of the dialectic, and the removal of the concrete of which it was formed will not remove the Wall from the mind.

Reality will forever rest on the memory of this eternal division. Such essential order, once split, can never be fully restored. There will remain forever a flaw, a chronic weakness, in the foundations of all constructions in this place. Toughened by an inheritance of opposition and negation, new landscapes must emerge – landscapes capable of building, on such a disturbed base, bridges across the wound of the future.

NOTES

ACHTECK 1

1. Though the influence came from France the surveyors and engineers for this and other projects in the new planning were Dutch.

2. Designed by the architect Mansart and renamed Place Vendome after the revolution.

3. This material was developed from many different sources, but the major references were: Jethro Bithell, *Germany: A Companion to German Studies* (London: Methuen, 1962); Hermann G. Pundt, *Schinkel's Berlin* (Cambridge: Harvard, 1972); *Berlin Und Die Antike*, Katalog II (Berlin: Deutsches Archäologisches Institut, 1979).

4. Gilly's father, David Gilly, came to Berlin in 1788 and established himself as favorite architect of the Court.

5. The Royal Commission proposed that the monument be built on Unter den Linden, the great public street of the new city.

6. The Temple of Serapis in Possuoli.

7. Reitdorf, Alfred, *Gilly Wiedegeburt der Architektur*. Translation by Josephine Budell and the author (Berlin: Hans von Hugo Verlag, 1940), 52.

8. Johann Winckelmann (1716-1768). His major work, *Geschichte der Kunst des Altertums* (History of the Art of the Ancients), published in 1764, was widely influential.

9. Winckelmann, Johann, in Irwin, David, ed., *Winckelmann: Writings on Art*, (New York: Phaidon, 1972), 72.

10. Reitdorf, *Gilly Wiedegerburt der Architektur*, 52.

11. In his report to the Royal Commission, Gilly described the experience of the monument:
    "The magnitude of the style would fix in the eyes of visitors an attitude with respect to all the other buildings of the city . . . . The base would be dark. Vaulted archways would open the view through the base of the gate to the level of the street. Inside there would be a great arch – a place for a sarcophagus – thus giving the monument even more significance. Above the sarcophagus in the middle of the vault would be a circle of stars getting light from above. The temple would be constructed in a light-colored material for effect against the sky: it would be of the Doric order like the Greek temple without ornamental niceties but with bas-reliefs in the pediments. Inside – a statue in a niche opposite the entry, on a great base and lit from above." From Reitdorf, *Gilly Weidegerburt der Architektur*, 61.

12. Irwin, *Winckelmann: Writings on Art*, 133.

13. Ibid., 146.

14. Gilly's father was a prominent member of the Huguenot community in Berlin. They were driven from France with the revocation of the Edict of Nantes in 1658. Huguenots were an estimated twenty percent of the population of Berlin at the end of the eighteenth century.

15. *Friedrich Gilly 1772-1800*, Katalog, Berlin Museum/IBA (Berlin: Verlag Willmuth Arenhovel, 1984).

16. Irwin, *Winckelmann: Writings on Art*, 93.

17. Karl Friedrich Schinkel (1781-1841) became the most prolific and influential architect in the court of Friedrich Wilhelm III. A brilliant draftsman and topographic painter, his designs touched all aspects of Berlin's cultural life, from furniture to theater design to the creation of the modern city. Rational and romantic, his neo-classical visions were as idealized as his gothic was sublime.

18. Schinkel was later to apprentice with Friedrich's father, David Gilly.

19. These events led to the abdication of the king of Austria, and to the dissolution of the Holy Roman Empire.

20. Johann Gottlieb Fichte (1762-1814). The most respected pedagogue in Prussia, Fichte turned Kantian philosophy in the direction of subjective idealism. He was the teacher of Hegel.

21. Fichte, Johann Gottlieb, *Addresses to the German Nation* (New York: Harper & Row, 1968), 215.

22. Expediency forced the court into a clear realization of fundamental weaknesses in the social and political culture of Prussia. The absolute and centralized power of the king and his court and his defeated army had little support within the mass of the populace. It was recognized that only by promoting civil and political freedom could the people be mobilized in the common service of the state. Broad political reforms were begun even during the French occupation; towns were allowed to become self-governing; serfdom and forced labor were abolished; the majority of the populace who had been dependent subjects were called, for the first time, free citizens and given the right to choose trades and occupations; and the army was restructured to reduce the influence of the aristocracy.

23. Johann Wolfgang von Goethe (1749-1832). Among the greatest of all German writers and thinkers, Goethe was a poet, playwright, lawyer, botanist, politician, painter, and cultural impresario.

24. Johann Wolfgang von Goethe, *Goethe on Art*, Gage, John, ed. and trans. (Berkeley: University of California Press, 1980), 108.

25. Ibid., 105.

26. Ibid., 108.

27. Ibid., 117.

28. It is difficult to appreciate now the idea of "German-ness" in relation to the Cathedral of Strasbourg. Its significance was heightened by the continual dispute over Alsace-Lorraine.

29. The architect of Strasbourg Cathedral was Erwin von Steinback. The foundation stone from 1277 is inscribed "In Die Beati Urbani Hoc Opus Gloriosum Inchoavil, Magister Ervinus de Steinback." Recent scholarship casts doubts on it being a work of Germanic culture.

30. It can be seen in the underlying character of *Faust* where the medieval alchemist becomes the disturbed romantic scholar.

31. Schinkel, Karl Friedrich, in *Karl Friedrich Schinkel: Architecktur Malerei Kunstgewerbe* (Berlin: Verwaltung der Staatlichen Schlösser und Gärten und Nationalgalerie Berlin, 1981), 100. Translations in this volume by Josephine Budell and the author.

32. Great quantities of documents were destroyed in World War II and the surviving Schinkel drawings are divided between collections in the East and the West. The only record of this project is in the East German collection.

33. Gage, *Goethe on Art*, 11.

34. Fichte, *Addresses to the German Nation*, 58.

35. Schinkel, *Karl Friedrich Schinkel*, 100.

36. This invention reemerged through his pupils in several public buildings throughout nineteenth-century Europe, in the Parliament House in Budapest, for example, and into the twentieth century in the "Rheinhalle" of Wilhelm Kreis.

37. To place such symbolic thinking within the spirit of the time it should be recalled that one of the first public acts in the weeks following the French Revolution was the attempt to remove the idea of God from the Cathedral of Notre Dame. A great banner was hung across the façade declaring it the "Temple of Reason."

38. Schinkel was the most accomplished scenic painter of his age, creating throughout his life public paintings, dioramas, and stage sets of great theatricality and imagination.

39. Hegel's lectures on *The Science of Logic* appeared between 1812 and 1816.

40. Schinkel, *Karl Friedrich Schinkel*, 254.

41. Fate drew a great many connections between *Truimphbogen* and Hitler's Triumphal Arch, conceived for this very place as a memorial to the millions who would die to achieve his purpose.

42. Schinkel, *Karl Friedrich Schinkel*, 253.

43. In a career spent reshaping the public center of Berlin for a court less autocratic than Gilly had known, Schinkel's architecture restated with increasing austerity the denatured form of Gilly's abstractions, and his strongest influence on his pupils was the emphasis on essential form in the rational character of their construction.

44. This was so not just in Berlin but throughout Europe, in Frankfurt, Prague, Vienna, Budapest, Rome, Venice, Milan, Palermo, and in many other smaller cities, but most dramatically in Paris. London and Britain in the Reform Act of 1832 diffused the problem by granting limited representation.

45. Semper had to flee the country because of his actions. In London he became closely involved with the design projects of Queen Victoria's husband, Prince Albert, which led to the Great Exhibition and to the museums in South Kensington.

46. Beginning in the 1840s, Berlin had become a center for heavy industry with the manufacture of locomotives and carriages, and by the end of the century it had attracted the most powerful of the manufacturers of the products of scientific research, AEG and Siemens.

47. From a population of 150,000 in 1800, Berlin grew to 450,000 in 1848, to 800,000 in 1870, to two million in 1900.

1. Benjamin, Walter, *Reflections* (New York: Harcourt, Brace Jovanovich, 1978), 75.

2. Ibid, 152. The observation is a paraphrase from Walter Benjamin's essay, "Paris, Capital of the Nineteenth Century." He offers potent insights into the transformation of the idea of the propagation of goods by means of world expositions: ". . . they create a framework in which commodity's intrinsic value is eclipsed. They open up a phantasmagoria that people enter to be amused. The entertainment industry facilitates this by elevating people to the level of commodity. They submit to being manipulated while enjoying the alienation from themselves and others. The enthronement of merchandise, with the aura of amusement surrounding it, is the secret scheme . . . . This is reflected in the discord between its utopian and cynical elements. Its subtlety in the presentation of inanimate objects corresponds to what Marx calls the 'theological whims of goods.'"

3. Ibid, 154. Again, a quote from Benjamin: ". . . living space becomes, for the first time, antithetical to the place of work. The former is constituted by the interior; the office is its complement. The private person who squares his accounts with reality in his office demands that the interior be maintained in its illusions. This need is all the more pressing since he has no intention of extending his commercial considerations into social ones. In shaping his private environment he represses both. From this springs the phantasmagoria of the interior. For the private individual the private environment represents the universe. In it, he gathers remote places and the past. His drawing room is a box in the world theater."

4. The Völkerschlacht memorial designed by Schmitz was built in Leipzig between 1898 and 1913. It was constructed to celebrate the Battle of the Nations in 1813 and spiritually completes the project begun by Schinkel in 1814.

5. Ernst Ludwig Kirchner (1880-1938) arrived in Berlin in 1910. Four years earlier in Dresden in 1906 he founded Die Brücke (The Bridge), a group of avant-garde artists. They came together out of a bitter reaction against industry and materialism.

6. The kaiser left Germany for the Netherlands where he remained until his death in 1941.

7. The displacement of the kaiser from the center of power brought, in the immediate aftermath of the war, violent conflict between the Socialists and the conservatives and liberals who were united by industrial capital.

8. Inflation peaked in 1923 when the German mark was valued at 4.2 trillion to the dollar, and the cost of a dozen eggs, it was said, could have bought the whole of Berlin before the war.

9. Benjamin, *Reflections*, 30. Benjamin reflected on life in this new city: "I wish to write of this afternoon because it made so apparent the kind of regimen our cities keep over imagination, and why the city, where people make the most ruthless demands of one another, where appointments and telephone calls, sessions and visits, flirtations and the struggle for existence, grant the individual not a single moment of contemplation, indemnifies itself in memory, and why the veil it has covertly woven of our lives shows the images of people less than those of the sites of our encounters with others or ourselves."

10. An early modernist presence on Potsdamer Platz was the Telschow Haus, completed in 1928 by the brothers

Luckhardt and Alfons Anker. The Luckhardts were the only architects of the period whose commercial work equalled the sophistication of their contemporary, Erich Mendelsohn, whose landmark Columbus Haus would emerge on Potsdamer Platz four years later. Telschow Haus, immediately adjacent to the Pschorr brewery, contained a spine that complemented the beer hall's tower and an elegant and fluid curving wall dedicated to the text it carried. It brought a new form of perceptual tension to Potsdamer Platz. Just visible on the right in the photograph is the first modernist project to arrive in the square: the renovation of a corner building on Potsdamerstrasse in 1927 by the architectural polemicist Herman Muthesius, who refaced the structure with continuous strip balconies from the newly-emerging modern idiom.

11. Among them were Walter Benjamin, Erich Mendelsohn, Walter Gropius, and Georg Grosz. None of the major figures in the Berlin avant-garde of the 1920s came from the working class.

12. I am indebted for this material to an as yet unpublished doctoral dissertation by Roger Jonathan Green from the University of Chicago, *Haus Vaterland, Berlin: Pleasure Architecture as a Mirror of Conflicts in German History 1912-1961*, 1987. With its forced purchase by the Nazi government the Kempinski name was removed from the walls. The legal complications in settling claims on the assets have continued into the 1980s.

HITLER **3**

1. Hitler would have shared power with Erich Ludendorff as so-called dictator. Ludendorff had been chief of staff to General Paul von Hindenburg, the supreme commander of German forces in the First World War and German President from 1925 to 1932.

2. Hitler, Adolf, *Mein Kampf* (Boston: Houghton Mifflin, 1971), 265-66.

3. Albert Speer (1905-1985) joined the National Socialist Party in January of 1931, and came to Hitler's attention first in 1932 when he refurbished the Party's district headquarters on Voss Strasse in Berlin. The following year he was asked to help stage the Party Rally in Nuremberg. Increasingly thereafter he became a favorite and confidant of Hitler's. Through two books, *Inside the Third Reich* and *Spandau Diaries*, he became the most celebrated survivor of the Third Reich and strongly influenced public perception of it.

4. Speer, Albert, *Inside the Third Reich* (New York: Macmillan Company, 1970), 96.

5. Hitler, *Mein Kampf*, 35.

6. Adolf Hitler from a speech given in 1933 and published in *Deutsche Kunst*, September 1, 1933. From Taylor, Robert R., *The Word in Stone* (Berkeley: University of California Press, 1974), 39.

7. *Hitler's Secret Conversations 1941-1944* (New York: New American Library, 1961), 77-78. Intro by H.R. Trevor-Roper.

8. Ibid., 75-76.

9. Ibid., 423.

10. Maser, Werner, ed., *Hitler's Letters and Notes* (New York: Harper & Row, 1974), 331.

11. Nietzsche, Friedrich, *The Will to Power*, translated by Kaufman and Hollingdale (New York: Vintage Books, 1968) 365.

12. Schiller, Friedrich "Über die ästhetische Erziehung des Menschen in einer Reihe von Briefen" in *Werke*, 1795 (Frankfurt: Insel Verlag, 1966), 4:200.

13. Joseph Goebbels (1897-1945) joined the National Socialist Party in 1924 and in the beginning belonged to its left wing. He founded the newspaper *Der Angriff* and became the Nazi's leading propagandist. Hitler named him Minister of Propaganda in 1933 and for the next ten years he dominated and shaped German cultural life.

14. Goebbels, Joseph, "Brief an Wilhelm Furtwangler vom 1. April 1933," quoted in Brenner, Hildegard, *Die Kunstpolitik Nationalsozialismus* (Hamburg: Rowohlt, 1963), 178.

15. Speer, *Inside the Third Reich*, 75.

16. Ibid., 74.

17. Moser, *Hitler's Letters and Notes*, 371.

18. Speer, *Inside the Third Reich*, 103.

19. Ibid., 103.

20. Ibid., 113.

21. Ibid., 114.

22. Political significance equalled the theatrical for Speer, who claimed to have collected almost all the military searchlights in the nation to produce the effect which became for the rest of Europe another ominous sign of Germany's increasing military strength.

23. *Hitler's Secret Conversations*, 451.

24. Heinrich Himmler (1900-1945), a Nazi leader and fanatical racist, became head of the SS in 1929 and assumed control of the entire German police system after 1933.

25. *Hitler's Secret Conversations*, 82.

26. Ibid., 81.

27. The plan included a vast square plaza to the west of Leipziger Platz and the rebuilding of the west side of Potsdamer Platz.

28. Speer, *Inside the Third Reich*, 74.

29. The Berlin Academy of Arts housed the display of Gilly's project for the Monument to Frederick the Great and Fichte gave his "Addresses to the German Nation" here.

30. Speer, *Inside the Third Reich*, 132-33.

31. Speer's plans involved, in the last years of his life, the well-respected German architect Peter Behrens (1868-1940), a herald of modernism and the mentor of Le Corbusier and Mies van der Rohe.

32. Hermann Goering (1893-1946) was the most celebrated flying ace of the First World War after Baron von Richthofen.

An early member of the Nazi Party, he was elected to the Reichstag in 1928 and became its president in 1932. With Hitler in power he became Air Minister and Prime Minister of Prussia where he founded the Gestapo.

33. Speer, *Inside the Third Reich*, 136.
34. Ibid., 137.
35. Ibid., 136-37.
36. After Speer, Sagebiel was the favorite architect of the Party. He was the designer of Tempelhof Airfield, one of the most spectacular projects of the Hitler years.
37. Lochner, Louis L., ed., *The Goebbels Diaries 1942-1943* (New York: Doubleday, 1948), 374.
38. Speer, *Inside the Third Reich*, 55-56.
39. Speer, *Inside the Third Reich*, 153.
40. Ibid., 141.
41. Ibid., 153.
42. Ibid., 144.
43. Slave labor was of primary importance to Speer after 1942 in his role as head of the Ministry of Munitions and Armaments.
44. *Hitler's Secret Conversations*, 61.
45. Adolf Hitler, extract from his will of 1938: "2nd May 1988 *My Testament*. Upon my death, it is my wish that 1. My body be taken to Munich where it is to lie in state in the Fedherrnhalle and then buried in the right temple of the Eternal Watch. (that is the temple next to the Führer Building) My coffin is to be similar to all the rest . . . ." From Maser, *Hitler's Letters and Notes*, 151.
46. Speer, *Inside the Third Reich*, 152-53.
47. Himmler, Heinrich, quoted in Bezymenski, Lev, *The Death of Adolf Hitler* (New York: Harcourt, Brace, and World, 1968), 76-77.
48. *Hitler's Secret Conversations*, 61.
49. Speer, *Inside the Third Reich*, 160.
50. Speer was tried at Nuremberg with the other senior figures in Hitler's Reich and sentenced to twenty years in prison. Goering was sentenced to death but committed suicide before execution.
51. Construction began on the Triumphal Arch with the building of an immense concrete plug to carry the immense weight of the arch. It still stands in a sedate housing project in West Berlin, south of the central city, too massive to be easily destroyed.
52. Speer, *Inside the Third Reich*, 429.
53. Ibid., 430.
54. Ibid., 431.
55. Ibid., 485.
56. Maser, *Hitler's Letters and Notes*, 350-52. Hitler dictated his will at the same time. Extract: "My Private Will - Because, in the years of my struggle I thought it irresponsible to enter into marriage I have now, before the end of my life on earth, decided to take that girl for my wife who after many years of sincere friendship freely entered the beleaguered city to share her fate with mine. It is her expressed wish to join me in death as my wife. It will recompense us both for what both of us have sacrificed through my work and the service of my people.

   I myself and my wife have chosen death rather than suffer the disgrace of dismissal or capitulation. It is our wish to be burnt at once at the very place I have done the major part of my daily work in the service of my people during the past twelve years.

   Berlin, 29th April, 1945, 4 a. m. Signed Adolf Hitler Witnesses Martin Borman, Dr. Goebbels, Nicholas von Below." From Maser, 205.
57. Ibid., 120.
58. Bezymenski, Lev, *The Death of Adolf Hitler* (New York: Harcourt, Brace, and World, 1968), 35-36.

1. Mendelsohn, Erich, extract from lecture to the Berlin Arbeitsrat für Kunst, 1919. From Conrads, Ulrich, *Programs and Manifestoes on 20th Century Architecture* (Cambridge, Mass: MIT Press, 1964), 54.
2. Von Eckardt, Wolf, *Erich Mendelsohn* (New York: George Braziller Inc., 1960), 16.
3. Ibid, 23.
4. Mendelsohn originally used the word "blood," but one translator replaced it with the word "vision" because, we must assume, its meaning has changed since the passage was written.
5. Beyer, Oskar, ed., *Erich Mendelsohn: Letters of an Architect* (London: Abelard-Schuman, 1967), 61.
6. Von Eckardt, *Erich Mendelsohn*, 14. At the end of the 1930s, Sigfried Giedeon, the most influential polemicist for the new architecture and the new order, inexplicably failed to mention Mendelsohn in his formative series of lectures given at Harvard entitled *Space, Time and Architecture*. These lectures were the single most important influence on American modernism. The reason why no mention is made of Mendelsohn has not been examined to my knowledge. The thesis of the work, which seems to stem directly from Mendelsohn, was that modern art and architecture also had discovered a fourth dimension in time, a discovery complementing and conceptually enlarging Einstein's theory of relativity. Around 1940, Mendelsohn sent the book to Einstein with the appropriate pages marked and received the reply: "Dear Mr. Mendelsohn, The passage you sent me from the book *Space, Time, and Architecture* has inspired me to the following reply: It's never hard some new thought to declare If any nonsense one will dare. But rarely do you find that novel babble is at the same time reasonable. Cordially yours, Albert Einstein. P.S. It is simply bull without

any rational basis."

7. Beyer, *Erich Mendelsohn: Letters of an Architect*, 94-95.

8. Mendelsohn aligns architectural order with a metaphysical-political vision in much of his writing. See Beyer, *Erich Mendelsohn: Letters of an Architect*, 62.

9. Dean, Andrea Oppenheimer, ed., *Bruno Zevi: On Modern Architecture* (New York: Rizzoli International Publications, 1983), 155. From the essay "Hebraism and the Concept of Space Time and Art."

10. Ibid., 157. Zevi has a deep critical interest in the architecture of Erich Mendelsohn. However his development of the themes of Hebraism becomes caught up in issues of contemporary philosophy, but they are stimulating nonetheless: "Hebraism in art emphasizes the anti-classical, the expressionistic de-structuring of forms; it rejects the ideological fetishes of golden proportions and celebrates relativity; it denies the authoritarian rules concerning what is beautiful, and opts for the illegality and disorderliness of what is true." In the concluding paragraph (p.165) he characterizes the essence of Hebraic reality in this century: "Expressionistic and rigorous; it applies Einstein's concept of "field"; it is multidimensional; it extols space by demolishing all fetishes and tabus concerning it, by rendering it fluid, articulated so as to suit man's ways, weaving a continuum between building and landscape. In linguistic terms, this means a total destructuring of form, denial of any philosophical apriori, any repressive monumentality: action architecture, aimed at conquering ever more vast areas of freedom for human behavior."

11. Beyer, *Erich Mendelsohn: Letters of an Architect*, 126.

12. He first moved to Holland, where he joined in the birthday celebration for the Belgian architect Henry Van de Velde. In June 1933, he moved to England.

13. The SS Schutzstaffel, or the Black Shirts, the protection detachment formed by Himmler in 1925 from Hitler's shocktroops.

14. Krausnick, Helmut, et al., *Anatomy of the SS State* (London: Collins, 1968), 408.

15. Whittick, Arnold, *Erich Mendelsohn* (London: Faber & Faber, 1940), 111.

16. At the center of the photograph is the little building refaced in the modern idiom by the architect Herman Muthesius in 1927. The first presentation of modernism on Postdamer Platz, it is a world apart from the confidence of Columbus Haus.

17. Noakes, Jeremy and Geoffrey Pridham, eds., *Documents on Nazism, 1919-1945* (New York: Viking Press, 1974), 285-86. Also discussed in Krausnick, *Anatomy of the SS State*, 433.

18. Krausnick, *Anatomy of the SS State*, 436. Military historians have called the Columbus or Columbia Haus prison a concentration camp.

19. Ibid., 434.

20. Beyer, *Erich Mendelsohn: Letters of an Architect*, 169.

21. It is significant that the official view of Einstein's Theory of Relativity counted it as "Jewish speculations." Philip Lenard, a leading Nazi physicist, wrote in 1936: "'German physics?' you will ask. I could have said 'Aryan physics' or 'physics of the Nordic Type,' physics of explorers of reality, the truth seekers. Physics of those who founded scientific research. You will want to object: 'Science is international and always will be!' But that is based on error. In reality, science like everything that people produce is racially conditioned. . . ." From Noakes, *Documents on Nazism, 1919-1945*, 348.

22. Mendelsohn, Erich, *Russland Europa Amerika: Ein Architecktonischer Querschnitt* (Berlin: Rudolf Mosse Buchverlag, 1929), 217. Translation by Michael Bullock.

23. Ibid., 217.

1. Brett-Smith, Richard, *Berlin '45 The Grey City* (New York: Macmillan, St Martin's Press, 1975), 75.

2. Boyle, Kay, *The Smoking Mountain: Stories of Postwar Germany* (New York: McGraw-Hill, 1950), 169.

3. *Baukunst und Werkform* (Heidelberg, 1947), 1:148. From Conrads, Ulrich, *Programs and Manifestoes on 20th Century Architecture* (Cambridge, Mass.: MIT Press, 1987), 148.

4. Among the other names were Otto Bartning, Egon Eiermann, Willi Baumeister, and Max Taut.

5. This arrangement remains substantially in effect at the time of this publication.

6. Construction of the monument began even before the Allies had met to discuss the future of the city. By July, the memorial was being constructed in what had become the British area of occupation. It remains an object of veneration for the Soviet army, but a second memorial was subsequently constructed in the eastern district of Treptow. An object of vast proportions, its base was constructed from the rubble of the Chancellery.

7. The texts of tourist guides to East Berlin continue to sustain the myth: "Contemporary Berlin is a flourishing city. One of the preconditions for her emergence from the debris of Second World War was her liberation by the Soviet army. When her wounds were still fresh and the scars of war had not yet healed, the Soviet people encouraged Berlin to start a new life by offering their fraternal assistance. That is something which the people of Berlin will never forget."

8. Before the war, only the British Embassy to the west lay between the Soviet Embassy and the Brandenburg Gate.

9. Discussed in *Joseph Stalin: Selected Writings* (Westport, Conn.: Greenwood Press), 1970.

10. Lenin, V.I., *Materialism and Empirio-Criticism* (New York: International Publishers, 1927), 377.

11. Its capital, the modest town of Bonn, was far from the front line.

12. Hoffman, Ernst, "Ideologische Probleme der Architektur," in *Deutsche Architektur* 1 (Berlin, 1952), 20.

13. What is remarkable about such criticism is that Berlin and Prussia had seen themselves as crucibles of modernism. The Bauhaus, which became the formative center of modernism in the world, was based in Weimar and Dessau,

cities close to Berlin and served by Berlin artists. It evolved a modernism based in socialism, in accord with the teachings of its most influential director, Walter Gropius. This led to its closure by the National Socialist Party.

14. Hoffman, *Deutsche Architektur*, 20. So immediate are these concerns that one wonders about the Marxist dimension of this post-modern project.

15. Minerwin, G., "Die Leninsche Theorie der Widerrspiegelung und die Fragen der Theorie des Sozialistischen Realismus," in *Deutsche Architektur* 3 (Berlin, 1953), 114.

16. Ibid., 114.

17. Ibid., 114. The Russian-English pioneer of modern British architecture, Berthold Lubetkin, commenting on the ideological rejection by the Communist Party of Soviet modern art, wrote: "all this romantic symbolism, all these petty bourgeois metaphysics could not hope to survive for long in the atmosphere of socialist realities." From the *Architectural Review* 92 (November, 1942), 111.

18. Ibid., 114.

19. Ibid., 114.

20. Lenin, *Materialism and Empirio-Criticism*, 380. Lenin, in a footnote to *Materialism and Empirio-Criticism*, suggested what for him was the poetic power of the dialectic in the shaping of reality: "Dialectics as a *living*, many-sided knowledge, (with the number of sides eternally increasing) with an infinite number of shadings of every sort of approach and approximation to reality, – here we have an immeasurably rich content as compared with "metaphysical" materialism, the fundamental misfortune of which is its inability to apply dialectics to the theory of reflection, to the process and development of knowledge."

21. The role of individuals in shaping this work was reduced in favor of the collective. However, there are names associated with both the master plan and with the design of Stalin Alle. They are H. Henselmann, E. Hartmann, R. Paulick, K.W. Leucht, H. Hopp, and K. Souradny, all apparently German. It is of interest to wonder where they learned to work within an architectural language whose nature was antithetical to the prevailing forms of Western post-war architecture.

22. In the closing days of war the Luftwaffe made their last stand on foot far from the center of Berlin in the western suburb of Wannsee. As the Russian forces moved toward the Chancellery, these streets were empty and offered no resistance. Unconfirmed British reports suggested that it was deliberately saved to provide the Russians with a base of operations at the heart of the city they were so anxious to control.

23. This revived the prewar concern with resolving traffic congestion that led to the creation of the North/South Axis.

24. *Architecture d'Aujourdhui* 29 (October, 1958), 40-47.

25. Le Corbusier's political positions were always in the service of his architecture. During the war he became associated with the Vichy government because "the opportunity was present for the first time in my life, being always rejected by administration and therefore deprived of official data, to be able to know the general data at the national level and thus the power of organization on a scale hitherto inaccessible to me. On the 27th of May 1941, a decree signed by Marshal Petain gave me a temporary mandate for the creation of a state organization, The Committee for Housing and Real Estate." Le Corbusier was sent by the Vichy government in 1942 to develop a plan for the city of Algiers. The CIAM architects did not welcome him because of his connections with Petain who was, for many, merely Hitler's aging puppet. The city government of Algiers, on the other hand, was concerned about his alleged communism. The mayor of Algiers let it be known that he intended to arrest him as a Bolshevik agent. Le Corbusier quickly left the country and returned to France. His remaining war years were spent in poverty and neglect. "Some men," he wrote, "have original ideas and are kicked in the ass for their pains." Quotations discussed in Jencks, Charles, *Le Corbusier and the Tragic View of Architecture* (London: Allen Lane), 1973.

26. Le Corbusier, *Charte d'Athenes* (New York: Grossman Publishers, 1973). The majority of the recommendations emerged from a meeting of the Congrès Internationaux d'Architecture Moderne (CIAM) held aboard the steamship Patris as it sailed from Marseilles to Athens in 1933, hence the name for the Athens Charter. The subject had been the Functional City, and subsequently Le Corbusier assembled the findings into a book published in France in 1941.

27. Le Corbusier, *Charte d'Athenes*, 93-105.

28. Ibid., 101.

29. In 1947 Le Corbusier published a little book entitled *Concerning Town Planning* (London: The Architectural Press, 1946). It was shaped by questions put to him by the editors of a new English magazine concerning the problems of rebuilding after the destruction of war. He was asked where to begin rebuilding. He replied: "Wherever bombs have done their work verdure flourishes and upon the wide green spaces will rise new buildings. Road alignments and their resulting interior courts are abolished. And this is a paramount decision which will be well understood one day!" The "paramount decision" was the removal of the dense centers of the old cities which had been the source of much urban misery and disease. He was asked to comment on the problem of compensation. He replied: "The law of the land is that it shall support houses, and not that it shall support the unmerited ascension of private fortunes." He was asked if the new quarters to be built in the destroyed towns should be in harmony with old buildings that may have been spared. He replied: "The questioner sees the dilemma and the necessity of choosing between harmony (safety), and change (danger), although the history of man, and particularly of architecture, shows us in all times and places how this particular dilemma can be avoided when harmony is provoked by the true expression of the spirit of an epoch . . . the Whiteners of Sepulchers are sent to the devil!" In *Concerning Town Planning*, 11.

30. Here and there are those elemental machines for living and working developed in the Paris projects of the 1920s and 1930s: the Assembly Building in Chandigarh, the Mundaeum, the Art Museum in Tokyo, and even a fragment from the Palace for the Soviets.

Similar pronouncements appear throughout Le Corbusier's writings in the pre-war years. In *The Radiant City*, he wrote: "The primary form of life consisted of cells that could reproduce by themselves, dividing themselves up,
31. multiplying, and forming an amorphous quivering, but purposeless mass. Then an intention appeared, an axis began to form in the center of this motionless agglomeration. A current, a direction, became apparent. An organism was born." From *The Radiant City* (New York: Orion Press, 1967), 81.

Le Corbusier, *Concerning Town Planning*, 23.

Boesiger, W., ed., *Le Corbusier 1957-1965 Oeuvre Complete* (New York: George Wittenborn, 1965), 230.

32. In the last years of the war while out of work, Scharoun produced a series of drawings that combined dynamic
33. modern forms with ominous Wagnerian landscapes. The dominant theme was of great staircases cutting through
34. man-made mountains, in which nature and architecture are intertwined, reaching for ecstasy.

From 1945 to 1947 he was Berlin's city planning officer. In 1946, he founded the Berlin Planungskollektiv. In 1946, he was appointed senior professor of Town Planning at the Technical University in Berlin, an appointment he held until
35. 1958. In 1947, he was appointed head of Berlin's Institute for Building Studies. In the immediate postwar years he was respected equally in the East and West, producing in 1949 the first plan for housing south of Stalin Allee.

Pfankuch, Peter, *Scharoun Hans Bauten, Entwürfe, Texte*. Schriftenreihe der Akademie der Kunst, 10 (Berlin: Mann Verlag, 1974), 257.

36. Ibid., 257.

Heidegger, Martin, "Building Dwelling Thinking," in *Poetry Language Thought* (New York: Harper & Row, 1971), 153.

37. *Architecture d'Aujourdhui* 17 (February 1960), 31.

38. According to the documents, the work had been carried out the previous year. It raises the question of why there was
39. such a lengthy delay before publishing such an important project.

40.

Gerhardt, Uta, "The Uprising of June 17," in *The Plebians Rehearse the Uprising: A German Tragedy* (New York: Harcourt, Brace, and World, 1966), 113-22.

1. Schneider, Peter, *The Wall Jumper* (New York: Pantheon Books, 1983), 52-53.

The foreigners' gate to East Berlin had just been reconstructed in recent months to soften its prison-like atmosphere
2. and create a more open relationship with the West. In response, a construction worker drove his truck filled with
3. gravel at full speed through the barriers and, in a hail of bullets, escaped to the West. The gate was reinforced. The view was closed.

Pfankuch, Peter, *Scharoun Hans Bauten, Entwürfe, Texte*. Schriftenreihe der Akademie der Kunst, 10 (Berlin: Mann Verlag, 1974), 257.

1. To the degree to which architecture can carry the weight of philosophy, Scharoun's later work is marked by a hard critical confidence derived from Heidiggerian existentialism and phenomenology.

2. Heidegger, Martin, "Poetically Man Dwells," in *Poetry Language Thought* (New York: Harper & Row, 1971), 227.

Scharoun, Hans, quotation in English from publicity material prepared for the opening, in Blundell, Peter Jones, *Hans*
3. *Scharoun* (London: Gordon Fraser, 1978), 36-37.

4. Pfankuch, *Scharoun Hans Bauten, Entwürfe, Texte*, 268. See also Haring, Hugo, "The House as an Organic Structure," in Conrads, *Programs and Manifestoes on 20th Century Architecture*, 126-27.

5. Scharoun, Hans, quotation in English from publicity material prepared for the opening, in Jones, Peter Blundell, *Hans Scharoun* (London: Gordon Fraser, 1978), 36-37.

6. One other work by Scharoun, the Prussian State Library in Berlin, in progress from 1964-77, must be considered in this context. It was to be his last work and with his death in 1972 the construction lacked the imposition of his will. It is a
7. work of circumstance and informal association on a vast scale. It was conceived in relation to a highway in the east that was never built. Appearing like a stranded ship, it is a mess of ill-assorted places presented in the same silent form as in the Philharmonic but without climactic gesture. The interior makes decoration out of conflicting layers of order in the sub-activities of the institution. The outside fails to convey any of this. In its circumstantial nature it seems more confused and inept than essential. Though the work sits in a mess of roads in Scharoun's mind's eye, it would become an object in and of nature, and placed in the informal landscape of his plan for 1957 it becomes meaningful.

It was demolished late in the summer of 1966, just a short time after Albert Speer was released from prison. The drive from prison took him, he wrote, past the ruin and it was this event that made the scales fall from his eyes and made
8. him aware of the megalomania of Hitler's project.

The others were Frank Lloyd Wright, Le Corbusier, and Alvar Aalto. This was not an invention of the author Peter Blake, who wrote monographs on each of them, but was and remains a consensus view within Western architectural
9. culture.

Late in the 1920s, at the time of Mendelsohn's Columbus Haus, he designed an office block named Adam Haus for Leipzigerstrasse. It was not built.

10. Schulze, Franz, *Mies Van Der Rohe: A Critical Biography* (Chicago: University of Chicago Press, 1985), 127.

Schulze, *Mies Van Der Rohe: A Critical Biography*, 172-73.

11. Mies van der Rohe, Ludwig, acceptance address on receiving the AIA Gold Medal of Honor, in *AIA Journal* (June
12. 1960), 91.

13. Mies van der Rohe, Ludwig, "Address to the Illinois Institute of Technology," 1952, quoted in Johnson, Philip C., *Mies Van Der Rohe* (New York: Museum of Modern Art, 1978), 203-04.

14. Spengler, Oswald, from *The Decline of the West*, quoted in Schulze, *Mies Van Der Rohe: A Critical Biography*, 92.

16. Mies' architecture from the pre-war period was much less zealous. The architectural historian Manfredo Tafuri described it as having the same critical character as the works of Mies' friend, the artist Kurt Schwitters, in that his architecture only became meaningful when reflecting the chaos and disorder of reality. They were the reflections of "Merz."

17. Though disbanded in 1987, a number of projects are still in development.

18. Arnell, Peter and Ted Bickford, eds., *James Stirling: Buildings and Projects* (New York: Rizzoli International Publications, 1985), 283.

19. Stirling, James, in *James Stirling, AD Architectural Design Profile* (London: Academy Editions/St. Martin's Press, 1982), 64.

20. Eisenman, Peter, in *Contemporary Architects* (New York: St. Martin's Press, 1980), 231.

21. Ibid.

22. Eisenman, Peter, in *The Charlottesville Tapes* (New York: Rizzoli International Publications, 1985), 140.

23. Ibid., 140-41.

24. Ibid., 141.

25. Ibid., 145.

26. Achleitner, Friederick, on Hans Hollein in *Contemporary Architects* (New York: St. Martin's Press, 1980), 369.

S E L E C T E D   B I B L I O G R A P H Y

Arnell, Peter, and Ted Bickford. *James Stirling: Buildings and Projects*. New York: Rizzoli International Publications, 1985.

Benjamin, Walter. *Reflections*. New York: Harcourt, Brace, Jovanovich, 1978.

Beyer, Oskar, ed. *Erich Mendelsohn: Letters of an Architect*. London: Abelard-Schuman, 1967.

Canetti, Elias. *The Torch in My Ear*. New York: Farrar, Straus, and Giroux, 1982.

Dearstyne, Howard. *Inside the Bauhaus*. New York: Rizzoli International Publications, 1986.

Gay, Peter. *Weimar Culture: The Outsider as Insider*. New York: Harper and Row, 1968.

Helmer, Stephen D. *Hitler's Berlin: The Speer Plans for Reshaping the Central City*. Ann Arbor, MI: UMI Research Press, 1985.

Kleihues, Josef P., and Heinrich Klotz, eds. *International Building Exhibition Berlin 1987: Examples of a New Architecture*. New York: Rizzoli International Publications, 1987.

Krier, Leon. *Albert Speer: Architecture 1932-1942*. Brussels: AAM Editions, 1985.

Lane, Barbara Miller. *Architecture and Politics in Germany 1918-1945*. Cambridge, MA: Harvard University Press, 1968.

Pundt, Hermann G. *Schinkel's Berlin: A Study in Environmental Planning*. Cambridge: MA: Harvard University Press, 1972.

Roters, Eberhard. *Berlin 1910-1933*. Secaucus, NJ: Wellfleet Press, 1982.

Schinkel, Karl Friedrich. *Collection of Architectural Designs*. New York: Princeton Architectural Press, 1989.

Schneider, Peter. *The Wall Jumper*. New York: Pantheon Books, 1983.

Schulze, Franz. *Mies van der Rohe: A Critical Biography*. Chicago: University of Chicago Press, 1985.

Speer, Albert. *Architektur: Arbeiten 1933-1942*. Berlin: Propylhaen, 1978.

Inside the Third Reich. New York: Macmillan Company, 1970.

Taylor, Robert. *The Word in Stone: The Role of Architecture in the National Socialist Ideology*. Berkeley: University of California Press, 1974.

Willett, John. *Art and Politics in the Weimar Period: The New Sobriety 1917-1933*. New York: Pantheon Books, 1978.

Zevi, Bruno. *Erich Mendelsohn*. New York: Rizzoli International Publications, 1985.

Italicized numbers indicate illustrations.

Akademie Der Künste
[2.11], [5.18-19]

AP/Wide World Photos
[8.1]

Architectural Review
[4.6, 4.8-11, 14], [7.28, 30-31]

L'Architecture d'Aujourd'hui
[5.16-17], [7.29]

Balfour, Alan
[4.38], [5.9], [5.11], [6.20-21],
[6.25-32], [7.27]

Berlin: 1910-1933
(Secaucus, NJ: Wellfleet Press,
1982)
[2.25]

Berlin in Abriss
[1.2, 4-5, 25]

Bildarchiv Preussischer
Kulturbesitz
[7.10]

Berlin-Schloss Charlottenburg
[1.22]

The Death of Adolph Hitler
(New York: Harcourt, Brace,
and World, 1968)
[3.42-43]

Deutsche Architektur
[5.7-8, 20-22]

Deutscher Kunstverlag, Berlin
[1.19-21, 24]

Les Editions d'Architecture
Artemis Verlag, Zurich
[5.12-13]

Eisenman Architects
[7.22-26]

Fondation Le Corbusier
[5.14]

Garland Publishing
[5.14]

Gilly Wiedegeburt der Architektur
(Berlin: Hans von Hugo Verlag,
1940)
[1.6-12, 14]

Global Architecture
[7.4-5]

Harvard Theatre Collection
[2.21]

Hitler
(New York: Harcourt, Brace,
Jovanovich, 1973)
[3.36]

Hollein, Hans
[7.28, 30-31]

Korab, Balthazar
[7.16]

Kunstbibliotek Preussischer
Kulturbesitz
[1.18], [4.2, 5, 7], [6.23]

Landesbildstelle
[2.1, 3, 5, 16, 18-20, 22-24],
[3.4-5, 7-8, 10-11, 18, 37-41, 44],
[4.12-13, 15-16, 18-19, 21, 23, 25-32,
34-37], [5.3-4, 5], [6.3-5, 8-19, 24],
[7.3, 6-9, 11-12]

Landesluftbilt Archiv
[7.1]

Mendelsohn Archive
[4.3-4]

The Museum of Modern Art
[2.12, 14]

Neue Deutsches Baukunst
(Berlin: Volk und Reich Verlag,
1943)
[3.19-20, 28-30, 34]

The New York Times
[1.1]

Reidemeister, Andrea
[2.4]

*Schinkel's Berlin: A Study in
Environmental Planning*
(Cambridge, MA: Harvard
University Press, 1972)
[1.3, 15-17]

Senator for Bau-und
Wohnungswesen
[6.2], [7.32]

Albert Speer Archive, Heidelberg
[3.1, 12-13, 21, 25-26, 31-33, 35],
[4.22]

Albert Speer
(Oldenburg: Gerhard Stalling
Verlag, 1943)
[3.23]

Albert Speer: Architecture 1933-1942
(Brussels: Aux Archive
d'Architecture Moderne, 1985)
[3.22, 24]

Staatliche Museen, Berlin
[1.23]

Stadtelsches Kunstinstitut
[2.6]

Stahl Und Form
[7.14-15, 17]

*James Stirling: Buildings and
Projects*
(New York: Rizzoli
International Publications, 1985)
[7.18-21]

Ullstein Bilderdienst
[2.2, 7-8], [3.6, 9, 15, 17], [4.17,
24, 33], [5.2, 10], [6.6-7]

Uppercase
[5.15]

V.E.B. Deutscher Verlag
[2.10]

V.E.B. Tourist Verlag
[6.1]

An important influence in the development of the photographic evidence
for this book comes from Janos Frecot and Helmut Geisert's *Berlin in Abriss*
(Berlin and Vienna: Berlinische Galerie/Medusa, 1981).